本书出版由国家社会科学基金项目"汉语 SLI 儿童移位结构与论元结构习得研究"（14CYY013）资助。

于浩鹏 著

Relative Clauses
in Mandarin Children
with Specific Language Impairment

汉语特殊型语言障碍儿童
关系从句习得研究

SLI

中国社会科学出版社

图书在版编目（CIP）数据

汉语特殊型语言障碍儿童关系从句习得研究 = Relative Clauses in Mandarin Children with Specific Language Impairment：英文 / 于浩鹏著 . —北京：中国社会科学出版社，2021.9

ISBN 978-7-5203-9042-2

Ⅰ.①汉…　Ⅱ.①于…　Ⅲ.①儿童—汉语—语言障碍—干预—研究—英文　Ⅳ.① H018.4

中国版本图书馆 CIP 数据核字（2021）第 176982 号

出 版 人	赵剑英
责任编辑	刘凯琳
责任校对	沈丁晨
责任印制	王　超

出　　版	中国社会科学出版社
社　　址	北京鼓楼西大街甲 158 号
邮　　编	100720
网　　址	http://www.csspw.cn
发 行 部	010-84083685
门 市 部	010-84029450
经　　销	新华书店及其他书店

印　　刷	北京君升印刷有限公司
装　　订	廊坊市广阳区广增装订厂
版　　次	2021 年 9 月第 1 版
印　　次	2021 年 9 月第 1 次印刷

开　　本	710×1000　1/16
印　　张	15.5
字　　数	251 千字
定　　价	86.00 元

凡购买中国社会科学出版社图书，如有质量问题请与本社营销中心联系调换

电话：010-84083683

Contents

List of Figures

List of Tables

List of Abbreviations

Asp	Aspect
CL	Classifier
C	Complementizer
CP	Complementizer Phrase
DCH	Derivational Complexity Hypothesis
DCM	Derivational Complexity Metric
DLD	Developmental Language Disorder
DREAM	Diagnostic Receptive and Expressive Assessment of Mandarin
EFs	Edge Features
EFUH	Edge Feature Underspecification Hypothesis
Foc	Focus
FUH	Feature Underspecification Hypothesis
G-SLI	Grammatical specific language impairment
IP	Inflection Phrase
IQ	Intelligence Quotient
LA	Language Age
LF	Logical form
LTM	Long-term Memory
Object RCs	Object Relative Clauses
p	significance probability
PIC	Phase Impenetrable Condition
PDH	Procedural Deficit Hypothesis
PPVT-R	Peabody Picture Vocabulary Test- Revised Chinese Version
Q	Question
Rel	Relative

RCs	Relative Clauses
RelP	Relative Phrase
RDDR	Representation Deficit for Dependent Relations
RM	Relativized Minimality
RSPCLD	Rating Scale for Pre-school Children with Language Disorder
SD	Standard deviation
SLI	Specific language impairment
Spec	Specifier
Subject RCs	Subject Relative Clauses
STM	Short-term Memory
Syn-SLI	Syntactic Specific Language Impairment
TCCM	Taiwan Corpus of Child Mandarin
Top	Topic
TD	Typically Developing
TDA	Typically Developing Age-matched
TDY	Typically Developing Younger
SPSS	Statistic Package for Social Science
S-Structure	Surface Structure
UPR	Universal Phase Requirement
VP	Verb Phrase
WPPSI-IV	Wechsler Preschool and Primary Scale of Intelligence
(CN)	(Chinese version)

Introduction

This study is the first attempt at exploring the acquisition of Relative Clauses (RCs for short) in Mandarin-speaking children with Specific Language Impairment (SLI for short) by probing the comprehension, production and repetition of RCs in this population. Although the literature in cross-linguistic researches is replete with evidence that the difficulty in RC acquisition is a hallmark of SLI, the hypotheses accounting for the source of the weakness seen in the population do not converge. Additionally, to date, few studies have been conducted on Mandarin-speaking children with SLI.

The current study informs the debate over the sources of the difficulty in the acquisition of RCs by Mandarin-speaking children with SLI by examining their ability to acquire restrictive subject, object and passive object RCs, with the purpose of determining whether there are discrepancies in the acquisition of the three types of RCs by children with SLI, and to investigate whether and to what extent the performances of children with SLI diverge from those of typically developing (TD for short) children, and finally to elucidate the relationship between the possible delay in RC acquisition and the nature of the deficits in children with SLI. We hypothesize that both representational and processing limitations underlie the grammatical deficiency seen in children with SLI. We further propose the Edge Feature Underspecification Hypothesis (EFUH for short) to account for the deficits at the representational level.

Two production tasks, two comprehension tasks and a repetition task were set up following recent researches on the investigation of RCs acquisition to test 47 children, which consists of 17 preschool children with SLI (age range: 4; 5[①]

---

① 4;5 means 4 years and 5 months.

-6; 0), a group of 15 TD children age matched with the SLI children (age range: 4; 3-5; 8) (TDA for short) and a group of 15 younger TD children (age range: 3; 2-4; 2) (TDY for short), in order to obtain a picture as panoramic as possible of factors underlying the deficits in children with SLI, thereby facilitating the development of effective methods of assessment and intervention of children with SLI.

The main findings are threefold. The first finding pertains to the sequence of RC acquisition in children with SLI. To begin with, we found that an advantage of reversible subject RCs holds for children with SLI in comprehension and production[1]. The subject over object RC primacy is captured by Relativized Minimality (RM for short) (Rizzi 1990, 2004) and EUFH, according to which difficulty seen in the acquisition of object RCs originates from the structural intervention of the embedded subject between the relative head and its copy. However, the distinction is not so crisp in all cases. For example, no asymmetry of subject and object RCs was detected in the repetition task. We propose that the symmetric performances of the participants in this task are due to the fact that in object RC task, the structural intervention arises, as predicted by the RM and EUFH, but in subject Relative Clause task, the linear intervention counts more. The imitation task diverges from the production and comprehension task in that the former is more heavily dependent on memory and processing factors. In addition, the SLI children performed similarly in the production of irreversible subject and object RCs. The relative easiness in producing irreversible object RCs has a causal relation with the disappearance of irreversible subject-object RC asymmetry in production. Lastly, the children with SLI had similar performance in the comprehension and production of object RCs and passive object reversible RCs, which is due to the fact that although passive object RCs do not involve RM effect[2], they are costly for children with SLI to compute, as predicted by EFUH.

---

[1] Unless specified otherwise, the RCs in the following part of this dissertation are semantically reversible RCs.
[2] RM effect refers to the intervention effect in the case of object RCs.

Secondly, we have identified the fact that the performances of children with SLI in the tasks were attenuated compared to TD children. The children with SLI performed more poorly than the TDA children in all the tasks, and in most of the tasks, they performed even worse than the TDY children, who are one and a half years younger than them.

Thirdly, the contrast between language profiles of children with SLI and those of TD children reveals that the children with SLI exhibit severe deficiency in the acquisition of RCs, which is imputed to both representational and processing deficit. Manifestations of the representational deficit are as follows. In the first place, in both production and comprehension tasks, children with SLI exhibited a clear subject-object reversible RC asymmetry, whereas TDA children performed equally well on both the subject and object reversible RCs in the two types of experimental tasks, and the TDY children exhibited the subject-object reversible RC asymmetry only in the production tasks. The findings indicate that the language development of children with SLI deviates from the typical trajectory. Next, the incorrect responses of children with SLI in the experiments are repercussions of their inability to assign thematic roles to the moved elements, and to project the fully-fledged object RCs. Lastly, in the priming production task, the children with SLI did not exhibit the priming effect, suggesting that they are not endowed with an intact syntactic representation of object RCs.

The processing deficit mainly manifests itself in the repetition task. First of all, more errors pertaining to the complementizer in children with SLI might suggest that there is a severe processing limitation in children with SLI, which has verified the Surface Account (Leonard 2014a:288-294). Secondly, the results indicate the children with SLI performed significantly worse in imitating subject RCs with greater linear distance between the head and its copy, suggesting that when the processing burden increases, their performance is more likely to be negatively affected. Lastly, in the production of subject RCs, the accuracy of the children with SLI was significantly lower than that of the TDA and TDY children, and in the comprehension of subject RCs, the children with SLI performed worse than the TDA children. These disparities possibly lie in their decayed processing capacities.

To wrap up, the results of the current research demonstrate that children with SLI exhibit poor performances in the production and comprehension of RCs, and the source of the impairments locate in both decayed syntactic representation and limited processing capacity, which corroborates the research hypothesis of this dissertation.

Chapter 1
General Introduction

Specific language impairment (SLI) refers to a significant deficit in language ability that cannot be attributed to hearing loss, low nonverbal intelligence, or neurological damage (Leonard 2014a: 3). Children with this language impairment are often given the label 'Specific language impairment children' (SLI children for short). The present study attempts to explore the acquisition of the Relative Clauses (RCs for short) by Mandarin-speaking children with SLI aiming to present a panoramic description of the profiles of SLI children's mastery of RCs and to locate the underlying factors that may contribute to the language impairment in them. This is the first study to examine the comprehension, production and repetition of RCs in Mandarin-speaking children with SLI, and to compare the profiles of RC acquisition in SLI children with those of their typically developing (TD) peers.

The organization of the first chapter is as follows. Firstly, a brief background of the research is provided. Next, the significance of the study is elaborated on. Subsequently, research questions are presented. And finally, the structure of this dissertation is outlined.

1.1 Background of the research

It is well documented that SLI children present with delays in language development, for example, in phonological representation (Coady 2013; Edwards and Lahey 1996, 1998; Ramus, Marshall, Rosen and van der Lely 2013), argument structure (Grela and Leonard 1997; van der Lely 1994),

5

morphosyntax (Friedmann and Novogrodsky 2004; Hesketh 2006; Menyuk 1964; Owen and Leonard 2006; Schuele and Dykes 2005; van der Lely and Battell 2003), and narratives (Guo, Tomblin, and Samelson 2008; Ukrainetz and Gillam 2009). Among these aspects, the deficits in morphosyntax are very notorious. Extensive studies have been conducted to explore the SLI children's acquisition of non-canonical structures, which require the movement of the sentential element, as in the case of passive sentences (Marshall, Marinis and van der Lely 2007; van der Lely 1996), *Wh*-questions (Marinis and van der Lely 2007; van der Lely and Battell 2003) and RCs (Friedmann and Novogrodsky 2004; Jensen de López, Sundahl Olsen and Chondrogianni 2014; Novogrodsky and Friedmann 2006). Among the constructions, RCs, in particular, have been reported to pose severe challenges for children with SLI in both comprehension and production, as in English (Frizelle and Fletcher 2014; Schuele and Dykes 2005; Schuele and Nicholls 2000; Schuele and Tolberrt 2001; van der Lely and Battell 2003), Hebrew (Friedmann and Novogrodsky 2004; Novogrodsky and Friedmann 2006), Danish (Jensen de López *et al.* 2014), Swedish (Håkansson and Hansson 2000), Italian (Contemori and Garraffa 2010), Greek (Stavrakaki 2001; 2002) . To date, there are only two studies investigating the comprehension and production of RCs by Mandarin-speaking children with SLI (He and Yu 2013; Yu, He and Wang 2017).

The present study seeks to examine the production, comprehension and repetition of RCs in Mandarin speaking children with SLI, for the purpose of discovering whether and to what extent their performance differs from that of TD children. The detailed examination will shed light on the underlying factors leading to the difficulties that SLI children experience in the acquisition of RCs.

Semantically, RCs can be divided into restrictive RCs and non-restrictive RCs.[1] The restrictive RCs can be further classified into Argument RCs and

---

[1]   In the literature, many scholars have examined the restrictiveness of RCs in Mandarin (Chao 1968, Huang 1998, Lin 2003, Tsai 1994). In this dissertation, we assume with Lin (2003) that all Mandarin RCs are restrictive, except when the relative head is a proper name or a pronoun.

Adjunct RCs. We will focus on the acquisition of restrictive argument RC in Mandarin SLI children, as in (1). Note that for the sake of simplicity, we use the term RCs in the rest of the dissertation to refer to 'restrictive argument RCs' unless otherwise specified.

(1) Zhangsan xihuan de shu
    Zhangsan like   DE book
    'the book that Zhangsan likes'

1.2 The significance of the research

The significance of the research is two-fold. Theoretically, Mandarin is a language with head-final RCs, which is very rare typologically. Therefore, Mandarin is an ideal language for the assessment of different theories of RC acquisition in SLI children and the exploration of the question whether language-specific properties influence language acquisition and development.

Practically, through the detailed examination of the performances of children with SLI in RC acquisition, the study may contribute to a better understanding of the language characteristics of RCs in Mandarin SLI children, which might shed light on more accurate methods of identification and more effective intervention strategies. Numerous overseas studies have revealed that Morpho-syntactic difficulties are important clinical markers for SLI children (Rice, Wexler and Hershberge 1998). However, Mandarin is a morphologically impoverished language, and thus, it is arduous to identify Mandarin SLI children by resorting to the morphosyntactic cues. Frizelle and Fletcher (2014) proposed RCs may distinguish between older English children with SLI and younger TD children. Thus, the current study will possibly be instructive to the diagnosis of Mandarin SLI children.

1.3 Motivation of the research

Accumulating evidence shows that in languages with head initial RCs, children's performance on subject RCs is better than that on object RCs. However, the findings in Mandarin children studies are inconsistent. The reasons for the discrepancy possibly lie in the fact that Mandarin RC is head final. Thus, the studies of Mandarin RCs in TD children and in SLI children can evaluate the various theories in the literature, most of which are solely based on data obtained from children speaking languages with head initial RCs.

The results of the previous studies on Mandarin-speaking children's comprehension of RCs are contradictory. Chang (1984) found that there is no difference between the comprehension of SS and SO RCs, and between OO and OS RCs, which suggests that there is neither subject RC advantage nor object RC advantage.[①] However, Lee (1992) examined the comprehension of SS, SO RCs by 61 Mandarin-speaking children and found that there is a clear subject RC advantage across ages. The above pattern was recapitulated by Hu, Gavarró, Vernice, and Guasti (2016), in which they examined the comprehension of subject and object RCs in 120 Mandarin-speaking children. On the contrary, He and Yu (2013) investigated the comprehension of RCs in Mandarin-speaking SLI children using a sentence-picture matching task and found that while Mandarin-speaking SLI children comprehend object RCs around the age of 4;0, they are still at chance level in subject RCs at that age.

The findings from the production studies in Mandarin children are also inconsistent. Some researchers found that there is a subject RC preference in the production, which is consistent with the pattern found in the languages with head-initial RCs (e.g. Cheng 1995, Hsu et al. 2009, Hu et al. 2015). On the other hand, other studies revealed that there is no asymmetry in the production of subject and object RCs (e.g. Su 2004; Yang 2013: 262-268). There are other studies indicating that object RCs are acquired earlier and with more easiness (e.g. Chen and Shirai 2015; Wang 2009). There is only one study investigating the acquisition of RCs

---

① SS indicates that the head noun functions as subject both in the main clause and the relative clause. SO indicates that the head noun functions as the subject of the main clause but the object of the relative clause. OO indicates that the head noun functions as the object both in the main clause and the relative clause. OS indicates that the head noun functions as the object of the main clause but the subject of the relative clause.

by using the sentence repetition task. Hsu (2014) tested 50 Mandarin-speaking children with a sentence repetition experiment and found that while the younger children exhibited inconsistent patterns, the 5-year-olds consistently had better performance in subject RCs than in object RCs.

In summary, to date, there is no agreement on whether there is a subject or object RC advantage in young Mandarin-speaking children. The results vary depending on different tasks adopted, and on different modalities (comprehension, production, or sentence repetition) assessed. And many studies above-mentioned are problematic in design. There are only two studies on the Mandarin SLI children's acquisition of RCs (He and Yu 2013; Yu *et al.* 2017), which suggest that there is deficiency in the knowledge of RCs of Mandarin-speaking children with SLI.

Therefore, it is of necessity to conduct a comprehensive study to assess the acquisition of RCs in Mandarin-speaking children with SLI. In this dissertation, we aim to address the following specific research questions: 1). Is there a subject over object RC advantage in Mandarin-speaking children with SLI? 2). Are the performances of children with SLI in RC acquisition attenuated compared to their typically developing peers? 3). What factors underlie the difficulty encountered by children with SLI in producing and comprehending RCs?

1.4 Organization of the book

The organization of the book is as follows. Chapter one provides a general introduction to the current research, including the significance and motivation of this study.

Chapter two concerns the theoretical issues, in which we will first discuss the syntactic features of Mandarin RCs. Then we proceed to present various theories accounting for the sources of SLI children's impairment, and then propose the research hypothesis of this dissertation.

Chapter three reports the design and results of production tasks, followed by discussion. In this chapter we will report one elicitation production experiment and one priming production experiment to probe the nature of the possible deficits seen in children with SLI.

Chapter four presents the design and findings of the comprehension tasks and the discussion. In this chapter we will first report results of a sentence-picture matching task, which turns out to be invalid to assess the comprehension of children. Subsequently, we will adopt a more effective task (character-picture verification task) to examine the comprehension of RCs.

Chapter five is about the design and results of a sentence repetition task and the discussion. The results of RC repetition task in this chapter suggest that the difficulty encountered by the children with SLI can be partially accounted for by their syntactic deficit, partially by their processing limitation.

Chapter six is a general discussion, where we will address the three research questions based on the findings of the experiments, attempting to come up with a rational explanation for the language impairment in children with SLI.

The conclusion wraps up the findings and presents the contributions and the limitations of the current research.

Chapter 2
The Theoretical Issues

This chapter provides a syntactic analysis of Mandarin RCs and outlines the theoretical issues behind the experimental research. There are two approaches to the derivation of Mandarin RCs, namely the movement analysis, the non-movement analysis. In section 2.1, we will review the two approaches and arrive at the conclusion that that the head-raising analysis can best capture syntactic features of Mandarin RCs. In 2.2, we will present accounts for the deficit in children with SLI, which are roughly divided into representational accounts and processing accounts. In section 2.3, based on previous studies, we will propose the hypothesis of this dissertation. We assume that children with SLI exhibit both the representational and processing deficit and that the representational deficit is targeted on the Edge Features (EF). Section 2.4 summarizes this chapter.

2.1 The syntax of Mandarin RCs

RCs are so-called because they relate to the constituent (the relative head), which is extracted from an internal position of the clause.[①] Being different from English, Mandarin is an SVO language with head-final RCs, namely the RC linearly precedes the relative marker *De* and the relative head, as exemplified in (1).

---

① Note that the relative head is different from the so-called head of a phrase in the generative grammar.

(1) a. Subject RC

    [t$_i$ qin baba de] xiaopengyou$_i$

      kiss father DE child

    'the child that kissed the father'

  b. Object RC

    [baba qin t$_i$ de] xiaopengyou$_i$

    father kiss DE child

    'the child that father kissed'

We assume a raising analysis of RCs following Chen (2007: 183), according to which, the derivation of Mandarin RCs is composed of two steps: raising the relative head to the Spec of CP to check the uninterpretable feature of [Rel] of the head C and further raising the IP into the Spec DP or GenP for different interpretations. The first step of the derivation is sketched in (2).[1][2][3] The second step is irrelevant to our discussion; therefore, we omit it to save space.

(2) a. Subject RC

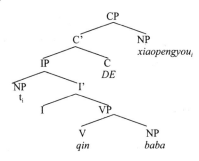

---

① Chen (2007: 49) dubbed the CP as RelP. In this dissertation, we use the more traditional term CP for convenience of discussion.

② For more discussions of the [Rel] feature, see Rizzi (2004, 2006) and Zwart (2000).

③ Chen (2007) did not examine the status of *De* in detail. In this dissertation, following the tradition, we assume that the RC marker *De* occupies the complementizer position (Hu 2014: 19; Ning 1993: 66; Pan 2016: 107).

b. Object RC

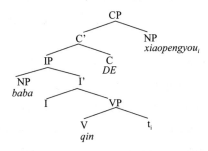

In the literature, there are two broad approaches to the derivation of Mandarin RCs, namely the movement analysis (Del Gobbo 2003; Simpson 2001, 2002; Xiong 2005) and the non-movement analysis (Comrie 2002; Yang 2008; Zhou and Han, 2012). [1][2] In what follows, we summarize previous studies and evaluate the evidence raised by both of the two groups of researchers.

The first piece of evidence supporting the head-raising analysis of RCs is the interpretation of idioms and anaphors. English exhibits reconstruction effects in respect to idiom chunks and binding of anaphora (Hulsey and Sauerland 2006), as in the case of (3).

(3) a. Mary praised the headway that John had made.

---

[1]   The movement analysis has another version, which is called operator movement analysis, also known as Adjunction Analysis and Matching Analysis in the literature. According to this analysis, the head of the RC is base-generated, and the RC adjoins to the head, as shown in (i). The co-indexation between the head and the trace inside the RC is achieved by the relative operator, which can bridge the gap between them. The relative operator can be instantiated as either a Wh-word or a null operator (Ning 1993).
(i)[CP Opi[c'[ta xihuanti][C0de]]]shui
        he like   DE book
        'the book that he likes'   (Ning 1993: 67)
[2]   According to Zhou and Han (2012), the Mandarin relative clause is DeP formed by modifier marker *De* and the relative clause complement left adjoining to the head of the phrase, and the gap in the relative clause is special base-generated empty category, as illustrated in (ii).
(ii) [DP D [DeP[CP C[TP Zhangsan xie e]][De de]][NPshu]]
                Zhangsan write   DE   book
                'the book that Zhangsan wrote'   (Zhou and Han: 31)

b. The portrait of himself that John likes is on the wall.

(cited from Han 2013:321)

In (3a), the idiomatic meaning coming from *make headway* is preserved, suggesting that *headway* originated in the object of the relative clause, before moving to the head noun position. In (3b), the antecedent of *himself* is *John*, which indicates that the head noun *portrait of himself* must have originated in the object position of the verb *likes* where *John* c-commands *himself*.

According to Aoun and Li (2003), the movement analysis of Mandarin RC is also supported by reconstruction effects in respect to idiom and anaphor, as shown in (4)[1]. The argumentation goes like this. In (4a), a part of the idiom is the relative head, and the idiomatic meaning coming from *Chicu* (to be jealous) is preserved, which means that *Cu* (vinegar) must have originated as the object of the verb *Chi* (eat). This is called the reconstruction of idiomatic expression. In (4b), the reflexive *Ziji* (himself) contained in the relative head can be bound by an antecedent within the relative clause. The antecedent of *Ziji* (himself) is *Meigeren* (everyone), which indicates that the relative head *Ziji de chezi* (the cars of their own) must have started out in the object position of the verb *Quan* (persuade), where *Meigeren* (everyone) c-commands *Ziji* (himself).

(4) a. [[Ta chi t_i de] cu$_i$]   bi   shei duo da. (Aoun & Li, 2003, p. 138)
          he eat   DE vinegar compare others all big
          'Lit. The vinegar he eats is greater than anyone else's.'
          'His jealousy is greater than anyone else's.'
     b. [[Wo jiao zhangsan quan   meigeren$_i$ kai lai   de]
          I   ask zhangsan persuade everyone-CL-person drive come DE
          ziji$_i$ de chezi]
          self DE car
          'self's car that I asked Zhangsan to persuade everyone to drive over'

---

[1]   See Yang (2013: 73-75) for a different analysis of the reconstruction effects of idiom and anaphor in Mandarin RCs.

The fact that the derivation of Mandarin RCs is subject to the Island condition is also compelling evidence for the movement analysis. The movement analysis predicts that a gap cannot occur inside an island in a relative clause. Some researchers assumed that a gap cannot occur inside an island in Mandarin RCs (e.g. Aoun and Li 2003; Chen & Wen, 2013; Huang, Li, and Li 2009 among many others). Examples given in (5) indicate that the sentences are ungrammatical because an element is relativized from islands: the subject clause island in (5a), the relative clause island in (5b) and the adjunct island in (5c).

(5) a. Subject clause island

　　　*Lisi mei kan zhen　qiguai　　de na ben shu

　　　Lisi not read really surprising DE that CL book

　　* 'The book x [that [that Lisi has not read x] is very surprising]'

　　　　　　　　　　　　　　　　　　　　　(Huang 1998: 326)

　　b. Relative clause island

　　　*kanjian de xuesheng laile　　de　nage　ren

　　　see　　DE student　come-Asp DE that-CL person

　　*'the person x [that [the students that saw x] came]'

　　　　　　　　　　　　　　　　　　　　　(Huang 1998: 324)

　　c. adjunct island

　　　*ruguo ta　chi, wo hui hen shengqi de cu

　　　if　　he eat, I will very angry　DE vinegar

　　　'the vinegar x [that [if he eat x], I will be very angry]'

　　　　　　　　　　　　　　　　　　　　　(Li 2002: 8)

However, Yang (2013: 77) assumed that there is no island constraint in the derivation of Mandarin RCs, as illustrated by (6). In (6a) the subject clause island constraint is violated, in (6b) the relative clause island is violated and in (6c) the adjunct island constraint is violated.

(6) a. Subject clause island

ni   zheme   huida bu heshi   de nage   wenti

you in-this-way answer not proper DE that-CL question

the question x [that [that you answered x in this way] is not proper]

b. Relative clause island

kanjian de xuesheng bu duo   de nage   ren

see   DE student   not many DE that-CL person

'the person x [that the students [that saw x] are not many]'

c. Adjunct island

zhiyao ta kan, ta baba   zhun hui shengqi de naben   shu.

if   he read, his father surely will angry   De that-CL book

'the book x that [if he read x], his father must be angry'

(Yang 2013: 77)

The data presented by Yang (2013) seemingly support the assumption that the derivation of Mandarin RCs is not subject to island constraint. However, under closer scrutiny, the assumption does not hold water. Hsu (2008) and Chen and Wen (2013) posit that some RCs, which seemingly violate the Island constraint, are derived from topic-comment structures, in which topics are base-generated. Therefore the target of relativization is located out of the island in the underlying structure, and the derivation does not violate the island condition. Hsu (2008) examined RCs deriving from the relative clause island, as exemplified in (7).

(7) a. [[[e_i chuan t_j de] yifu$_j$] hen   piaoliang de] nage   nühai$_i$

wear   DE dress very pretty   DE that-CL girl

'[the girl x that [the dress [x wears] is very pretty]]'

(Hsu 2008: 32)

The author proposed that (7) is derived from a topic-comment structure, as illustrated in (8).

(8) Nage   nühai$_i$, [[pro_i chuan t_j de] yifu$_j$] hen piaoliang.

that-CL girl   wear DE dress very pretty

16

'As for the girl$_i$, the dress she$_i$ wears is pretty.'

(Hsu 2008: 32)

The analysis is supported by two pieces of evidence. Firstly, the sentential adverb can occur after the first NP in (8), suggesting that the first NP *Nage nühai* (that girl) is not a part of the relative clause modifying the matric subject *Yifu* (dress), as illustrated in (9).

(9) Nage   nühai$_i$, **xianrandi**, [[*pro$_i$* chuan t$_j$ de] yifu$_j$] hen piaoliang.
      that-CL girl   obviously   wear   DE dress very pretty
      'That girl$_i$, obviously, the dress she$_i$ wears is pretty.'

(Hsu 2008: 32)

Secondly, the empty category can be replaced by a lexical NP, which indicates that the empty category is not a gap, because the gap is not replaceable by the lexical element, as shown in (10).

(10) Nage   nühai$_i$, [[ta$_i$-de pengyou chuan t$_j$ de] yifu$_j$] hen piaoliang.
      that-CL girl   her   friend   wear   DE dress very pretty
      'As for that girl$_i$, the dress her$_i$ friend wears is very pretty.'

(Hsu 2008: 32)

Nevertheless, not all such RCs are acceptable, as illustrated in (11).

(11) * [e$_i$ bangmang t$_j$ de] xiaojie$_j$ mai-le   yixie shu   de   nage   ren$_i$.
        help   DE lady   buy-ASP some book DE that-CL person
      '[the man x such that [the lady who [x helps] bought some books]]'

(Hsu 2008: 39)

In line with the above analysis, the possible underlying structure for (11) is a topicalization structure in (12).

(12) * Nage   ren$_i$, [[*pro$_i$* bangmang t$_j$ de] xiaojie$_j$] mai-le   yixie shu.

       that-CL person,   help   DE lady   buy-ASP some book

       'As for that person x, the lady who x helps bought some books.'

(Hsu 2008: 39)

Hsu maintained that in RCs as (11), the target of the relativization is not a topic NP in the underlying structures because the possible underlying topic structure is ungrammatical, which is attributed to the pragmatic factors. Hsu posited that the topic structure in (12) is not acceptable because the topic NP in it cannot be clearly characterized by the following clause, following the Characterization Condition for [NP, S] Construction (Hsu 2008: 44), according to which S can characterize the NP if and only if at least one pragmatically natural property to be readily derived. In (12) no natural property of the NP *ren* (person) can be easily derived, because a person is not usually characterized by the other person who he helps. Therefore, in such RCs, the relative heads are derived from a relative clause island.

    There is another kind of RC involving the relative clause island, in which the relativized head is extracted from the relative clause modifying an object, as shown in (13).

(13) * wo xihuan chuan de yifu   de nage   ren

       I   like   wear DE dress DE that-CL person

       'the person x that I like the dress that x wears'

(Hsu 2008: 34)

Hsu (2008) proposed such RC is ungrammatical in that it violates the island constraint because the possible underlying topic-comment structure of (13) is ungrammatical, as exemplified in (14).

(14) *Wo xihuan, nage   ren$_i$, [[*pro$_i$* chuan t$_j$ de] yifu$_j$].

       I   like   that-CL person   wear   DE dress

       'I like the dress which the person wears.'

(Hsu 2008: 34)

We turn to the subject clause island, which has been explored by Chen and Wen (2013). Following Hsu (2008), they assert that some RCs, in which the relative heads are extracted from the subject clause islands, are acceptable, if the underlying structures are topic structures, as shown in (15a) and (15b).

(15) a. [[Zhangsan kan t_i] bu heshi] de naxie shu$_i$

Zhangsan read   not proper DE those books

'the books x that [that Zhangsan read x is not proper]'

b. Naxie shu,   Zhangsan kan bu heshi.

those books, Zhangsan read not proper

'Those books$_i$, [that Zhangsan read t_i] is not proper'

(Chen and Wen 2013: 145)

Chen & Wen (2013) further asserted that some RCs, which seemingly violate the adjunct island condition, are grammatical for the same reason, as illustrated in (16).

(16) ruguo meigeren dou yao kan t_i, Zhangsan hui hen gaoxing de   naben

if   everyone all want read,   Zhangsan will very happy DE that-CL

taziji   de shu$_i$

himself DE book

'the book x written by Zhansan himself, such that if everyone wants to read x, Zhangsan will be very happy'

(Chen and Wen 2013: 145)

The data presented above provide solid evidence that when Mandarin RCs are formed, island constraints are observed. Even when the extraction out of islands is permissible, the island constraints are not violated, because the target of relativization is located out of the islands in the underlying structure. Hsu (2008) and Chen and Wen (2013) put Yang's (2013) assumption that derivation of Mandarin RC is not subject to the Island constraint in serious doubt. As posited by

Chomsky (1977) and Huang *et al.* (2009: 39), the fact that the formation of RCs is subject to Island constraints is a piece of diagnostic evidence for the existence of movement. Therefore, we can safely arrive at the conclusion that syntactic movement is involved in the derivation of Mandarin RCs.

To wrap up this section, we have raised evidence with respect to the reconstruction effect of idiom and anaphor and the island constraints to support the assumption that Mandarin RCs are derived through syntactic movement[①]. As noted by Chen (2005), the operator movement analysis is both theoretically undesirable and empirically inadequate. Therefore in this dissertation, we will not adopt this analysis. Thus for the remainder of the study, we will assume that the relative head starts out internal to the relative clause and that the gap in the relative clause is a copy of the relative head.

2.2 Accounts for the deficit in children with SLI

In this section we will present explanatory hypotheses accounting for the deficit in children with SLI. Generally speaking, two broad competing theoretical perspectives have been proposed, attempting to explain SLI. Problems with Morpho-Syntax are notorious in children with SLI, and therefore some researchers postulate that the disorder is specific to the domain of language, specifically to the impaired knowledge of particular rules, principles or constraints, which underlie the combination of words into complex structures. However, previous studies have also revealed that children with SLI present with subtle non-linguistic weakness, and therefore other scholars assume that the deficit in children with SLI is traceable to the limitation in general information-processing capacity (Leonard 2014a: 271), which is claimed to compromise the possibility to put in use the knowledge of grammar.

---

① According to Chen & Wen (2013), syntactic movement is involved in RCs, in which an argument, a topic and a time or place adjunct is relativized; and no movement is involved in RCs, in which an adjunct of other types or a sloppy constituent is the relative head. This dissertation only examines the acquisition of RCs in which arguments are relativized, therefore we will stick to the movement analysis for the remainder of the dissertation.

This section is organized as follows. In 2.2.1 we will present the representational accounts, which assume that the deficit in children with SLI lies in the grammatical knowledge impairment. In 2.2.2, the processing accounts will be discussed, which posit that the deficit is attributable to processing limitations in these children. In 2.2.3, we will elaborate on the Procedural Deficit Hypothesis, according to which the deficit in children with SLI can be imputed to a deficit in the procedural memory system.

2.2.1 Representational Accounts

Many researchers posit that the linguistic problems seen in children with SLI may arise from grammatical deficiencies. Various theories have been proposed to account for the impaired knowledge of the verb reflections reflecting subject-verb agreement, auxiliaries and copular forms in children with SLI, such as the Agreement/Tense Omission Model (Schütze and Wexler 1996), the Extended Optional Infinitive account (Rice and Wexler 1996), the Extended Unique Checking Constraint Account (Wexler 2003) and the Grammatical Agreement Deficit Account (Clahsen 1999).

In previous studies on the acquisition of RCs by SLI children, a substantial asymmetry arises between subject RCs and object RCs: the latter being more compromised than the former. The widely-assumed subject RCs advantage in acquisition is established on the easier acquisition of subject RCs, such as (17a), compared to object RCs in (17b).One of the hotly-debated questions in the literature of RC acquisition is how to account for the subject over object RCs advantage in children with SLI speaking languages with head-initial RCs.

(17) a. the girl$_i$ [that t$_i$ kissed the father]

  b. the girl$_i$ [that the father kissed t$_i$]

Also hotly debated is the question what factors contribute to difficulties with RC acquisition in children with SLI. Most of the previous studies have demonstrated that children with SLI suffer from a protracted delay in the acquisition of RCs compared to their TD peers.

Many representational theories have been developed attempting to account for the profile of children with SLI in acquiring RCs, and address the issues of the nature and locus of the impairment. All representational accounts converge on the assumption that the deficit in children with SLI lies in the linguistic representation. However, there is substantial disagreement regarding the nature of the impairment. In this section, we will review the accounts explaining the deficit of children with SLI in the acquisition of RCs, namely the Thematic Role Assignment Deficit Account (Cromer 1978; Friedmann and Novogrodsky 2004), the Representational Deficit for Dependent Relationship Theory (RDDR for short) (van der Lely 1996), the Functional Category Deficit Account (Håkansson and Hansson 2000; Leonard 2014a: 246-248), and the Relativized Minimality Account (Jensen de López *et al.* 2014).

2.2.1.1 The Thematic Role Assignment Deficit account
The first theory attributes the deficit in children with SLI to their inability to assign thematic role to moved elements in RCs, namely the relative head. Cromer (1978) proposed that children with SLI interpret RCs solely relying on the linear order of the sentential elements, because they do not possess the intact syntactic representation required for the assignment of thematic roles. Namely, children with SLI will regard the first noun phrase in RCs as the agent of the action, and the second noun phrase as the theme (or patient). The interpretation of English subject RCs like (17a) by using such a strategy will lead to the correct interpretation because the first noun phrase happens to be the agent and the second noun phrase is the theme. However, if they use such a strategy to interpret object RCs, they will get a reversed interpretation of the sentence. For example, when interpreting the object RC (17b) '*the girl that the father kissed*', children with SLI will regard the first NP '*the girl*' as an agent and the second NP '*the father*' as a theme (patient), and thus, consistently getting the reversed interpretation. According to this theory, children with SLI perform well on subject RCs, but consistently badly on object RCs.

However, this conclusion was questioned by many researchers. For example, in a study examining the comprehension of RCs in Hebrew children with syntactic

SLI, Friedmann and Novogrodsky (2004) found that the children with syntactic SLI performed at chance level on object RCs in the binary sentence-picture matching task, which is contrary to the prediction of Cromer's theory, which wrongly predicts consistent role reversal, namely, a below-chance performance in the task. Moreover, the predictions of linear assignment theory of Cromer are articulated in terms of comprehension, but it is unclear what the predictions would be in terms of production.

Novogrodsky and Friedmann (2006) posited that the deficit in production of RCs by children with SLI is also related to their inability to assign thematic roles to moved constituents. They examined the production of RCs in Hebrew-speaking children with SLI by using a preference task and a picture description task and found that the Hebrew-speaking children with SLI had more accuracy on subject RCs than object RCs in both tasks. The most frequent errors detected in children with SLI in the object RC elicitation tasks consisted of thematic errors and reduction of thematic roles. Similarly, Jensen de López et al. (2014) explored the production of subject and object RCs in Danish-speaking children with SLI by adopting a preference task. They found that in object RC tasks, children with SLI opted for simple sentences, passive object relatives, fragments and RCs with thematic role reversals. Following Novogrodsky and Friedmann (2006), Jensen de López and his colleagues hold that the deficiency in children with SLI is related to the assignment of thematic roles. Riches (2017) also found that children with SLI have difficulties with thematic role assignment in sentence repetition.

Although this theory may provide satisfactory account of the errors with respect to the thematic role assignment in children with SLI, it cannot capture all the linguistic characteristics of children with SLI in acquiring RCs. As will be shown in 2.2.1.3, many researchers have found that SLI children committed more errors of complementizer omission than the TD children and that this error assumes a large percentage in the incorrect responses. This being so, this conclusion renders less plausible the view that the deficit in children with SLI is only reduced to the thematic role assignment.

2.2.1.2 The Representational Deficit for Dependent Relationship theory

The Representational Deficit for Dependent Relationship Theory (RDDR) was developed aiming to account for the broad range of deficits found in children with Grammatical-SLI (G-SLI for short), according to which the receptive and expressive language of G-SLI could be accounted for by a deficit in dependent structural relationships between constituents. (van der Lely 1994, 1998; van der Lely and Stollwerck, 1997). According to RDDR, the core deficit responsible for G-SLI grammar involves treating movement as optional, rather than obligatory. More specifically, in the grammar of TD children, the basic grammatical operation Move is obligatory whereas in the grammar of children with G-SLI it is optional. Thus, RDDR predicts that children with G-SLI would have problems with constructions involving movement. The prediction has been confirmed in both the comprehension and production of *Wh*-questions in studies by van der Lely and Battell (2003).

In a similar vein, the comprehension of RCs, which involves the *Wh*-movement, will also be problematic, as predicted by RDDR. However, it is hard to predict the exact performance of the children with SLI in the RC comprehension because it is difficult to infer the results of treating movement as optional in comprehension of RCs, which involves movement of a noun phrase (Friedmann and Novogrodsky, 2004). Based on the theory proposed by Grodzinsky (1990) for individuals with agrammatic aphasia, Friedmann and Novogrodsky (2004) deduced an exact prediction.

Grodzinsky contended that the deficit in movement leads to the inability to assign thematic roles to noun phrases (NPs) that undergo movement from their original sentential position. NPs that do not move retain their thematic roles in the grammar of the children with SLI. When children with SLI cannot assign a thematic role to the NP undergoing movement, they will adopt a non-syntactic strategy to interpret this NP. More precisely, if the NP lacking a thematic role is the first NP, it is interpreted as the agent according to its position in the sentence; whereas if the NP lacking a thematic role is the second NP, it is interpreted as the theme (or patient). For example, when children with SLI encountered a subject RC (e.g. *the girl*$_i$ *[that t*$_i$ *kissed the father]*), where the role-less NP *the girl* is the first NP of the sentence and also an agent, and thus they would interpret the sentence correctly, though not necessarily by using normal syntactic knowledge. However, when children with SLI processed the object RC, they would meet troubles because in object RCs (e.g. *the girl$_i$ [that the father kissed t$_i$])* , the NP lacking a thematic role is '*the girl*', which is a theme, and the children with SLI will mistakenly interpret it as an agent according to its position in the sentence. Given the fact that the sentence contains a real agent, which retains its agent role because it has not moved, the hearer was forced to guess who the agent is. Thus, the prediction of a movement deficit, together with the interpretation strategy discussed above, will lead to constantly correct interpretation of subject RCs and chance-level performance on object RCs. The prediction has been endorsed by Friedmann and Novogrodsky (2004), in which the children with SLI consistently performed well on subject RCs (98.5%), whereas they had chance-level performance on object RCs (62%).

Interestingly, according to this theory, children with SLI speaking a language with head-final RCs, such as Mandarin, will exhibit a reversed pattern in interpreting the RCs. In Mandarin object RCs (18b), the moved NP is *nühai* (the girl), which is the second NP in the sentence, the children with SLI will interpret it as a theme by using the strategy illustrated above. This interpretation happens to be correct. However, when they encountered a subject RC (18a), in which the role-less NP is an agent, they will interpret it as a theme. If they adopt a guessing strategy, they will have a chance-performance on the subject RC comprehension task.

(18) a. Subject RC

      [t$_i$ Qin baba de] nühai$_i$

         kiss father De girl

         'the girl that kissed the father'

    b. Object RC

      [baba qin t$_i$ de] nühai$_i$

      father kiss De girl

      'the girl that the father kissed'

This prediction has been confirmed by He and Yu (2013). They reported an object over subject RC advantage in a study investigating the comprehension of RCs in Mandarin-speaking children with SLI. However, as will been shown in chapter 4, the methodology adopted in the study in problematic, and hence the results of this study may not be reliable. Hu *et al.* (2016) tested 120 Mandarin-speaking TD children (age range 3;0-8:11) on their interpretation of subject RC and object RC by adopting the character-picture verification task. The results show that up to seven years of age, Chinese children showed a subject RC preference when asked to select a character. If we adopt the view that the linguistic characteristics in children with SLI are comparable to those of their younger TD peers (Leonard 2014: 41), it naturally follows that the children with SLI will also exhibit a subject RC preference in RC comprehension. Obviously, RDDR cannot provide a satisfactory account of the pattern.

Regarding production of RCs, the RDDR and the deficit in thematic role assignment predict that children with SLI will commit errors related to thematic roles (Novogrodsky and Friedmann, 2006). However, Novogrodsky and Friedmann found that children with SLI in their study prefer to produce subject RCs, with role reversal errors, instead of the target object RC. This finding remains unaccountable under RDDR. To be more precise, the theory fails to explain why movement from subject positions is easier than movement from object positions. The second prediction of the RDDR would be that children with SLI will have chance performance in terms of accuracy on RC production, given the assumption that they treat movement as optional. But the findings in Jensen de López et al. (2014) did not corroborate this prediction, as the children with SLI had very low accuracy on object RCs production.

2.2.1.3 The Functional Deficit Account

Many grammatical elements concerning functional categories constitute significant areas of weakness for children with SLI (Leonard 2014a: 246), which raises the question whether these children have troubles with the functional categories. This assumption is not fresh in literature of first language acquisition.

Several researchers have proposed that in the earliest stage of the grammar development in young TD children, the functional categories are absent (Guilfoyle and Noonan 1992; Radford 1988, 1990). Given the fact that the functional categories appear later than the lexical categories in TD children's grammar, it is reasonable to suspect that the difficulty seen in SLI might be attributable to the slow development of the functional categories (Leonard 2014a: 247).

Some scholars have attributed the difficulty seen in children with SLI in producing RCs to a structural deficit (Håkansson and Hansson 2000; Meisel and Mü-ller 1992). More specifically, SLI children's knowledge of functional categories, including complementizers (C), is impaired and thus projecting a fully-fledged clause structure is difficult for them. Previous studies of preschool children with SLI proved that the proposal is on the right track because errors in production of RCs by children with SLI are mainly related to C omission.

For example, Håkansson and Hansson (2000) investigated the production of subject RCs in Swedish children with SLI and found that those children committed more errors of C omission than the TD children and that this error assumes a large percentage in the incorrect responses. A similar finding is presented in Contemori and Garraffa (2010), in which they examined the production of RCs by Italian preschoolers with SLI. The production is severely impaired in the children with SLI and in terms of errors committed, they omitted the complementizer more frequently than TD children, who never committed such errors. The evidence for the structural deficiencies has also been found in spontaneous data of English children with SLI. Schuele and Dykes (2005) and Schuele and Tolberrt (2001) found that the onset of RCs in children with SLI was at the age of 4;8 years. The majority of RCs are subject RCs with omitted relative markers (*that* or *Wh*-pronouns). The few object RCs also involved omissions of obligatory relative markers.

Some criticisms should be levied to the functional deficit account. Firstly, this account failed to capture the well-attested subject over object RC asymmetry in children with SLI. If the children with SLI cannot project a fully-fledged clause structure of RCs, as predicted by the functional deficit account, the knowledge of the subject and object RC in them will be equally impaired, which is contrary to the fact. Secondly, because this theory is proposed mainly relying on the production data of children with SLI, it is unclear what the predictions would be in terms of comprehension of RCs in this population.

2.2.1.4 The Relativized Minimality Account

The Relativized Minimality (RM for short) was first postulated as a theory of syntactic locality on constraints governing extraction from Syntactic Islands (Rizzi 1990, 2004). In the configuration of (19), a local relation between X and Y cannot hold if the intervener Z is similar in structure to X.

(19) a. X . . . Z . . . Y

      b. Z intervenes between X and Y if and only if Z c-commands Y and Z does not c-command X.

                                                     (Rizzi 2004: 225)

There are many studies examining RM effect in normal children's first language acquisition (Belletti, Friedmann, Brunato and Rizzi 2012; Friedmann, Belletti and Rizzi 2009; Grillo 2009; Hu *et al.* 2016; Hu, Gavarró, & Guasti 2015). Friedmann *et al.* (2009) proposed that a dependency between the relative head and the trace is hard to establish for young children if there is a qualified element intervening between them. For example, in the object RC (20b), the intervener is the subject (the father) of the embedded clause because it c-commands the trace of the relative head and does not c-command the relative head. However, in the English subject RC (20a), there is no intervener between the relative head and its trace, because the potential intervener, the object (the father) in embedded clause, does not c-command the trace of the moved element.

(20) a. the girl$_i$ [that t$_i$ kissed the father]

      b. the girl$_i$ [that the father kissed t$_i$]

It should be noted that the intervention effect is based on the feature configuration of the NPs involved. Under a raising analysis, the relative head is supposed to bear the feature [+Rel, +N] whereas the subject, which is the intervener, bears the feature [+N] in (20b). According to RM, the subject NP cannot block the dependency between the relative head and the trace, because the subject and the relative head do not bear same features. Therefore, for adults and elder TD children, their performances on object RCs will not be impaired.

But the scene is different in young children and children with SLI. Although the relative head and the intervener do not share the same feature set, they have one shared feature, namely, [+N]. Thus, the intervener has a subset of the features of the relative head. To interpret the object RC, one has to compute the subset–superset relation. Friedmann et al. (2009) proposed that limited computational resources sometimes prevent younger children from making this computation. Thus, RM will block chain formation, as a consequence, it is impossible to assign correct thematic role to each argument, which ultimately results in poor comprehension of object RCs.

Jensen de López *et al.* (2014) extended this account to RC acquisition in children with SLI. They found that children with SLI were sensitive to the same intervention effects as their TD peers, which gave rise to the subject over object RC advantage in both comprehension and production. They also found that RM can explain the avoidance strategies adopted by SLI children in the case of object RC production tasks.

To date, the RM approach is the most plausible account of the nature and cause of SLI because it can accommodate very well recent findings obtained from the studies on both the two modalities, namely the comprehension and the production. For instance, it can capture more linguistic features of children with SLI, such as avoidance strategies adopted by SLI children in the case of object RC production tasks, which is out of the reach of other theories. However, this approach is far from being perfect for the following reasons. Firstly, it cannot provide satisfactory account of the deficits in children with SLI with respect to the functional categories, such as the complementizer omission, which is very prevalent in preschool children with SLI. Secondly, this theory is mainly based on the data obtained from the studies, which examined the children speaking a language with head-initial RCs. It is unclear what the results would be in terms of acquisition of Mandarin RCs by children with SLI. Thirdly, the methodology used in Jensen de López et al. (2014) to assess children's comprehension of RCs is not appropriate and therefore it is hard to determine whether the conclusion from the study can hold water.[①]

To summarize, we found that neither of the representational theories can accommodate all the linguistic features of children with SLI, exhibited in the acquisition of RCs. In section 2.3, we will put forward a novel representational account, attempting to accommodate all the linguistic features of children with SLI in acquiring RCs.

2.2.2 Processing accounts

Previous studies have revealed that the non-linguistic abilities of the children with SLI are also vulnerable, and therefore many researchers maintain that the problems in linguistic and non-linguistic areas reflect a limitation in information-processing capacities (Leonard 2014a: 271), especially in the processing speed and working memory. The shared assumption of processing accounts is that the language impairment in children with SLI has a causal relationship with a general or specific processing deficit. This key notion makes them distinguished from the representational accounts of SLI, which posit that the nature and cause of the impairment is at the level of linguistic representation per se.

There are many studies converging on the view that the poor performance in RC acquisition seen in children with SLI is due to the processing limitations. Riches, Loucas, Baird, Charman, and Simonoff (2010) assessed sentence repetition of RCs in adolescents with SLI. They found that the repetition of RCs in adolescents with SLI is severely impaired, partly owing to the limited working memory. Hestvik, Schwartz, and Tornyova (2010) showed that the locus of comprehension difficulties with RCs seen in children with SLI is at the level of processing mechanisms but not the grammatical knowledge. Garraffa, Coco, and Branigan (2015) adopted a structural priming paradigm to investigate the production of subject RCs. The results indicated that the magnitude of priming

---

① We will elaborate on this issue in Chapter 4.

effect in SLI children was the same as that in TD children, but that children with SLI showed a smaller cumulative priming effect than TD children. Therefore, they proposed that the language deficit of SLI children should be ascribed to impaired implicit learning mechanisms rather than the syntactic knowledge. Rakhlin, Kornilov, Kornilova, and Grigorenko (2016) investigated RC comprehension in Russian-speaking children with developmental language disorder (DLD).[1] They arrived at the conclusion that a key deficit in children with DLD is not attributable to syntactic component but to limitation in working memory resources.

Next, we will review theories addressing the sources of the processing limitations seen in children with SLI. Locke (1993, 1994) proposed that children with SLI exhibited a neuro-maturational delay, which is seen in the late appearance of several cognitive and motor milestones. Among them the lexical development is also delayed. According to Locke's account, a time-locked grammatical analysis mechanism (20-36 months) is activated on the condition that the lexical material is adequate. The delayed lexical development means that the activation of the grammatical analysis mechanism will be postponed. Thus, the development of grammar in children with SLI will be impaired. In Locke's theory, the conspicuous weakness in language seen in children with SLI is due to the delayed activation of the grammatical analysis mechanism. And the deficits in non-linguistic areas might be attributable to the fact that the children with SLI cannot resort to language mediation to facilitate non-linguistic reasoning.

Children with SLI often encounter difficulties on tasks requiring them to process the auditory stimuli, which are brief or presented in rapid succession. Tallal and his colleagues proposed that the difficulty with the brief and rapidly presented stimuli reflects a temporal processing deficit in children with SLI (Tallal and Stark 1981), among many others. In general, many studies have revealed that children with SLI performed well below the level of their age-matched peers on tasks involving briefly or rapidly appearing auditory stimuli (Leonard 2014a: 313-314). However, Leonard (2014a: 314) holds that this weakness seems to be less close to the core of SLI than other types of limitations.

---

[1]   Developmental language disorder is another label of Specific Language Impairment (SLI).

Processing approaches are not exempt from problems. Ullman and Pierpont (2005) posited that the processing-deficit hypotheses, which ascribe the impairments in SLI to a general processing deficit, are somewhat problematic. Firstly, some researchers have argued that theses hypotheses cannot easily explain certain types of linguistic impairments observed in SLI (van der Lely and Ullman 2001). Secondly, because these hypotheses claim that the deficits are quite general, they have difficulty accounting for the fact that the non-linguistic abilities in children with SLI are impaired selectively (Ullman and Pierpont 2005). Finally, a limited processing capacity account is too general, because nearly any kind of impairment could potentially be explained by processing limitations.

2.2.3 Procedural Deficit Hypothesis

To overcome the shortcomings of the previous accounts, Ullman and Pierpont (2005) proposed the Procedural Deficit Hypothesis (PDH). They argued that this hypothesis can explain the neural abnormalities found in SLI, as well as the consistency and heterogeneity in the linguistic and nonlinguistic deficits found in the disorder. According to PDH, various problems in children with SLI can be imputed to a deficit in the procedural memory system.

Pinker and Ullman (2002) made a distinction between the procedural memory system and declarative memory system. The former is related to learning and performance of skills involving sequences (linguistic, cognitive, motor skills). The latter is associated with semantic memory and episodic memory. Acquisition of the skills in procedural system is gradual, because the learning is based on multiple trials. In contrast, the learned skills generally apply quickly and automatically. The procedural system is composed of several interconnected brain structures, which are responsible for not only motor and cognitive skills, but also the function of grammar, lexical retrieval, dynamic mental imagery, working memory, and rapid temporal processing (Ullman and Pierpont 2005). They used the procedural system to refer to the entire system involved in the learning, representation and use of procedural memories.

In terms of language, a categorical distinction was made between lexicon and grammar in the hypothesis. Namely, the idiosyncratic mappings are stored in a 'mental lexicon', which involves the declarative memory, and whereas the learning and use of rule-governed computations depends on 'mental grammar' in procedural memory. The rules are a form of mental knowledge, which underlies the capacity to produce and comprehend complex forms.

The PDH predicts that aspects of grammar that involve rule-governed operations, should be impaired, in that such aspects of grammar are dependent on the procedural memory system. The hypothesis further predicts that the impairments are across domains of grammar, including the components of syntax, morphology, and phonology. The impairment in processing capacity is also predicted by the PDH, because evidence indicates that the brain structures that underlie the procedural system also are responsible for important aspects of timing and rapid temporal processing (Ullman and Pierpont 2005).

2.3 Research hypothesis

As discussed previously, although the grammar-deficit hypotheses have been quite successful in explaining many facets of the grammatical impairment prevalent in children with SLI, these hypotheses are also problematic to some extent. Firstly, few of those hypotheses can account for the full range of linguistic deficits exhibited in the RC acquisition, either within a given language or cross-linguistically (Leonard 1996). Moreover, such hypotheses positing only grammatical deficits cannot account for the non-linguistic weaknesses observed in children with SLI. As reviewed in 2.2.2, there are many researchers positing that the deficits in children with SLI lie in the general processing capacities. However, as noted by Ullman and Pierpont (2005), the processing accounts are also somewhat problematic. One of the most important issues typically raised by its opponents is related to the actual empirical coverage of the accounts. For example, some researchers have argued that theses hypotheses cannot easily explain certain types of linguistic impairments observed in children with SLI (Ullman and Pierpont 2005).

Based on the above observations, in this dissertation, we will accept the central claim of PHD, namely the deficit in SLI lies in both the representational and processing level. The hypothesis of this dissertation is formulated in (21).

(21) Hypothesis of the dissertation

The deficit in children with SLI lies at both the representational and processing levels.

As mentioned above, some scholars found that the deficits in children with SLI lie in specific linguistic principles (Rice, Wexler, and Cleave 1995; van der Lely 2004), whereas other researchers claimed that the deficit is a non-linguistic processing deficit in nature (Bishop 1992; Leonard, McGregor, and Allen, 1992; Norbury, Bishop, and Briscoe 2001)or the dysfunction of phonological working memory (Archibald and Gathercole 2007; Montgomery 1995). These accounts can capture some specific deficits of the empirical studies, but none of them can account for the disparate impaired functions of children with SLI easily.

Our hypothesis overlaps with the perspective that argues for a grammar-specific deficit because it also asserts that grammar itself in children with SLI is directly affected. However, our hypothesis differs from this view in that it acknowledges that the impairments manifest themselves not only in all domains of grammar but also in lexical retrieval and non-linguistic aspects.

Our hypothesis also bears resemblance to the processing-deficit hypotheses because it asserts that the processing capacities, including those of working memory and rapid temporal processing, are affected by non-linguistic deficits. However, it diverges from this view in that it holds that these impairments might result from an underlying dysfunction in procedural memory system, which is not restricted to the processing deficit, but has a causal relation with other impairments, including grammar, lexical retrieval and motor functions, following Ullman and Pierpont (2005).

In a word, unlike the main classes of competing explanatory hypotheses for SLI, which attribute the impairment uniquely to the grammatical deficit or the processing deficit, our hypothesis might cover all the linguistic and non-linguistic impairments exhibited in children with SLI.

Additionally, there is substantial disagreement with respect to the nature and locus of the representational impairment in children with SLI. In this dissertation, we propose a novel representational account aiming at a better explanation of the grammatical deficit. The hypothesis is dubbed as Edge Feature Underspecification Hypothesis (EFUH for short), as formulated in (22).

(22) Edge Feature Underspecification Hypothesis

The representational deficit in children with SLI is caused by the edge feature underspecification, which will in turn result in RM effect and errors related to the functional category.

In the following parts of this chapter, we will discuss EFUH in detail. In 2.3.1, we will discuss the central claim of this hypothesis. In 2.3.2, we will elaborate on the main reasons for assuming the hypothesis. And finally, we will specify what the specific predictions of EFUH are.

2.3.1 The edge feature underspecification hypothesis

Based on the above discussions, we found that neither of the representational accounts can accommodate all the linguistic features of children with SLI exhibited in the acquisition of RCs. In this subsection, we will put forward a novel hypothesis, namely EFUH, attempting to account for the deficits of children with SLI in acquiring RCs.

2.3.1.1 The Edge feature in RCs

In 2.1 we have reviewed studies on syntax of Mandarin RCs and concluded that head-raising is involved in the derivation of Mandarin RCs. Now we will elaborate on the question what feature drives the derivation of RCs. Reinhart (1998) argued that syntactic movement takes place only to satisfy some interface requirement. Rizzi (2006) further divided the interface into two types: the syntax-morphology interface, which is internal to the narrow computational system and the external interface with semantics, as in the case of left-peripheral A' movement. The examples in (23) all involve A' movement. In these sentences, there are two interpretations for the moved element [D book]: the first is the patient of the verb *read*, the second is related to the semantics, i.e. Interrogative, Topic and Focus.

(23) a. Which book should you read <which book>?

    b. This book, you should read <this book >.

    c. THIS BOOK you should read <this book>, (rather than something else).

(Rizzi 2006: 100)

Rizzi (2006) proposed that natural languages express this duality of interpretive properties by resorting to the syntactic movement. Firstly, elements are merged in a semantically selected position, where they are assigned thematic properties. Subsequently, they can be remerged in a position dedicated to scope-discourse semantics, where they get the semantic interpretation. Scope/discourse positions require Spec-head agreement with respect to features of the relevant class: Q, Top, Foc, R, etc. for Questions, Topic, Focus, Relatives, etc. Such features are also known as Edge features, which refer to features at the edge of the nominal, verbal and clausal domain.[1] Thus, in the version of generative grammar adopted here, movement operations are derived through feature matching between a probe and a goal in its c-command domain. In the example in (24) below, a C head endowed with an uninterpretable Edge-feature (R) search through its c-command domain and attracts the closest element bearing an interpretable Edge-feature (R).

(24) $[_{CP} [_{IP} t_i$ qin baba$]_C$ De xiaopengyou$_i]$

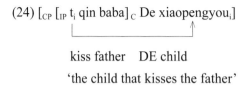

        kiss father   DE child

        'the child that kisses the father'

---

[1] The Edge feature was first proposed by Chomsky (2008) in explaining *wh*-movement. Chomsky (2008) has suggested that *wh*-movement is driven by an Edge Feature (= EF) on C which attracts an appropriate type of constituent to move to the edge of CP to become the specifier of C.

According to the essential notions and operations of the Minimalist Program (Chomsky 1995, 2000, 2001, 2004, 2008), movement operation is defined as: Agree + determine what is going to be moved with the features (i.e. Pied-piping of a lexical item) + Merge (Pan 2016: 81). Accordingly, the EF attached to the Probe (C) is uninterpretable and unvalued, whereas the EF on the goal is interpretable and valued. The Goal that bears valued EF will provide the EF attached to the Probe with a value through the operation of Agree.

At this juncture, we know that it is the EF of the probe that drives the syntactic movement in RCs. Therefore, we venture to propose that all the errors prevalent in children with SLI in the acquisition of RCs are relevant to the EF. The main reason for assuming the hypothesis is that it enables a natural explanation of all the representational deficits with RC acquisition in children with SLI. This hypothesis is intended to replace the more problematic generalizations such as those discussed in 2.2.1. In 2.3.2, we will elaborate on additional reasons for EFUH.

2.3.1.2   Deficits in Edge Features in children with SLI

EFUH is modeled on the Feature Underspecification Hypothesis (FUH), which was proposed by Grillo (2005, 2008:49, 2009) to account for comprehension deficits with non-canonical sentences in agrammatic aphasics. Grillo proposed that the comprehension deficits in this population stems from the fact that they cannot represent the scope-discourse features at the edge of the nominal, verbal and clausal domain. Many theories accounting for SLI have been borrowed from the studies of aphasics (eg. Friedmann and Novogrodsky 2004) .[1] Thus we tentatively develop our hypothesis on the basis of FUH.

The problems of children with SLI with EFs are notorious, which naturally leads to the conclusion that the locus of the deficits in children with SLI is in the EFs. Syntactic studies following the cartographic approach assume that the

---

[1]   In the history of SLI studies, the term of developmental aphasia has been employed to refer to SLI, which suggests that SLI and aphasia might share many similarities.

structural representation of the clause is organized in three different types of layers, as represented in (25).

(25) [CP Discourse-linked features [IP Inflectional/agreement features
[VP thematic features]]]

(Grillo 2008: 50)

The first is the lexical layer, encoding the basic relations between a predicate and its arguments. On top of the lexical layer are several functional heads responsible for the assignment of argumental features and the Tense and Aspectual heads. The third layer is the left periphery or edge of the clause, which hosts discourse-linked features (see Belletti 2004; Cinque 1999, 2002; Pollock 1989; Rizzi 1997 and much related work).

There is substantial evidence indicating that children with SLI exhibit difficulties with sentences, in which the discourse-linked features drives the derivation, such as Relatives (Håkansson and Hansson 2000; Schuele and Nicholls 2000), *Wh*-questions (van der Lely and Battell 2003), Topicalization constructions (van der Lely and Harris 1990; Yu 2016), Passives (van der Lely 1996).[1] The existing studies point to the generalization that features associated with the left periphery of the clause (the edge of the clause) is problematic for children with SLI. If the assumption that the locus of the deficit of SLI is in the syntax-discourse interface is on the right track, the problems observed in children with SLI in acquiring all the above constructions can be reducible to a common underlying deficit. It would certainly be advantageous to account for a set of seemingly unrelated problems with a single and unified explanation.

The assumption that the impairment of SLI is related to the features of the functional category is not fresh. Gopnik's (1990) Feature Blindness hypothesis (FBH) posits that developmental dysphasia can be reduced to a deficit in marking

---

[1] Gehrke and Grillo (2008) proposed that in passive constructions, a stative subevent of a structurally complex event is moved to a discourse-related position at the edge of the verb phrase.

a specific class of linguistic features.[1] The author further maintains that the impairments typical of developmental dysphasia result from a grammar, which is devoid of syntactico-semantic features. Gopnik (1990) presents data of a case study, showing that in this population there is no feature marking on number, gender, animacy, mass/count, proper name, person, tense, or aspect and that, as a consequence, a wide range of different surface manifestations concerning such features are compromised. In a similar vein, some researchers argue that the locus of the deficit in children with SLI is in non-interpretable features of functional categories (Mastropavlou and Tsimpli 2011; Tsimpli 2001; Tsimpli and Stavrakaki 1999). Functional categories involving any non-interpretable features are predicted to be impaired. Here, SLI is not caused by a maturational delay, but because children with SLI have not yet acquired features that do not have a semantic interpretation.

However, such theories are not exempt from problems. One criticism that has been levied against this account concerns the cross-linguistic differences. For example, many researchers have found that tense is not affected by SLI in some languages as much as in others (Clahsen, Bartke, and Gollner 1997; Clahsen and Dalalakis 1999; de Villiers 2003; Dromi, Leonard, and Blass 2003; Mastropavlou 2006; Tsimpli and Stavrakaki 1999). The second criticism against this theory is that the theory posits that the syntactico-semantic features are absent from the grammar of this population. One of the empirical consequences of this claim is that a wide range of surface manifestations controlled by such features are absent from the grammar of children with SLI. This prediction is in conflict with the fact that there are considerable variations concerning the language disruption in this population. For example, Leonard (1995) found that all the 10 English-speaking preschool children with SLI in his study showed evidence for using functional words (articles; determiners; pronominal possessive forms, etc), suggesting that functional categories are present in the grammar of these children and the differences are in degree of use. In other words, children with SLI have been found to use elements associated with functional categories with lower

---

[1] Developmental dysphasia is another term for SLI.

percentages in obligatory contexts.

Our hypothesis differs from FBH in two ways. Firstly, we postulate that the impairment in children with SLI results from the underspecification of edge features, which are claimed to be problematic in many typologically different languages. For example, relatives have been reported to be difficult to perceive and produce for children with SLI in English (Frizelle and Fletcher 2014; Schuele and Dykes 2005; Schuele and Nicholls 2000; Schuele and Tolberrt 2001), Hebrew (Friedmann and Novogrodsky 2004; Novogrodsky and Friedmann 2006), Danish (Jensen de López *et al.* 2014), Swedish (Håkansson and Hansson 2000), Italian (Contemori and Garraffa 2010), Greek (Stavrakaki 2001; 2002). It seems that the deficits concerning the edge features are universal and exist widely in the population of SLI. Our hypothesis is not formulated on the basis of linguistic evidence from a single language; thereby cross-linguistic variation might not constitute a serious challenge to it.

Secondly, we posit that the deficit of SLI results from the underspecification of edge features, but not the blindness of the features. According to the Gopnik (1990), the blindness of features will result in the impairment both "in the morphological form of the feature-marked word and constraints among items in the sentence that must have the same feature marking." It is natural to infer that according to this theory, the grammar of the children with SLI is devoid of all morphological form of the feature-marked words and the grammatical rules governing the feature marking. For example, Stavrakaki (2002) postulates that syntactic knowledge in children with SLI is altogether impaired. Following Paradis and Gopnik (1997) (cited from Stavrakaki 2002), Stavrakaki maintains that children with SLI follow a deviant pattern of linguistic development. Precisely, individuals with SLI use controlled processes to construct an utterance, whereas the children without language disorder employ the autonomous processes to generate sentences.

On the contrary, our hypothesis assumes that the underspecification of features does not necessarily mean the absence of the grammatical rules governing the feature marking. Our proposal is that the underspecification of edge features will result in the poor performances in the acquisition of the relevant constructions.

Our hypothesis can accommodate the variation, because the underspecification is not equal to being absent and null.[①] The prediction of our hypothesis is that the production and comprehension of RCs will be difficult but not impossible for children with SLI. Different degrees of underspecification could give rise to different patterns of disruption and impairment. Our hypothesis is well-grounded on empirical studies. For example, Adani, Stegenwallner-Schütz, Haendler, and Zukowski (2016) found that the *wh*-movement is not absent in the children with SLI. They examined the production of RCs in German-speaking children with SLI (4;7-10;11) and found that young children with SLI encounter substantial difficulty when producing RCs in general and their performance is poorer even than children matched to their language age. They arrived at the conclusion that although *Wh*-movement is hard for children with SLI, they did show some ability of producing adult-like embedded sentences derived by *Wh*-movement, which is at odds with the hypothesis that the *Wh*-movement is absent in children with SLI.

In summary, we maintain that the deficit in children with SLI results from the underspecification of EFs and that the underspecification varies in degree. The first advantage of our hypothesis is that variation in severity in this population can be accounted for by this hypothesis. The second advantage is that our hypothesis can provide a single and unified explanation for a set of seemingly unrelated problems.

2.3.2 Why the edge Features

In this subsection, we will elaborate on the question why the underspecification in children with SLI is targeted on edge features. There are two reasons for this phenomenon. The first one is that the edge features, which belong to the interface feature, are problematic for language learners, especially for those with language impairment. Secondly, the underspecification of EFs is possibly a processing

---

① According to Radford, Atkinson, Britain, Clahsen, and Spencer (2009: 361), the underspecification of features on functional categories means that functional category will be null where children have no suitable overt lexical item which can fill the relevant slot. One of the consequences of this underspecification is the omission of functional words.

derived deficit, i.e. it results from limited processing capacity.

2.3.2.1 The problematic discourse-syntax interface features

It is well established that the edge features, which belong to the interface feature, are problematic for language learners, especially those with language disorder. Garraffa and Grillo (2008) posit that underspecification of the aphasias follows a particular order: the deficits are more likely to be targeted on the representation of features that are accessed later in the derivation. As shown in (25), the structural representation of the clause is organized in three different types of layers, the EFs (Discourse-linked features) are hosted in the CP layer, which is the highest in the hierarchy. It is acknowledged that the representation of the higher functional field of the syntactic tree is hard to access for the population with language disorder (cf. Friedmann and Grodzinsky's Tree Pruning Hypothesis 1997). We can therefore expect that the representation of the syntax-discourse interface features in children with SLI will also be compromised.

In effect, the acquisition of the interface features are claimed to be problematic even for normal language learning, such as advanced second language acquisition (cf. Sorace and Filiaci's Interface Hypothesis 2006), and the bilingual first language acquisition (Sorace, 2011). According to Interface Hypothesis, the learners' knowledge of structures, in which an interface between syntax and other cognitive systems is involved, is more likely to be compromised. In other words, those structures are less likely to be acquired completely than other structures. The acquisition of such structures is characterized as optionality and instability. The difficulty is reducible to the fact that the syntax-discourse interface is a higher level of language use, requiring the integration of knowledge of syntax and pragmatics. When the language learners' syntactic knowledge is not fully developed, the syntax-pragmatics interface might constitute an area of weakness. For example, Hulk and Müller (2000) pointed out that young bilingual children, who have not fully acquired the C-domain, exhibited protracted delays in the structure involving syntax–discourse interface.

Given the fact that the acquisition of structures involving an interface between syntax and discourse poses challenges for normal language learners, we have good reason to expect that such interface features will also be problematic for children with SLI. The reason behind this assumption is that children with SLI have exhibited severe weakness in the area of syntax. It follows naturally that the underdeveloped syntactic capacity will result in the difficulties in coping with the syntax-discourse interface, which requires the integration of the component of syntax and pragmatics.

2.3.2.2 A processing derived deficit

The underspecification of EFs in children with SLI is possibly a processing derived deficit, resulting from limited processing capacity (cf. Grillo 2008). It has long been established that children with SLI have deficits in processing capacities. In the processing literature, researchers addressed the issue of limited processing capacity from two different perspectives: space or time (Kail and Salthouse 1994; Roediger 1980). The limitation of space refers to insufficient workspace. In other words, there is a restriction on the size of the computational region of memory. The limitation of time refers to the time restrictions dictated by the rate at which information can be processed. It is assumed that the information will be susceptible to faster decay or interference from the subsequent information, if it is not processed quickly enough (Leonard 2014a: 271).

The processing literature in children with SLI fell into two categories: studies investigating speed of processing and those examining processing capacity, primarily in terms of working memory. Accumulating evidence pointed out that the children with SLI exhibit limitations not only in processing time (processing speed) but also in processing space (working memory). Anderson (1965) has provided the earliest evidence available that children with SLI have slower processing speed than their same-age peers in a picture naming tasks (cited from Leonard 2014a). Since then, numerous studies have indicated that children with SLI have relatively slow response times (RTs) in various tasks (Kohnert, Windsor, and Miller 2004). Similarly, some studies directed at the storage components in children with SLI have found weaknesses in children with SLI in storage of visual-spatial information (Bavin, Wilson, Maruff, and Sleeman 2005; Hoffman and Gillam 2004).

In non-word repetition tasks, children with SLI were reported to exhibit weaknesses in the storage of phonological information (Estes, Evans, and Else-Quest 2007; Kamhi and Catts 1986). In addition, children with SLI performed well below the level of their typically developing age-matched peers on the task of Listening Span (e.g. Archibald and Gathercole 2006; Weismer, Evans and Hesketh 1999), which examines not only the storage component but also the mental manipulation of working memory. As noted by Leonard (2014a: 282), the processing speed and working memory are intimately connected—faster speed can ensure faster rehearsal, which in turn can give rise to more information retained in storage component. We can safely infer that slower speed can negatively affect the storage component and in turn result in the bad performances in processing information. It is often possible to discuss the same task in terms of some combination of them. For example, it might be assumed that certain types of lexical items are located deeper in memory stores than others. Retrieving these items, then, might require greater expenditure of energy and more time.

Based on the evidence that children with SLI exhibited slow processing rate in a wide range of linguistic and nonlinguistic tasks, Kail (1994) proposed the "Generalized Slowing" Hypothesis, which maintains that children with SLI should respond more slowly than TD children of the same age across all processing tasks. Given the fact that these children exhibited limitations in both the processing speed and working memory, it is not a large leap in logic to assume that they may encounter difficulties in processing syntactic information, which are accessed later in the derivation, namely the EFs. Following Grillo (2008) and Kolk (1998) among many others, we assume that there is an impoverishment of the featural make-up of syntactic elements in children with SLI because of the processing limitations in terms of space and time. Following Grillo (2008: 53), we assume that not all morphosyntactic features are activated at the same time; in other words, different types of features are accessed at different time points in the processing of a sentence. The syntax-discourse features (Edge Features) are accessed later in representation. It follows naturally that the slowed-down syntactic processing capacity will have severe effects on the representation of Edge Features, which belong to a higher type in the hierarchy in (25). To summarize, we maintain that the representation of features accessed later in the derivation is more likely to be compromised as a consequence of a reduction of syntactic system, which in turn will result in the slower activation of discourse/ contextual information.

The idea that processing limitations will possibly give rise to the disruption in the syntactic processing is not fresh in literature of language impairment and acquisition. According to Kolk (1998), the linguistic and processing approaches could well merge into an integrated theory of aphasic disorder of syntax. Such a theory should specify the question in what aspects of sentence processing capacity demand is higher than what is available to a particular group of patients. In the studies directed at the bilingual acquisition, Sorace (2011) maintained that "bilinguals are less efficient than monolinguals because their knowledge of or access to computational constraints within the language module is less detailed and/or less automatic than in monolinguals." One reason why bilingual speakers may be less efficient at processing structures at the syntax–pragmatics interface is that syntactic processing is less automatic for them, which may be due to less developed knowledge representations or to less efficient access to these representations.

According to our hypothesis, limitations in internal syntactic processing capacities are supposed to underlie the difficulties in language acquisition in children with SLI. The less efficient processing of syntactic information will result in the desynchronization of parts of the syntactic tree (cf. Kolk 1998). The synchrony will be more difficult to achieve in processing the complex phrase structures, in which the edge features are involved. Summing up, we assumed that children with SLI cannot represent the full array of morphosyntactic features associated with syntactic categories, especially the scope-discourse features, i.e. Edge features. The underspecification results from the reduction of the syntactic processing capacities in children with SLI.

2.3.3 Predictions of the hypothesis

In this subsection, we will discuss what are the predictions of our hypothesis in terms of the RC acquisition in mandarin-speaking children with SLI. We will present the predictions of our hypothesis concerning the three research questions, namely the sequence of RC acquisition, possible compromised performances of children with SLI and the nature of the possible deficits in this population.

2.3.3.1 The advantage of subject over object RC or the reversed pattern

The first research question that we will address in this dissertation is whether Mandarin children with SLI differ in the acquisition of subject RCs and object RCs. Regarding this question, our prediction is consistent with that of RM. As discussed earlier, according to RM (Rizzi, 1990, 2004), in the configuration of (19) (repeated in 26), a local relation between X and Y cannot hold if the intervener Z is similar in structure to X.

(26) a. X . . . Z . . . Y

b. Z intervenes between X and Y if and only if Z c-commands Y and Z does not c-command X

(Rizzi 2004: 225).

Friedmann *et al.* (2009) proposed that a dependency between a head and the trace is harder to establish for young children if there is a qualified element intervening between them. Following Chen (2007: 183), we assume that syntactic movement is involved in the derivation of Mandarin RCs. Precisely, the relative head is attracted by the head of CP bearing the feature [+Rel] to move to the specifier of CP. The subject and object RCs are shown in configuration (2) (repeated in 27). In (27a), there is no intervener between the target (specifier of CP) and the origin (place of extraction). In (27b), the subject NP is an intervener between the target and the origin. According to Friedmann *et al.* (2009), in the adult grammar, an intervener can block the establishment of a local A' relation only when the intervener and the attractor share the same featural specification, as in configuration (28), in which the relationship between the target and the intervener is identity.

(27) a. Subject RC

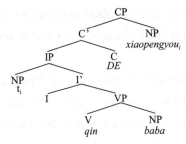

b. Object RC

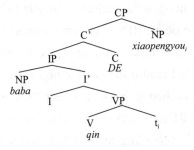

(28) +A . . . . +A . . . . <+A> *

If the attractor is more richly specified in formal features than the intervener, there is no blocking effect, as in configuration (29), in which the relationship between the target and the intervener is inclusion.

(29) +A+B . . . . +A . . . . . <+A+B> ok

The object RC is a case of (29), shown in (30). In this case, the attractor has a [+Rel] feature, which makes the attractor more richly specified. Thus in adult system, (30) is ruled in.

(30) [+Rel, +NP] . . . . . . [+NP] . . . . . <+Rel, +NP>

However, if EFUH is on the right track, SLI children's grammar cannot specify [Rel] feature in (30). It naturally follows that the relationship between the intervener and the target is identity, which will be ruled out by RM. Therefore, in such case, there will be intervention effect in object RCs for children with SLI, and such effect will in turn cause the subject RCs over object RCs advantage in acquisition.[1]

Note that this prediction can be borne out only in tasks in which the syntactic factors outweigh the processing factors[2], such as the elicitation production task and priming production task in chapter 3, and the character-picture verification task in chapter 4.

In 3.5 and 4.4, in addition to the subject and object RC, we will also examine the acquisition of passive object RCs in children with SLI. According to Belletti (2009), in object production tasks, children opted for the passive object RCs instead of the object RCs because the passive object RC does not involve RM effect. According to this theory, passive object RCs are easier for children to produce than object RCs. However, this conclusion seems run counter to the prediction of EFUH. According to EFUH, children with SLI will counter difficulties in acquiring structures, in which EFs are involved. Gehrke and Grillo (2008) assume that in passive constructions, a stative subevent of a structurally complex event is moved to a discourse-related position at the edge of the verb phrase. If this analysis is on the right track, we can safely predict that children with SLI will also have troubles in acquiring passive object RCs, even though such structure does not involve RM effect. Therefore, the prediction might be that children with SLI will have similar performances in acquiring object RCs and passive object RCs.

In 3.6, we will investigate the production of irreversible RCs in children with SLI. A sentence is reversible if, when the major noun exchange positions, the sentence still make sense (e.g. *"the boy that the father is kissing"* is reversible,

---

[1] Note that the reason of the blocking effect in children with SLI is different from that in young TD children. We will turn to this point in the subsequent chapters.

[2] Mandarin is a typologically rare language with the SVO main clause and the head-final RCs. The surface word order and structural factors pull in opposing directions: the surface word order favors the object over subject RC advantage, and whereas the structural factor favors the opposite.

but "*the flower that the boy is kissing*" is not.). We predict that the production of irreversible RCs will be improved compared to that of reversible RCs. Jensen de López *et al.* (2014) found that children with SLI were likely to commit the errors of thematic reversal in object RC production due to the RM effect. We predict that children with SLI will not commit such errors because in the irreversible object RC task, the agents of the event are always animate, the patients (themes) are always inanimate. We propose that the mismatch in terms of the animacy of the NPs involved in RCs will reduce the difficulty confronting the children when producing object RCs. According to PDH and EFUH, children with SLI are compromised in terms of the representation of EFs, but their ability to perceive the semantic features are preserved. Hence, we predict that in the irreversible conditions, no asymmetry of subject and object RCs can be detected because the feature of animacy might facilitate the production of object RCs.

2.3.3.2 The compromised performance of children with SLI

In this part we will elaborate on the question what are the possible non-target responses of children with SLI in different tasks, as predicted by the EFUH.

Firstly, EFUH assumes that the children with SLI cannot represent the full array of morphosyntactic features, especially the EFs. The natural consequence of this statement is that children with SLI cannot specify the EF on the head of CP, namely C. It follows that in the production tasks children with SLI will commit errors concerning the complementizer omission, which is quite prevalent in preschool children with SLI in other languages (Schuele and Dykes 2005; Schuele and Tolberrt 2001 among many others).

Secondly, children with SLI might be insensitive to the sematic function of RCs. As pointed by Quine (1960) (quoted in Heim & Kratzer 1998), restrictive RCs are noun modifiers, and they have the same function as the adjectival phrases and prepositional phrases. The restrictive RC functions to restrict the referent set given in the context. For instance, in order to interpret the RC in (31) the listener must understand that the embedded clause is a noun modifier and that the noun, in other words, being modified is the NP, '*boy*'. Kuno (1976) and MacWhinney (2005) also assumed that RCs must be about the referent of their head noun.

The RC describes a property of the head of the relative clause. In other words, it attributes a particular property to the head noun.

(31) the boy [that the father is kissing]

If children with SLI are insensitive to the EF on C, namely [Rel], they will encounter troubles in recognizing the fact that restrictive RCs are noun modifiers. One of the possible consequences is that children with SLI cannot differentiate SVO sentences and RCs. Therefore, in production tasks, in which they are required to produce RCs, they probably produce SVO sentences instead of the target structure. The second possible result is that in the character-picture verification tasks, in which they are obliged to point to the picture corresponding to the relative head, they possibly point to the picture corresponding to the NP in the embedded clause.

Thirdly, EFUH might predict that there is no priming effect in the case of object RC production in 3.7. Syntactic priming paradigm appears to be very telling about syntactic representation of speakers. It is firmly established that speakers have a tendency to reuse the structure, which they have produced or comprehended, in the subsequent production. According to EFUH, children with SLI might exhibit deficiency in reusing the structure they have heard, because children with SLI cannot specify the [Rel] feature, which means they are not fully equipped with the representation of RCs. In object RC priming production, we predict that there is no priming effect, because of the poor representation of RCs and RM effect; but in the case of subject RC production, the priming effect might be detected given the fact that in the latter no RM effect is involved.

2.3.3.3 Representational or processing deficits or Both
The hypothesis of this dissertation is that the deficits of children with SLI lie at both the representational and processing levels.

Firstly, the representation deficits will mainly exhibit in the production tasks in chapter 3 and comprehension tasks in chapter 4. Although the findings are mixed in the literature, based on the latest studies in RC acquisition in mandarin

TD children (Hu *et al.*, 2015; Hu *et al.*, 2016), we assume that the tasks in chapter 3 and chapter 4 are designed mainly to assess the structural factors in the acquisition of RCs and whereas the processing factor does not play very important role.[①] This assumption is based on the evidence that in such tasks a preference for subject RCs persists as children grow older (Hu *et al.*, 2016), which indicates that in such tasks the structural intervention count more than the linear intervention. If the above analysis is on the right track, according to our hypothesis, it is highly plausible that children with SLI might encounter greater difficulties compared to their TD peers.

Secondly, the processing deficits might manifest themselves in the repetition task adopted in chapter 5. Some researchers claimed that in addition to the syntactic representation, the sentence repetition also involves numerous cognitive processes: phonological STM to keep short-term phonological information, the Central Executive to deal with the exchange of information between STM and LTM, and phonological output processes (Rummer 2004; Willis and Gathercole 2001 among many others). In other words, in sentence repetition tasks, both the structural (syntactic factors) and the linear intervention (processing factors) will exert influence on the performance of children with SLI. The possible consequence of this scenario is that in sentence repetition tasks no asymmetry of the subject and object RC will emerge, because the syntactic and processing factors pulling in the opposing directions. Children with SLI will exhibit severe deficiency in sentence repetition because we assume that these children are impaired both in the representational and the processing level.

In addition, we predict that the children with SLI performed significantly better in imitating subject RCs with the adjective in the relative clause than subject RCs with adjective in the main clause, as the case of (32).

---

① In chapter 4, we will refine the comprehension tasks used in Hu *et al.* (2016). However, we still assume that in the new task, the subject RC advantage will exhibit.

(32) a. SRCM

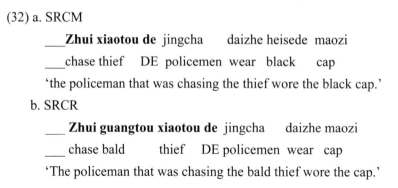

    ____**Zhui xiaotou de** jingcha   daizhe heisede maozi

    ____chase thief DE policemen wear black   cap

    'the policeman that was chasing the thief wore the black cap.'

    b. SRCR

    ____**Zhui guangtou xiaotou de** jingcha   daizhe maozi

    ____chase bald   thief DE policemen wear cap

    'The policeman that was chasing the bald thief wore the cap.'

The length of the dependency between the head and the gap is greater in subject RC with adjectives placed within the RC (SRCR) than in subject RC with adjectives placed in the main clause (SRCM). We anticipate that when the processing burden increased, the performance of children with SLI will be more likely to be negatively affected.

2.4 Summary

In summary, this chapter firstly presents the syntactic analysis of Mandarin RCs, which leads us to the conclusion that syntactic movement is involved in the derivation of Mandarin RCs. Then we proceed to discuss the competing theories accounting for SLI. In terms of the nature of the impairment in children with SLI, we hypothesize that what underlies the malfunctioning of grammar in children with SLI are the representational and processing limitations. We further propose EFUH to account for the representational deficits in such population, according to which the representational deficits are caused by their inability to fully specify the scope-discourse features. Finally, we discuss the predictions of our proposal. In the remaining parts of this dissertation, we will present the results of 5 experiments to testify the hypothesis proposed in 2.3.

Chapter 3
The Production of Relative Clauses

This chapter explores the production of subject, object and passive object RCs in children with SLI and their typically developing peers, by using a structured elicitation task and a priming production task, with the purpose of detecting linguistic characteristics of SLI children's production of RCs. By conducting the first experiment, we aim to answer the following specific questions: (I) whether there is asymmetry in the production of subject RCs, object RCs and passive object RCs in children with SLI; (II) whether children with SLI exhibit the wildly assumed syntactic impairment in the production of RCs; (III) whether the production of RCs by children with SLI is affected by the animacy of the NPs involved in RCs. The priming production experiment is designed with the goal of investigating whether the children with SLI possess the intact syntactic representation of subject and object RCs.

The chapter is organized as follows. In section 3.1 we briefly review previous studies on the production of RCs in TD children in languages with head-initial RCs. Section 3.2 is a review of studies on Mandarin-speaking TD children's production of RCs. Section 3.3 is devoted to the introduction to the production studies in children with SLI across languages. Section 3.4 and section 3.5 present the elicitation production experiment and the priming production experiment respectively. In section 3.6, we give a summary of this chapter.

3.1 Previous studies on the production of head-initial RCs in TD children

To have a better understanding of RC production in children with SLI, a brief review of the studies on the acquisition of RCs in typically developing children is indispensable. The focus of the literature in this aspect is whether there is a primacy for subject RCs or object RCs in production. Studies on languages with head-initial RCs unanimously found a preference for subject RCs in production, whereas the results on the languages with head-final RCs are mixed: a primacy for subject RCs, object RCs or no asymmetry in the production.

Extensive researches on many languages with head-initial RCs indicate that children produce subject RCs with greater easiness than object RCs, such as Arabic (Botwinik, Bshara, and Armon-Lotem 2015); Catalan (Gavarró, Cunill, Muntané, and Reguant 2012); English (Zukowski 2009); French (Labelle 1990, 1996); German (Adani, Shem, and Zukowski 2013); Hebrew (Arnon 2010); Italian (Contemori and Belletti 2014; Guasti and Cardinaletti 2003); Portuguese (Costa, Lobo, and Silva 2011); Spanish (Pérez-Leroux 1995). Many hypotheses have been put forward to account for the findings, which can be roughly divided into the usage-based approach, the processing account based on linear word order and the account based on syntactic structures.

Unfortunately, the three accounts usually converge in languages with head-initial RCs, all pointing to the subject over object RCs advantage. Under the multifactorial usage-based account for RCs acquisition (Brandt, Kidd, Lieven and Tomasello, 2009; Diessel 2009; Diessel and Tomasello 2000, 2005), children acquire RCs in a piecemeal fashion by producing new RC constructions based on simpler constructions, which have been deeply entrenched in their mind. As the examples in (1) illustrate, subject RCs maintain the canonical subject–verb–object order of English, whereas object RCs has an object-subject-verb order, which is different from the basic word order in English. According to Kidd, Brandt, Lieven, and Tomasello (2007) among many others, it is the canonical word order in subject RCs that facilitates the production of this kind of RCs.

(1) a. Subject RC

the boy [that _ is kissing the mother]

SUBJ   VERB OBJ

b. Object RC

the boy [that the mother is kissing _]

OBJ   SUBJ   VERB

To be more precise, the advantage of subject over object RCs is a result of a learning process. By expanding simple clause structure, e.g. the SVO structure, the English-speaking children may produce subject RCs earlier and with substantial easiness. Arnon (2010) also supported the assumption, suggesting that mastery of RCs emerges as a gradual expansion of uses, consistent with usage-based account.

The processing based accounts also correctly predict the subject over object RC advantage in English. Goodall (2004: 102) and Hawkins (2004: 173) proposed that filler–gap dependency places a burden on processing resources. Under this account, in order to integrate a filler (the relative head in the case of RCs) into the sentence, the human processor needs to maintain the filler in the working memory until the processor encounters a gap, at which time the dependency between the filler and gap can be established. As a consequence, RCs with greater linear distance between a gap and its filler are harder to process, because such RCs tax more on the processor. The account quantifies the distance between the gap and filler in terms of the number of elements with discourse referents (essentially, nouns and verbs) occurring between the filler and the gap (Gibson 1998, 2000; Grodner and Gibson 2005: 252; Lewis, Vasishth, and Van Dyke 2006; Warren and Gibson 2002). The establishment of filler–gap dependency in the subject RC (eg. *the boy [that _ is kissing the mother]*) is less demanding for working memory, because no element with discourse referents intervenes between the filler and the gap. On the contrary, there are two elements with discourse referents (the NP *the mother* and the verb *kiss*) intervening between the filler and the gap in the object RC (eg. *the boy [that the mother is kissing_]*).

Nevertheless, the subject-object RC asymmetry can also be accounted for by the theories capitalizing on structural distance between the filler and gap. O'Grady (1997) suggested that the structures with more deeply embedded gaps are more complex and thus more difficult for children to produce. More precisely, a structure's complexity increases with the number of XP categories intervening between the gap and the filler (O'Grady 1997: 136). In the same way, Hawkins (1999) proposed the Minimal Distance Hypothesis measuring the filler-gap distance based on the structural hierarchy. The distance between the filler and the gap is determined by counting all the nonterminal nodes (the phrasal nodes (XP) and the intermediate nodes (X0) in the tree structure) and terminal nodes (lexical items) in the hierarchical structure of the clause. Such theories correctly predict that children encounter substantial difficulties in producing English object RCs, in which the gap is more deeply embedded, as illustrated in (2). The object RC is more complex, in which three XP categories (CP, IP, and VP) intervene between the gap and the head noun (2a) whereas in the subject RC two XP categories (CP and IP) occur between the gap and the head noun (2b).

To summarize, the three accounts all correctly predict the fact that the acquisition of subject RCs is easier than the object RCs. The first two accounts capitalize on the surface word order, and the last one on the hierarchical structure. The surface word order and structural factors cannot be teased apart in head-initial RCs (e.g. English RCs).

(2) The structures of a subject-gapped RC and an object-gapped RC in English

a. Subject RC

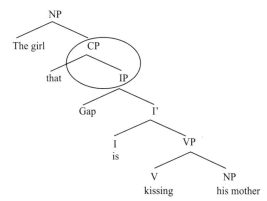

b. Object RC

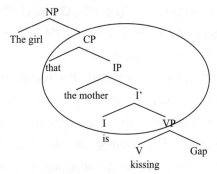

Mandarin is a typologically rare language with the SVO main clause and the head-final RCs, as in (3). The surface word order and structural factors pull in opposing directions: the surface word order favors the object over subject RC advantage whereas the structural factor favors the opposite.

(3) Subject RC: __Qin mama   de nühai

                kiss the mother DE girl

                'the girl that kissed the mother'

  Object RC: Mama   qin __ de nühai

                the mother kiss   DE girl

                'the girl that the mother kissed'

Thus the investigation of the acquisition of RCs in Mandarin is helpful to tease apart the various factors affecting RC acquisition.

3.2 Previous studies on the production of Mandarin RCs in TD children

The results of the production studies of Mandarin RCs in TD children are inconsistent. In total, there are three views on the sequence of RC acquisition in TD children: subject RC advantage, object RC advantage and no asymmetry.

  Some researchers found that there is a subject RC preference in the production by Mandarin-speaking children, which is in consistent with the pattern found in the languages with head-initial RCs. Cheng (1995) observed a subject RC preference (subject RCs vs. object RCs: 42% vs. 19%) by examining 27 children (aged 3;6 to 6;3) using an elicitation task.

In an elicited production task modeled after Hamburger and Crain (1982), Hsu *et al.* (2009) tested 23 Mandarin-speaking children (with a mean age of 4;8) and 10 adults. They manipulated both the gap position and the embedding. The subject-object RC occurs as free-standing DPs, left-branching RCs and center-embedded RCs. They found a subject RC advantage both in children and adults (children: subject RC 83.5% vs. object RC 38.9%; adults: subject RC 95% vs. object RC 79.5%) irrespective of the embedding context of the RC. In addition, the children also made more grammatical errors when they tried to produce an object RC than a subject RC. Interestingly, Hsu, *et al.* (2009: 350) attributed the poorer performance on object RCs to the fact that object RCs are less natural (in terms of a speaker's goals) as restrictive modifiers than subject RCs based on the Hypothesis of Message Planning Stage (Zukowski 2009).

Hu *et al.* (2015) explored the production of RCs in 125 Mandarin children (aged 3 years to 8 years, 11 months) and 20 adults by using a preference choice task modeled after Novogrodsky and Friedmann (2006). The results revealed a subject RC advantage in children of all ages and in adults. When attempting object RCs, the 8-year-old children and adults tended to transform the target object RCs into subject RCs through passives. They explained the results under the RM approach: in subject RCs, no structural intervener occurs between the relative head and its trace, whereas in object RCs, a qualified element (the embedded subject) intervenes between the relative head and its trace.

However, some materials were arguably problematic in both Hsu *et al.* (2009) and Hu *et al.* (2015). For example, as noted by Hu *et al.* (2015), in Hsu *et al.* (2009) some of the verbs in the subject RC could be used intransitively (e.g. *nage nühai zai huahua/changge* 'That girl is drawing /singing'), whereas in the object RC elicitation task, all verbs are transitive. The intransitive verb and the transitive verb are different in terms of the theta role assignment. For the intransitive verb, only one argument is required and the agent theta role is assigned. In contrast, for the transitive verb, two arguments are required and the agent or patient theta roles are assigned to them respectively. Thus, the verb choice in the subject RC condition may inflate the subject RC advantage.

In subject RC elicitation tasks of Hu *et al.* (2015), three of the verbs (*he* "drink," *chi* "eat," *mai* "buy") are problematic, in that semantically reversible RCs might not be built by using them. For example, one target subject RC is *he kele/ niunai de xiaopengyou 'the child that is drinking cola/milk'*, in which the head noun is animate and the embedded NP is inanimate, and thus the sentence **he xiaopengyou de kele/niunai '*the cola/milk that is drinking child'* is semantically awkward. The irreversible RCs are less demanding to children because they can be interpreted without the need for full recourse to syntactic processing (Kim and O'Grady 2016). However, all the stimuli in the object RC elicitation task are semantically reversible. Thus the choice of the verb in this study may also broaden the gap between the subject and object RC production.

On the other hand, some other studies revealed that there is no asymmetry in the production of subject and object RCs by Mandarin-speaking children. By using an elicitation task, Su (2004) tested two groups of children (older group: age range from 5;7 to 6;5; younger group: age range from 5;0 to 5;6) and 31 adults by adopting the elicitation method in Hamburger and Crain (1982) with minor revision. She manipulated the gap positions: the stimuli include subject, object, object of preposition, clausal complement and unextractable subject RCs. The results revealed that there is no difference between the subject and object RCs production in both the two groups of children and in adults (e.g., subject vs. object RCs: 84% vs. 88% for children aged 5;0–5;6; subject vs. object RCs: 78% vs. 83% for children aged 5;7–6;5; subject vs. object RCs: 98% vs. 89% for adults).

Similarly, Yang (2013: 262-268) examined 180 Mandarin-speaking children's production of RCs (aged from 3-6), by using a priming paradigm. Yang did not find any preference (subject vs. object RCs: 86% vs. 90%) in RC production. In addition, she found that in the object RC production, no child transformed the target object RC into passive object RCs. She also tested the production of passive object RC (e.g. *bei gou dale de zhu*, '*the pig that was beaten by the dog*') and found that the accuracy of the production is 63%, and that children tended to transform passive object RCs into object RCs (19%). To summarize, she found that the children aged 3 have had a mastery of RCs and there is no preference for the subject RC or object RC. She held that the absence of subject-object RC asymmetry can be accounted for under the assumption that in the derivation of Mandarin RC no syntactic movement is involved (Yang 2013: 145-146).

As noted by Hu *et al.* (2015), Su's results should be considered with some caution because the results were obtained with two trials for each sentence type. According to Thornton (1996), in elicited production task at least four tokens of each sentence type should be used. In Yang (2013), both the subject RC and object RC are not semantically reversible (The target subject RC: *xiang chi gutou de nazhi gou, 'the dog that wants to eat bone'*; the target object RC: *houjiejie zhai de tao 'the peach that the monkey plucked'*), which may reduce the difficulty of production (Kim and O'Grady 2016), and consequently may lead to the absence of the asymmetry. Interestingly, in the passive object RC tasks, the stimulus is a reversible sentence (*bei gou dale de zhu, 'the pig that was beaten by the dog'*), and thus it is hard to compare the performance of the children in the object RC and passive object RC conditions.

There are other studies suggesting that the object RCs are acquired earlier and with more easiness. Wang (2009) examined the production of RCs in 815 Mandarin-speaking children ranging in age from 2; 1 to 6; 11 by adopting a priming paradigm. The results revealed that there is a preference for the production of object RCs (subject RC vs. object RC: 54% vs. 77%).[1] She interpreted the results under the Canonical Word Order Hypothesis (Diessel and Tomasello 2005) and the processing account, which is based on the surface word order instead of the syntactic structure (Gibson 2000).

By analyzing the spontaneous production of four Mandarin-speaking children (aged 0;11–3;5), Chen and Shirai (2015) found a primacy of object RC over subject RC in early child speech.[2] The same pattern was also detected in the children's first ten RCs. They proposed that the fact

---

[1] The results are performances of all the age groups combined in the production task.
[2] The children produced 34 (18.6%) subject RCs and 78 (61.5%) object RCs.

that Mandarin object relatives exhibit the same typical SVO word order as canonical simple sentences may facilitate the production of object RCs. In addition, they also proposed that the object RC advantage may be influenced by the factor of input, because they found that in the parental speech during the interaction between the children and their caregivers, object RCs (58.6%) are more frequent than subject RCs (17.6%).

There are also problems in these two studies. In the study of Wang (2009), the target RCs are also not semantically reversible (e.g. the target subject RC: *xia baidan de ji* 'the hen that laid the white egg'; the target object RCs: *baiji xia de dan* 'the egg that the white hen laid'). As discussed above, processing such RCs does not need full recourse to syntactic processing, and thus the results from the study must be considered with some caution. Chen and Shirai's (2015) study revealed the early trajectory of Chinese children's RC production, but it also has some limitations. Firstly, the object RC advantage was established merely on a numerical basis. Secondly, the object RC primacy found in the parental speech is at odds with the results from several corpus studies, which consistently showed a subject RC advantage in Mandarin-speaking adults (Hsiao and Gibson 2003; Pu 2007; Wu, Kaiser, and Andersen 2010). Thirdly, as noted by Hsu (2014), the majority of the object RCs reported in Chen and Shirai (2015) are associated with the so-called 'cleft construction', which typically puts a particular constituent into focus, as illustrated in (4).

(4) (shi) baba   mai de
    (SHI) father buy DE
    'It is father who bought (the book)'

Children tended to omit SHI and drop the head, which accounts for the overwhelmingly large number of the headless, object-gap, cleft related RCs found in the corpus. She found that when such structures were removed, the object RC advantage disappears.

Also crucial is the fact that in all the previous studies reviewed above, there is limitation in the coding system. According to Liu (2005), the demonstrative can function as the relative marker in Mandarin, as in (5).

(5) Tiyi   wa jing ne gongren zao   zou   le.

     propose dig well that worker   early leave ASP

     'The worker that proposed to dig a well had left long before'

                                         (Liu 2005: 5)

There are two reasons supporting the assumption. The first one is that with the presence the demonstrative, the relative marker DE can be omitted, as shown in (5). The second one is that when the demonstrative is deleted, the relative marker must be added, otherwise, the sentence is ungrammatical, as shown in (6).

(6) *Tiyi   wa jing gongren zao   zou   le.

     propose dig well worker   early leave ASP

If we accept the assumption, we must consider the RCs with demonstrative as the relative marker as the target responses in coding the responses from children. Neglecting the fact that Mandarin RC has various markers will lead to the underestimation of the RC production in children, because the RCs with demonstrative as relative marker may be regarded as simple SVO sentences (*mama qin nage nühai* 'the girl that the mother kissed') or uninterpretable sentences (*qin mama nage nühai* 'the girl that kissed the mother').

     To summarize, because the design and the coding system in the above-mentioned studies are problematic, it is difficult to interpret the results. We can hardly evaluate which preference holds in Mandarin RC acquisition and which is the source of difficulty in the production of RCs. In current study, we will test the production of RCs by using the semantically reversible RCs on the one hand and by using the non-reversible RCs on the other hand, which may provide a more comprehensive understanding of the production of RCs in Mandarin-speaking children with SLI and their TD peers. In coding the responses, we will take the RCs with demonstrative as relative marker into consideration.

3.3 Previous studies on the production of RCs in children with SLI

Being similar to the studies on the RC acquisition in TD children, the studies on children with SLI also concentrate on the question which RC is preferred in the production. Additionally, the researchers showed even greater interests in the question what factors contribute to the decayed ability in producing RCs in children with SLI, namely, the relationship between the syntactic impairment in children with SLI and the production of RCs.

There is now a fair amount of data amassed cross-linguistically on RC production by children with SLI. The extensive studies have shown that SLI children have severe deficits in the production of RCs across typologically different languages, e.g. English (Frizelle and Fletcher 2014; Schuele and Dykes 2005; Schuele and Nicholls 2000; Schuele and Tolberrt 2001; van der Lely and Battell 2003), Swedish (Håkansson and Hansson 2000), Hebrew (Novogrodsky and Friedmann 2006), Italian (Contemori and Garraffa 2010; Garraffa *et al.* 2015), Greek (Stavrakaki 2001, 2002), Danish (Jensen de López *et al.* 2014) and German (Adani et al. 2016), Mandarin (Yu *et al.* 2017). At the same time, Subject RCs have been shown to be easier to be produced compared to object RCs (Jensen de López *et al.* 2014 among many others). Nevertheless, the results of the previous studies vary depending on the children's age (Novogrodsky & Friedmann, 2006) and on different elicitation tasks.

In section 3.3.1 we review the studies on the younger children with SLI, which indicated that the nature of the deficit lies in the syntactic movement. Section 3.3.2 is devoted to the introduction of studies on school children with SLI, which attribute the deficiency to the thematic role assignment. In section 3.3.3, we introduce the studies assuming that the deficit of children with SLI is due to the implicit learning mechanisms. In section 3.3.4 and 3.3.5 we present the studies concerning the animacy of the NPs in RCs and the acquisition of passive object RCs respectively.

3.3.1 Impairment in syntactic movement

Extensive studies consistently showed that the decayed performance in producing

RCs by children with SLI lies in the impairment in syntactic component. Some researchers maintained that the syntactic movement is inaccessible to the children with SLI whereas others held that although the syntactic movement is hard, the children with SLI do possess the knowledge of syntactic movement.

For the preschool SLI children, the difficulty in relative clause production was attributed to the inability to project a fully-fledged clause structure. Severe impairment in elicitation tasks and in spontaneous speech has been shown in the studies investigating the production of RCs in SLI children at this age. The impairment manifests itself in omission of the obligatory complementizer and in a 2-year delay in the onset of relative clause production (Håkansson and Hansson 2000; Schuele and Dykes 2005; Schuele and Nicholls 2000; Schuele and Tolberrt, 2001).

Håkansson and Hansson (2000) proposed that children with SLI have difficulties with functional categories, including complementizers, and thus have problems projecting a fully-fledged CP, owing to structural deficiencies. It should be noted that the elicitation method used by Håkansson and Hansson (2000) seems to be problematic. Firstly, the method cannot tease apart the RC structural deficiencies and the possible impairment in negation, both of which may contribute to the impairment of RC production because the target responses are RCs with negation. The elicitation task is a sentence completion task in which there are two sets of pictures, one showing a person carrying out an action, the other showing the person, who was not carrying out the action. The experimenter first named all the pictures to the child, and then a lotto game was played, where RCs with negation were elicited from the child, as shown in (7).

(7) Prompt: 'Look, here is the girl who sleeps, and here is the girl …?'
Expected answer: 'who doesn't sleep'

The second problem is that the target sentences are irreversible, which does not need full syntactic processing (Kim and O'Grady 2016).

Schuele and Nicholls (2000) reported that when the English-speaking children with SLI begin to attempt subject RCs, they tend to omit the obligatory complementizers in subject RCs, suggesting the existence of linguistic vulnerabilities and children with SLI produce subject RCs as late as 5 or 6 years of age, indicating the delayed emergence of RCs. They maintained that the findings are consistent with Leonard's (1995) functional category deficits account, which posits that the omission of the obligatory complementizer indicates that there is a weaker representation of functional category in the underlying grammar of children with SLI.

Using a toy elicitation task (Crain and Thornton 1998), Stavrakaki (2002) tested Greek-speaking children with SLI (aged 5 to 9) and a group of Language Age (LA) matched controls. The overall accuracy of the RC production in TD children was much greater than that in children with SLI (children with SLI: 4.165%; TD children: 70.83%). The avoidance strategies employed by the children with SLI include simple active sentences (63.33%), coordinated structures (7.5%) and RCs with missing heads (12.5%). Stavrakaki argued that RCs with missing heads show that co-indexation between the variable bound by the operator in [Spec, CP] and the head cannot be established, which in turn proves the absence of the operator movement.[①] Stavrakaki also maintained that the decayed performance in RC production indicates that the knowledge of relativization is absent in the grammar of the children with SLI, though they produced few target-like RCs. At last, Stavrakaki concluded that the deficit in SLI seems to be due to the impaired syntactic component of language, more precisely, the severe impairment in non-interpretable features of grammar.

Contemori and Garraffa (2010) adapted Novogrodsky and Friedmann's (2006) tasks to test 4 Italian-speaking children with SLI (aged from 4;5 to 5;9), 4 typically developing children age-matched to children with SLI and 4 younger typically developing children (aged from 3;7-3;11). They found that the children with SLI performed more poorly than the control participants in both subject RCs

---

① As discussed in chapter 2, movement analysis has another version, which is called operator movement analysis in the literature. According to this analysis, the head of the RC is base-generated, and the RC adjoins to the head. The co-indexation between the head and the trace inside the RC is achieved by the relative operator, which can bridge the gap between them.

and object RCs elicitation tasks. Children with SLI either gave "no response" or produced a declarative clause in most of the cases where a RC was targeted. In addition, they concluded that the most widely attested atypical production in children with SLI was the omission of the complementizer, suggesting the absence of a CP layer in the grammar of children with SLI.

To summarize, all the studies mentioned above converge in terms of the source of difficulty of RC production, all pointing to the absence of the relativization in the narrow syntax of children with SLI.

However, Adani et al. (2016) proposed that the Wh-movement is not absent in the children with SLI. They examined the production of RCs in German-speaking children with SLI (4;7-10;11) and found that young children with SLI encounter substantial difficulty when producing RCs in general and their performance is poorer even than children matched to their language age. When they failed to produce the target structure, they adopted the avoidance strategies consisting of simple declarative sentences, nominal and prepositional phrases produced in isolation. The first conclusion of the study is that the results are in contrast to those accounts attributing the source of the impairment in SLI uniquely to slower processing (Deevy and Leonard 2004) or limited cognitive capacities (Leonard, Deevy, Fey, and Bredin-Oja 2013). This is because they found that children with SLI do not have a stronger disadvantage with center-embedding than TD children, which is widely assumed to be more demanding of the processing capacity than the right-branching RCs (Warren and Gibson 2002). The second conclusion is that *Wh*-movement is hard for children with SLI. They found that the children with SLI did show some ability of producing adult-like embedded sentences derived by *Wh*-movement, which is at odds with the hypothesis that the *Wh*-movement is absent in children with SLI. van der Lely and Battell (2003) proposed the RDDR claiming that the *Wh*-movement is incorrectly marked in the grammar of children with SLI as being optional. Adani et al. found that the children with SLI produced very few instances of filled object gap structures (RCs with in situ heads), which is in contrast to the view that the *Wh*-movement is optional in children with SLI.

Yu *et al.* (2017) examined the production of subject and object RCs by 12 Mandarin-speaking children with SLI (age range: 3;11-6;1) and 12 age-matched children (age range: 3;11-6;1) and 12 language-matched younger children (age range: 2;11-4;11) by using a preference task following Novogrodsky and Friedmann (2006). The results revealed a subject RCs (33.3%) over object RCs (15.3%) advantage in production by SLI children. The results also suggested that the production of RCs by SLI children is severely impaired compared to the TD children.[1] When the children with SLI failed to produce the target structures, the most frequently adopted avoidance strategies consist of declarative sentences and sentence fragments. They held that there is a deficiency in the grammatical knowledge concerning the functional category Complementizer. The SLI children's grammar cannot specify edge feature (EF) of the moved element, which may give rise to RM effect, and in turn cause the subject RCs over object RCs primacy in production.

3.3.2 Impairment in thematic assignment

Studies that examined the production of RCs in school children with SLI found that the deficit in SLI children should be attributed to thematic role assignment to moved constituents, and not to a structural deficit in projecting the fully-fledged structure (Jensen de López *et al.* 2014; Novogrodsky and Friedmann 2006).

Novogrodsky and Friedmann (2006) examined the production of RCs in 18 Hebrew-speaking children with SLI (aged 9;3–14;6) and 28 typically developing children (aged 7;5–11;0) by using a preference task and a picture description task. They found that the TD children produced both the subject and object RCs without difficulty (subject RC: 98%; object RC: 94%) whereas the children with SLI performed significantly more poorly than the control participants on both subject and object RCs and on both tasks (subject RCs: 94%, object RC: 60% in preference tasks; subject RCs: 83%, object RC: 46% in preference tasks). The children with SLI had greater accuracy on subject RCs than object RCs in both tasks. The most frequently errors detected in children with SLI in the object RC elicitation tasks consisted of thematic errors and reduction of

---

[1] The age-matched children's accuracy on subject RCs is 87.5%, and on object RCs is 86.1%. The language-matched children's accuracy on subject RCs is 63.8%, and on object RCs is 37.5%.

thematic roles (18%), no movement from object position (8%), and production of simple sentences instead of a RC (14%). Most importantly, they did not find that complementizer was omitted by children with SLI. They summarized that the deficit in children with SLI is mainly related to thematic role assignment to moved constituents, but not to a structural deficit in embedding.

Jensen de López *et al.* (2014) explored the production of subject and object RCs in 18 Danish-speaking children with SLI (aged from 5;0 to 8;4), 18 age-matched controls (aged from 5;0 to 8;2) and 9 language-matched controls (aged from 4;0 to 6;5) by adopting the preference task (Novogrodsky and Friedmann 2006). They found that the children with SLI had poorer performance than the two groups of TD children in producing the subject RC (age-matched TD=90.8%, language-matched TD=94.9%, SLI=58.6 %), whereas no significant difference was detected among the three groups in producing the object RCs (age-matched TD=64.1%, language-matched TD=63.9%, SLI=45.5 %). A preference for subject RCs was found in all the three groups. They attributed the subject-object RC asymmetry in production to the RM effect involved in the object RC following Friedmann *et al.* (2009). In the subject RC task, the predominant error type in the children with SLI was simple sentences. In the object RC task, children with SLI opted for simple sentences, passive object relatives, fragments and role reversals. No difference was found among the three groups of children in omitting the obligatory complementizer. Following Novogrodsky and Friedmann (2006), they held that the deficiency in children with SLI is related to the assignment of thematic roles, instead of the structural make-up of RCs.

Although both the two studies found that the deficiency in children with SLI is caused by the impaired ability of thematic role assignment, such inability is not restricted to the SLI children because the TD children also committed the errors of thematic role reversal, which suggests that the impaired thematic role assignment ability does not reflect the qualitative difference between children with SLI and TD children.

3.3.3 Impaired implicit learning mechanisms

Garraffa *et al.* (2015) adopted a structural priming paradigm to investigate the production of subject RCs in 19 Italian pre-school children with SLI (age range: 51-75 months) and 19 age-matched typically-developing children controls (age range: 50-77 months). Although TD children tended to produce more subject RCs in both the baseline condition (SLI children 14%; TD children 29%), and the priming condition (SLI children 35%; TD children 64%), the effect of priming was equivalent in both groups. In addition, they found that children with SLI showed a smaller cumulative priming effect than TD children. Based on the findings, they proposed that the language deficit in SLI children should be attributed to impaired implicit learning mechanisms and SLI children possess an abstract representation of subject RCs, which facilitates the production.

However, Marinellie (2006) found that it is difficult to prime RCs even in 7-8-year-old children with SLI and proposed that the absence of the priming effect might be due to the syntactic dependency involved in RCs and the low frequency of RCs in input. Also important is the fact that in the priming paradigm Garraffa *et al.* (2015) only examined the production of subject RCs, which is widely assumed to be easier than object RCs. Thus, the question whether children with SLI have abstract representation of RCs remains unclear.

3.3.4 The Animacy of the Relative Clause head

The role of animacy of the RC head in the production of RC is controversial. In a sentence imitation task, Kidd *et al.* (2007) found English-speaking TD children (aged 3;1-4;9) performed in object RCs with inanimate head and animate embedded NP as well as in subject RCs, suggesting that such object RCs are acquired with more easiness than object RCs with the animate head and the animate embedded NP. In an adult processing experiment, Mak, Vonk, and Schriefers (2002) and Traxler, Morris, and Seely (2002) found that the object RC with an animate head and inanimate embedded NP is easier to be processed than object RCs with two animate NPs.

Zhou, Zheng, Shu, and Yang (2010) manipulated the animacy of the NPs in the RC in the comprehension study of 2 Mandarin-speaking aphasic patients. They found that the patients were at chance level when they comprehended the object RCs with two animate NPs (e.g. *nanren qin de nüren daizhe maozi, 'the women that the man kissed wore a hat'*), whereas when they comprehended the object RCs with animate head NP and inanimate embedded NP (e.g. *gou yao de piqiu shi heise de 'the ball that the dog bit was black'*), they reached the ceiling level. It seems natural to arrive at the conclusion that the difficulty associated with object RCs is greatly reduced when the two NPs in the RCs are not matched in animacy.

However, Jensen de López *et al.* (2014) found that the animacy of the RC head did not affect the production of RCs in the Danish-speaking SLI children. Following Novogrodsky and Friedmann (2006), they adopted a preference choice task to assess SLI children's production of RCs, in which there were reversible sentences and irreversible sentences on per condition (subject RC and object RC). In the reversible sentences, both the participants of the events encoded by the RC were always animate, whereas in the irreversible ones, one participant is animate, while the other one is inanimate. The results suggested that the participants did not differ in terms of the accuracy in producing reversible and irreversible RCs

It is not clear whether the animay of the NPs in RC head will affect the production of RC in Mandarin-speaking preschooler with SLI because no previous study has been conducted to address this question.

3.3.5 The passive object relative clause

The previous studies have found that in the object RC elicitation task, children opted passive object RCs for object RCs. For example, Novogrodsky and Friedmann (2006) found that the Hebrew children with SLI avoid producing object RCs, sometimes by replacing target object RCs (e.g. *'The father that the boy catches.'*) with the passive object RCs (e.g. *Ha-aba she-nitfas al-yedei ha-yeled 'The father that is caught by the boy.'*). Jensen de López *et al.* (2014) had a similar finding in the production of RCs by Danish-speaking TD children.

Contemori and Belletti (2014) tested the production and comprehension of RCs in Italian-speaking typically developing children and adults. In the elicitation task (adapted from Novogrodsky and Friedmann 2006), they found an overwhelming preference for passive object RCs in the adults' productions (90%) when an object RC is targeted and the older children also opted for passive object

RCs in the tasks (5-year-old children: 11.3%; 6-year-old children: 13%; 7-year-old children: 4.7%; 8-year-old children: 46.3%). In the comprehension task, the participants were required to comprehend the object RC and the passive object RC. A primacy for the passive object RC was detected: the children aged from 6;5 to 8;10 were more accurate on passive object RCs than object RCs. They proposed that passive object RCs are easier to produce and comprehend than object RCs because the former does not involve RM effect.

However, the proposal seems to be implausible for two reasons. Firstly, the proposal cannot account for the adults' preference for passive object RC in the object RC task. According to Friedmann *et al.* (2009), the adults, with mature grammar system, are not subject to RM restriction. In other words, the overwhelming preference for passive object RCs in adults seemingly has no causal relationship with the RM effect. Contemori and Belletti (2014) also mentioned that they cannot provide a reasonable account for the phenomenon. Secondly, according to the Derivational Complexity Hypothesis (DCH for short) (Jakubowicz 2005, 2011), children prefer more economical derivations and young children tend to avoid using movement because it is costly.[1] Thus passive object RCs will be more difficult to produce than object RCs given the fact that the former involves one additional movement: the passivation. In a word, the two theories pull in opposite directions.

Although many studies revealed that children opted for passive object RCs, instead of the target structures in the object RC elicitation task, to date, no study has compared the production of passive object RCs and object RCs directly. We wonder whether the opposite pattern will be found in the production of passive object RCs, in other words, whether in the task the children will opt object RCs for passive object RCs. Therefore, in this chapter, we will compare the production of the two RCs directly by using the preference task (Novogrodsky and Friedmann 2006). If there was a passive object RCs over object RCs advantage, we can conclude RM effect will override the derivational cost.

---

[1] In 3.5.4, we will give the definition of DCH.

Based on the previous studies reviewed in the preceding subsections, by using the preference task in the experiment 1, the specific research questions that we will address are (1) whether or not Mandarin children with SLI differ in the production of subject RCs and object RCs; (2) whether or not Mandarin children with SLI differ from their TD peers in their production of RCs (3) whether or not children with SLI adopt same avoidance strategies as TD children, when they failed to produce the target relative clause? (4) whether or not Mandarin children with SLI differ in the production of object RCs and passive object RCs? (5) whether or not the animacy of the RC head affects the performance of RC production in children with SLI? By using the priming tasks in the experiment 2, we seek to examine whether or not the Mandarin children with SLI possess the intact syntactic representation of RCs.

To date, no other studies have examined the production of subject and object RCs in Mandarin children with SLI by using the preference task and the priming paradigm at the same time. This study might enable us to ascertain the nature of the deficits seen in the children with SLI. We also compare the production of the object RC and passive object RC in the study for the first time in the studies on children with SLI, which might further provide empirical evidence for the RM effect. In addition, we employ similar methodologies used in previous studies on children with SLI (Garraffa *et al.* 2015; Novogrodsky and Friedmann 2006), this continuity in the methodology permits to investigate whether or not the difficulty reported for other languages manifests itself in Mandarin-speaking children with SLI.

3.4 Condition 1 of experiment 1: Reversible subject and object RCs

3.4.1 Method

3.4.1.1 The Participants

Forty-seven monolingual Mandarin-speaking children aged from 3; 2 to 5; 11 participated in the present study. Both the children with SLI (N=17) and the TD children (N=30) were recruited from normal kindergartens. For all children, we asked their parents to give their consent for the participation.

The children with SLI ranged in age from 4;5 to 6;0 (Mean=62.4 months; SD=6.04 months). The recruitment of the children with SLI consisted of the screening phase and the testing phase. In the screening phase, the parents and kindergarten teachers were required to fill in *the Specific Language Impairment Checklist for Pre-school Mandarin-speaking Children* (He 2010) to select the suspected subjects. In this stage, those children who do not meet the criteria for SLI as described in Leonard (2014a: 14-15) were excluded. To be more precise, all the subjects have normal hearing ability, no otitis media with effusion, no neurological dysfunction history, no structural anomalies, no oral motor dysfunction or no symptoms of impaired reciprocal social interaction.

In the testing stage, the language ability of suspected children with SLI was tested by two standardized tests. The first test is *Peabody Picture Vocabulary Test– Revised Chinese Version 1990* (PPVT-R for short), which can be employed to test the Mandarin-speaking children's receptive vocabulary with considerable validity and high reliability (Sang and Miao 1990). The second one is *Diagnostic Receptive and Expressive Assessment of Mandarin* (DREAM for short) (Ning, Liu, and de Villiers 2014), which is assumed to hold promise as a diagnostic test of Mandarin language impairment for children aged 2;6 to 7;11 (Liu *et al.* 2017).

The children's performance IQ was assessed with Wechsler Preschool and Primary Scale of Intelligence-- Fourth Edition (WPPSI-IV (CN) for short), which was developed by King-May Psychology Assessment, Ltd. with the license by NCS Person, Inc.. All children had non-verbal IQ within the normal range and got at least two of the six scores in the language tests (DREAM and PPVT-R) at least 1 SD below the mean for their age, among which the scores on the syntax in DREAM are at least 1 SD below the mean for their age. All the children with SLI in the current study exhibit the syntactic impairment, and thus we name them as children with Syntactic-SLI (SLI for short subsequently). Table 3-1 presents the scores of children with SLI on PPVT (R) and DREAM.

Table 3-1   **Detailed profiles of the three groups of children**

Child ID	Sex	Month	PPVT (R)	DREAM				
				Total	REC	EXP	SEM	SYN
SLI 1	female	68.2	22	76	76	71	81	70
SLI 2	male	63.5	27	85	86	80	86	85
SLI 3	female	57.4	15	75	76	68	81	69
SLI 4	male	63.2	25	83	84	78	86	79
SLI 5	male	59.5	32	90	94	69	98	81
SLI 6	female	61.7	26	89	92	75	98	80
SLI 7	male	66.6	22	85	86	81	86	85
SLI 8	female	59.9	22	93	96	77	102	83
SLI 9	male	59.5	19	91	95	74	97	85
SLI 10	male	56.1	17	82	84	70	89	74
SLI 11	male	68.3	56	83	86	67	91	75
SLI 12	male	68.7	21	95	100	71	106	84
SLI 13	male	50.5	11	78	80	73	76	81
SLI 14	male	68.3	20	83	86	71	93	74
SLI 15	male	71.1	58	84	87	65	93	75
SLI 16	female	63.8	24	81	84	68	88	75
SLI 17	female	52.5	16	93	97	76	104	83

Child ID	Sex	Month	DREAM				
			Total	REC	EXP	SEM	SYN
TDA 1	female	68.5	109	109	109	114	105
TDA 2	male	63.4	121	121	118	124	118
TDA 3	female	56.4	119	119	118	133	104
TDA 4	male	62.7	106	110	85	116	96
TDA 5	male	59.9	120	121	113	132	108
TDA 6	male	65.5	115	117	102	123	107
TDA 7	male	65.9	110	110	110	117	103
TDA 8	female	60.9	115	118	102	130	100
TDA 9	male	66.8	113	117	95	125	102
TDA 10	female	60	121	122	118	127	116

Continued

Child ID	Sex	Month	DREAM				
			Total	REC	EXP	SEM	SYN
TDA 11	male	60.1	101	100	106	94	107
TDA 12	male	56.3	126	128	117	136	117
TDA 13	male	67.3	95	94	98	96	93
TDA 14	male	67.7	119	121	108	125	113
TDA 15	male	51.3	123	123	120	121	124

Child ID	Sex	Month	DREAM				
			Total	REC	EXP	SEM	SYN
TDY 1	female	51.2	119	120	117	129	109
TDY 2	male	45.8	120	119	123	126	114
TDY 3	female	38.5	131	134	112	141	120
TDY 4	male	45.4	127	129	119	137	117
TDY 5	male	42.5	125	127	116	133	118
TDY 6	male	47.6	116	116	116	123	109
TDY 7	male	49.2	125	126	124	140	111
TDY 8	female	44.6	132	134	124	136	129
TDY 9	male	49.6	131	132	121	137	124
TDY 10	female	42.4	126	127	123	125	127
TDY 11	male	40.6	131	135	112	142	120
TDY 12	male	39	131	133	117	138	124
TDY 13	male	50.5	106	106	108	107	105
TDY 14	male	49.5	125	126	122	133	117
TDY 15	male	38.8	122	124	112	127	116

Note. REC=Receptive; EXP=Expressive; SEM=Semantics; SYN=Syntax

With the purpose of answering question 1 of this chapter, we recruited two groups of TD children to participate in the experiment, which allows us to ascertain the possible discrepancy between the children with and without SLI. One control group of fifteen children (Age range: 4;3-5;8; Mean=62.1 months, SD=4.97 months) was selected to serve as TDA children. The remaining fifteen children were TDY children (Age range: 3;2-4;2; Mean: 45 months, SD: 4.5 months). A one-way ANOVA test showed that there is significant difference among the three groups in terms of age (F (2;46)=55.4, $p<.01$) and the post-hoc comparisons with Bonferroni correction shows that the TDA and SLI group do not differ in age (MD=0.27, p=.884>.05) and there is significant difference in age between the TDY and SLI group (MD=17.4, $p<.01$). Four children with SLI (SLI 14-SLI 17) did not fulfill the production tasks in experiment 1 and 2, the remaining children with SLI do not differ with TDA children in age (MD=-0.403, p=.832>.05) and the TDY children and the remaining SLI group differ in age (MD=16.76, $p<.01$).

The TDA and TDY group also received a standardized language test (DREAM) and their scores are within the normal range. All the TDA and TDY children are mentally and physically healthy and with normal language proficiency.

We examined whether there is difference between the children with SLI and TDA children in terms of the language proficiency, which we obtained from the results from DREAM[1]. The independent T-test revealed that there is significant difference between the children with SLI and the TDA children in total scores (17 children with SLI as a group T=-11.197, $p<.01$; 13 children with SLI as a group T=-10.031, $p<.01$) and in scores of syntax (17 children with SLI as a group T=-10.527, $p<.01$; 13 children with SLI as a group T=-10.07, $p<.01$) in DREAM.

We further examined whether there was any difference between the children with SLI and the TDA children in terms of the scores of working memory and the processing speed obtained from two subtests of WPPSI-IV (CN). The independent T-test revealed that there is significant difference between the two groups in processing speed (17 children with SLI as a group T=-3.594, p=.001<.05; 13 children with SLI as a group T=-2.722, p=.010<.05). No significant difference

---

[1] We have not examined the question whether there is difference between the children with SLI and TDY children in terms of the language proficiency, working memory and processing speed because the scores form DREAM and WPPSI-IV (CN) are standardized ones, which cannot be compared between children of different age.

was detected between the two groups in working memory (17 children with SLI as a group T=-1.159, p=.256<.05; 13 children with SLI as a group T=-1.052, p=.302>.05).

3.4.1.2 Materials for condition 1 (The reversible subject and object RCs)
We adopted a preference choice task to assess the production of RCs in Mandarin children following Novogrodsky and Friedmann (2006). The child was required to choose one s/he preferred between two options presented to them. The task was designed to ensure that the response would have to be formulated as a relative clause. The task consisted of twenty trials: half of them elicited subject RCs, the rest object RCs. All the targeted subject RCs and object RCs are reversible, in which the participants were always animate. The examples are given in (7).

(7) a. Reversible subject RCs

Experimenter: You liang-ge xiaopengyou, yi-ge xiaopengyou zai tui baba, yi-ge xiaopengyou zai tui mama. Ni xihuan na-ge xiaopengyou?

'There are two children. One child is pushing the father. The other is pushing the mother. Which child do you like?'

Target response: Wo xihuan tui baba\mama de xiaopengyou

'I like the child who is pushing the father\mother'

b. Reversible object RCs

Experimenter: You liang-ge xiaopengyou, baba zai tui yi-ge xiaopengyou, mama zai tui yi-ge xiaopengyou. Ni xihuan na-ge xiaopengyou?

'There are two children. The father is pushing one children. The mother is pushing the other children. Which child do you like?'

Target response: Wo xihuan baba/mama tui de xiaopengyou

'I like the child who the father/mother is pushing'

All the nouns and verbs used in the tasks are familiar to the children aged 4-6. To build up our stimuli, we used 10 transitive verbs, including *tui* 'push', *la* 'hold hands', *yao* 'bite' , *bao* 'hug', *ti* 'kick' , *zhua* 'scratch', *bei* 'carry on back', *qin* 'kiss', *zhuang* 'bump', and *zhui* 'chase'. A total of fifteen nouns were employed to depict the animate characters (*baba* 'father', *mama* 'mother', *didi* 'younger brother', *meimei* 'younger sister', *yeye* 'grandpa', *nainai* 'grandma' , *xiaomao* 'cat', *xiaogou* 'dog' , *xiaozhu* 'pig', *xiaoyang* 'sheep', *xiaoniu* 'calf' , *xiaolu* 'deer', *laohu* 'tiger' , *shizi* 'lion' , *xiaoxiong* 'bear'). Experimental items were randomized and presented in the same order to all children. All the test sentences were between nine and eleven words.

3.4.1.3 Procedures

Participants were tested in a quiet room in the kindergarten. They were examined individually in ten 30-minutes sessions. The relative clause task and many other tasks made up a large-scale study on Mandarin-speaking children with SLI. Only the tasks relevant for this study are reported in this dissertation. Before the experiment, there was one trail for practice to ensure that the participants understood the task. In the practice trial, the correct answer was presented to the participants, who failed to produce the target sentence. All the elicited sentences were audio-recorded and later transcribed based on the recordings. The coding was checked for agreement by two researchers.

3.4.1.4 Coding and Scoring

Various types of responses elicited were grouped into three categories: target RC responses, non-target RC responses, and other responses. The coding for the responses is exemplified in (8) to (17).

> (8) Target subject RC
> Tui   mama   de   xiaopengyou
> push mother DE   child
> 'the child who pushes the mother'

(9) Target object RC

    Mama tui   de xiaopengyou

    mother push DE child

    'the child that the mother pushes'

Sentences (8), (9) are the target responses for subject RCs, object RCs respectively. According to Liu (2005), the demonstrative can function as the relative marker. In consequence, sentences with demonstrative Na (that) as complementizer, as in (10), were also considered as target responses.

(10) Demonstrative as complementizer RC

    Tui   mama   na-ge   xiaopengyou

    push mother that CLA   child

    'the child who pushes the mother'

In addition, the headless RCs were also regarded as target responses, as exemplified in (11).

(11) Headless RCs

    Tui   mama de

    push mother DE

    ' (the child) who pushes the mother'

The second category of responses are called non-target RCs. In the object RC condition, the non-target RCs include passive object RCs (12), RCs with resumptive NPs (13), subject RCs with thematic role reversal (14), complementizer omission RCs (15). Although (15) is identical to a declarative sentence in terms of word order, we coded it as a complementizer omission RC. Because the experiment is designed to answer the question *Ni Xihan Nage Xiaopengyou*, '*which child do you like*', when the children started with *Wo Xihuan* 'I like', they intended to complete the sentence with an NP object. Thus, it is reasonable to believe that when the declarative sentences follow *Wo Xihuan* 'I like', they should be coded as a complementizer omission RC.

(12) Passive object RCs

　　Bei　Mama　tui　　de　　xiaopengyou

　　BEI　mother　push　DE　　child

　　'the child that is pushed by the mother'

(13) RCs with resumptive NPs

　　Xiaopengyou$_i$　zai　qin　mama　de　　xiaopengyou$_i$

　　Children　　　　Asp　kiss　mother　DE　that-classifier

　　'the child who is kissing the mother'

(14) Subject RCs with thematic role reversal[①]

　　Tui　　mama　de　xiaopengyou

　　push　mother　DE　child

　　'the child that pushed the mother.'

(15) Complementizer omission RC

　　mama　　tui　　(xiaopengyou)

　　mother　push　　(child)

　　' (the child) (that) pushed the mother'

The third kind of responses are named as other responses, which includes the simple sentence (16) and sentence fragment (17), which occurred across the two conditions.

(16) Simple sentences

　　Baba　tui　　yi-ge　　xiaopengyou

　　Father　push　one-CL　child

　　'The father pushed a child.'

---

①　The intended RC is the object RC in (9).

(17) Sentence fragment

Baba

Father

'the father'

3.4.2 Results

A total of 860 responses were elicited in condition 1. Half of the responses resulted from the condition of subject RCs, the rest from the object RCs elicitation task. We will present the target responses, the non-target RC responses and other responses from the three groups.

3.4.2.1 The analysis of the target responses

The results revealed a subject over object RCs advantage in production by SLI children as shown in the Table 3-2 and Figure 3-1. The percentages, raw scores, means and standard Deviation of target responses in each group are shown in Table 3-2.

Table 3-2   Percentage (%), raw scores (N), means (M) and standard
deviation (SD) of target responses in each group

Groups	Subject RCs				Object RCs			
	%	N	M	SD	%	N	M	SD
SLI	30	39/130	3.00	3.39	18	24/130	1.84	2.26
TDA	93	140/150	9.33	1.11	80	120/150	8.00	1.60
TDY	76	115/150	7.67	2.72	48	72/150	4.80	3.57

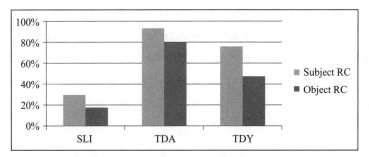

Figure 3-1 Production of subject RCs and object RCs in each group

Figure 3-1 shows the comparison of the production of target subject RCs and object RCs in the SLI group to that of the TDA and TDY groups. For all the three groups, subject RCs were more frequently produced than object RCs. For children with SLI, the accuracy on subject RC (30%) was greater than the object RC (18%). The same pattern is also found in TDY children: they produced more subject RCs (76%) than object RCs (48%). For TDA children, there was also difference in the performance on the subject RC (93%) and object RC (80%), although they were nearly at the ceiling level on both of the two conditions.

Our observation was partly confirmed by the statistical analysis by using SPSS 20.[①], as illustrated in table 3-3. The results of Wilcoxon Signed Ranks Test indicated that there is an asymmetry in SLI children's production of subject RCs and object RCs (z=-2.264, p=.024<.05). A similar asymmetry was also found in the TDY children (z=-2.944, p=.003<.05). For the TDA children, there is no significant difference (z=-1.918, p=.055>.05). Thus the answer to the first research question of this chapter is that the children with SLI exhibited a primacy for the subject RC in the elicitation production.

Table 3-3   **Wilcoxon Signed Ranks Test for production of the target
subject RC and object RC in the three groups**

Groups	SLI	TDA	TDY
Z	-2.264	-1.918	-2.944
Asymp.Sig.	.024	.055	.003

We turn to seeking the answer to the second research question: whether or not the children with SLI differed from the TD children in the production of RCs. As expected, there were differences in the production of target RCs in the three groups. The statistical data was summarized in table 3-4 and table 3-5. On the production of target subject RCs, SLI children's performance significantly differed from that of the TDA and TDY children (SLI vs. TDA: U=7.500, p<.01; SLI vs. TDY: U=7.500, p<.01). At the same time, there was also significant

---

① In this dissertation, all statistical analysis was conducted by using the SPSS 20. 0.

difference between the TDA and TDY children (U=62.000, p=.026<.05).

On the production of object RC, the TDA and the TDY children produced significantly more target RCs than the children with SLI (SLI vs. TDA: U=2.500, p<.01; SLI vs. TDY: U=46.000, p=.016<.05). There was also significant difference between the TDA and TDY children (U=55.500, p=.017<.05). To summarize, the children with SLI produced significantly less target subject and object RC than both the TDA and TDY children.

It is worth noting that the headless RCs account for a large proportion in the target responses by all the three groups, as shown in Table 3-6.

Table 3-4   **Mann Whitney U Test for production of the target subject RC in the three groups**

	SLI VS. TDA	SLI VS. TDY	TDA VS. TDY
Mann-Whitney U	7.500	7.500	62.000
Asymp. Sig.	.000	.000	.026

Table 3-5   **Mann Whitney U Test for production of the target object RC in the three groups**

	SLI VS. TDA	SLI VS. TDY	TDA VS. TDY
Mann-Whitney U	2.500	46.000	55.500
Asymp. Sig.	.000	.016	.017

Table 3-6   **Number (N), percentage (%) (Headless RCs/target RCs) of the headless RCs in each group**

Groups	Subject RCs			Object RCs	
	N	%		N	%
SLI	14/39	36%		13/24	54%
TDA	63/140	45%		26/113	23%
TDY	46/115	40%		39/72	54%

3.4.2.2 The analysis of the non-target RC responses

The analysis in 3.4.2.2 and 3.4.2.3 will provide the answer to the third question of this chapter. A total of 67 non-target RCs were produced in condition 1. In the subject RC elicitation task, there were 8 RCs with resumptive NPs. The rest 59 responses were produced in the object RC tasks. Among them, there were 34 subject RCs with thematic role reversal, 15 Passive object RCs, 8 Complementizer omission RCs and 2 RCs with resumptive NPs. A summary of the results were provided in Table 3-7. Given that the amount of non-target RCs was not abundant, we did not conduct any statistical analysis.

For SLI children, the two most frequently occurring non-target RCs were complementizer omission RCs and subject RCs with thematic role reversal. While for the TDA children, Passive object RCs and subject RCs with thematic role reversal were more produced than other non-target RCs. For TDY children, the subject RCs with thematic role reversal ranked first, and other responses were rarely produced.

Table 3-7   **Numbers (N), percentage (%) (non-target RCs/all responses) of the non-target RCs in each group**

Groups	RCs with thematic role reversal		Passive object RCs		Complementizer omission RCs	
	N	%	N	%	N	%
SLI	6/130	4.6%	1/130	0.7%	7/130	5.3%
TDA	9/150	6%	14/150	9.3%	1/150	0.6%
TDY	19/150	12.6%	0/150	0%	0/150	0%
Total	34/430	7.9%	15/430	3.4%	8/430	1.8%

Groups	Object RCs with Resumptive NP		Subject RCs with Resumptive NP	
	N	%	N	%
SLI	1/130	0.7%	7/130	5.3%
TDA	1/150	0.6%	1/150	0.6%
TDY	0/150	0%	0/150	0%
Total	2/430	0.4%	8/430	1.8%

3.4.2.3   The analysis of other responses

The experiment yielded 283 sentences, which belonged to other responses. Table

3-8 provides the number and percentages of other responses produced by all the three groups.

**Table 3-8   Numbers (N), percentage (%) (other responses/all responses)
of other responses in each group**

Groups	Subject RCs				Object RCs			
	Simple sentences		Fragment		Simple sentences		Fragment	
	N	%	N	%	N	%	N	%
SLI	18	14%	68	52%	19	15%	72	55%
TDA	5	3.3%	3	2%	2	1.3%	3	2%
TDY	22	14.6%	12	8%	20	13%	39	26%

Firstly in the subject RCs elicitation task, children with SLI produced much more fragments than that obtained from the TDA and TDY children (SLI vs. TDA: 52% vs. 2%; SLI vs. TDY: 52% vs 8%). The statistical analysis confirmed the observation, as shown in Table 3-9. Significant differences were detected both between the SLI children and TDA children (U=10.500, p<.01) and between them and the TDY children (U=21.000, p<.01). As shown in Table 3-10, there was no significant difference in the production of simple sentences between the SLI and TDA children (U=81.000, p=.357>.05), and between the children with SLI and TDY children (U=90.000, p=.701>.05).

**Table 3-9   Mann Whitney U Test for production of fragments
in subject RC tasks in the three groups**

	SLI VS. TDA	SLI VS. TDY
Mann-Whitney U	10.500	21.000
Asymp. Sig. (2-tailed)	.000	.000

**Table 3-10   Mann Whitney U Test for production of simple sentences
in subject RC tasks in the three groups**

	SLI VS. TDA	SLI VS. TDY
Mann-Whitney U	81.000	90.000
Asymp. Sig. (2-tailed)	.357	.701

Secondly in the context of object RCs, much more fragments were also obtained from the children with SLI than from other two groups (SLI vs. TDA: 55% vs. 2%; SLI vs. TDY: 55% vs 26%). As illustrated in Table 3-11, there were significant differences in children with SLI and TDA children (U=2.000, p<.01) and in children with SLI and TDY children (U=21.000, p<.01).

Table 3-11　　Mann Whitney U Test for production of fragments
in object RC tasks in the three groups

	SLI VS. TDA	SLI VS. TDY
Mann-Whitney U	2.000	21.000
Asymp. Sig. (2-tailed)	.000	.000

As shown in Table 3-12, there was no significant difference in the production of simple sentences between the SLI and TDA children (U=66.000, p=.079>.05), and between the SLI and TDY children in the object RCs tasks (U=78.000, p=.342>.05).

Table 3-12　　Mann Whitney U Test for production of simple sentences
in object RC tasks in the three groups

	SLI VS. TDA	SLI VS. TDY
Mann-Whitney U	66.000	78.000
Asymp. Sig. (2-tailed)	.079	.342

3.4.2.4 Summary of the findings

What follows is a brief summary of the findings from condition 1 of experiment 1. Firstly, there was a subject RCs over object RCs advantage in the production by the children with SLI and the TDY children; whereas no subject-object RCs asymmetry was detected in the production task by the TDA children. Secondly, compared to the TDA and TDY children, children with SLI encountered more difficulties in producing RCs. To be more precise, the children with SLI produced significantly less target subject and object RCs than both the TDA and TDY children. Thirdly, when the children with SLI failed to produce the target structure, they were more likely to adopt the sentence fragments as avoidance strategy than their typically developing peers. In terms of the non-target RCs, the children with

SLI produced 7 RCs without complementizer. The TDA children adopted passive object RCs to take the place of target object RCs. All the three groups produced subject RCs with thematic role reversal in the object elicitation tasks.

3.4.3 Discussion

In this section we will try to provide the explanation of the findings reported in 3.4.2. Firstly we will account for the subject over object RC advantage in the production by the children with SLI and the TDY children. Secondly, we will explore the nature of the deficiency of children with SLI, which manifested itself in the production of RCs. Lastly, we will analyze the avoidance strategies adopted by the participants when they failed to produce the target structure.

3.4.3.1   The advantage of subject over object RCs in the production

The first research question that we addressed in this chapter was whether Mandarin children with SLI differ in the production of subject RCs and object RCs. Results showed that children with SLI performed better in the subject RCs task than the object RCs task. The question that arises at this point is which theory could provide reasonable explanation for the asymmetry observed in our experiment.

According to Linear Distance Hypothesis, it is the distance between the head and the gap in RCs that gives rise to the subject-object RC asymmetry in English RC acquisition (Gibson 1998, 2000; Hawkins 1989; Tarallo and Myhill 1983; Wanner and Maratsos 1978). In English subject RCs, there is only one intervening element (the complementizer *that*), as shown in (18a). On the other hand, three elements intervene between the head and gap (the complementizer *that*; the NP *the father* and the verb *kiss*) in object RCs, as shown in (18b). Therefore, object RCs pose greater difficulty to processing because of the greater distance between the gap and the head compared to that in subject RCs.

(18) a. Subject RC: the girl **that** __ kissed the mother. (1 intervening word)

b. Object RC: the girl **that the mother kissed** __. (4 intervening words)

However, this theory cannot account for the findings of our experiment. The reason is that Mandarin is a language with head-final RCs. In Mandarin Chinese, there are more intervening words in subject RCs than that in object RCs (Subject RC vs. object RC: 3 vs. 1), as shown in (19).

(19) a. Subject RC: __**Qin mama** de nühai (3 intervening words)
                kiss the mother DE girl
                'the girl that kissed the mother'
      b. Object RC: Mama qin __ de nühai (1 intervening word)
                the mother kiss DE girl
                'the girl that the mother kissed'

This theory predicts that Mandarin subject RCs are more difficult to process because of the greater distance between the gap and the head compared to that in object RCs, which is contrary to our findings.

The second theory is called Canonical Word Order Hypothesis, according to which the difficulty in English object RCs arises from its non-canonical word order (Diessel and Tomasello 2000, 2005; Kidd *et al.* 2007; MacDonald and Christiansen 2002). As shown in (20), the object RC has a non-canonical word order, namely SOV; while the subject RC has a similar word order to simple sentences (SVO) (omission of the complementizer). In a word, the similarity or dissimilarity to canonical word order can assist or hinder the production and comprehension of RCs.

(20) a. Subject RC: the girl that __ kissed the mother.
                    S   V   O
      b. Object RC: the girl that the mother kissed __.
                    S   O   V

However, this theory also predicts that Mandarin Chinese object RCs are easier to process than subject RCs, given the fact that object RCs have the same word order with the simple sentences and subject RCs have a non-canonical OVS order, as in (21). However, our findings did not corroborate this prediction.

(21) a. Subject RC: __Qin mama de nühai

     V O   S

     kiss the mother DE girl

     'the girl that kissed the mother'

  b. Object RC: Mama qin __ de nühai

      S V   O

     the mother kiss DE girl

     'the girl that the mother kissed'

Structural Distance Hypothesis (Collins 1994; O'Grady 1997) proposed a different explanation, which draws on the notion of structural distance between the head and the gap. The structural distance is determined by the number of XP nodes intervening between the head and the gap. If we adopt Chen's (2007) analysis, as shown in (22), it is self-evident that in the subject RC, there are less nodes between the gap and the relative head. In the subject RC, there is only one node between the head and the gap (TP). However, the object RC has two nodes between the head and the gap (TP VP). According to this theory, the gap in the object RC is more deeply embedded within the syntactic tree; therefore children will encounter more difficulty in producing object RCs. This prediction is borne out by our findings. However, this theory cannot provide adequate account of all the findings of our experiment. Firstly, it cannot account for the fact that there is no asymmetry in the production of RCs by the TDA children. Secondly, it fails to explain avoidance strategies that the children used, when they failed to produce the target RCs.

(22) a. Subject RC

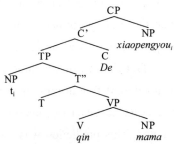

b. Object RC

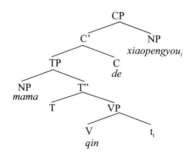

The fourth theory is called Frequency Hypothesis (Ambridge, Kidd, Rowland, and Theakston 2015). It is well known that the frequency with which particular patterns occur in the input often correlates with ease of production, comprehension, and acquisition (Ambridge *et al.* 2015). In adults' speech, subject RCs are reported to be used more frequently than object RCs in multiple corpora, including a Switchboard corpus, which collected data from telephone conversations (Roland, Dick, and Elman 2007). The findings are that while there were 9,548 subject RCs per one million NPs, object RCs were just about half-- 5,616 per one million NPs.

But the corpus studies on the input frequency of Mandarin children have yielded mixed results. Several studies have shown that subject RCs are more frequent than object RCs (Hsiao and Gibson 2003; Pu 2007; Wu *et al.* 2010). On the other hand, Chen and Shirai (2015) found that subject RCs are less than object RCs in the input of Mandarin children (subject RC 17.6% VS. object RC 58.6%). Given the mixed results, we cannot determine whether our findings can corroborate the prediction of Frequency Hypothesis.

The fifth one is Semantic Prominence Hypothesis (O'Grady 2011: 20). The hypothesis proposed that the more prominent a nominal's referent is within a RC, the more easily the processor can establish an aboutness relationship with that nominal. Given the fact that a referent functioning as subject within the RC is most prominent, a referent functioning as direct object is next most prominent, therefore the subject RC is easier to construe. Thus the subject-object RC asymmetry can be explained. This prediction was borne out by our findings.

However, this theory also failed to explain the avoidance strategies employed by our participants.

The last one is the RM. As discussed earlier, RM is postulated as a theory of syntactic locality on constraints governing extraction from syntactic islands (Rizzi 1990, 2004). In the configuration of (23), a local relation between X and Y cannot hold if the intervener Z is similar in structure to X.

(23) a. X . . . Z . . . Y

      b. Z intervenes between X and Y if and only if Z c-commands Y and Z does not c-command X

(Rizzi 2004: 225)

Friedmann *et al.* (2009) proposed that a dependency between a relative head and its trace is harder to establish for young children if there is a qualified element intervening between them. Following Chen (2007) among many others, we assume that Mandarin RCs are derived by movement. Precisely, the head noun is attracted by the head (Rel) bearing the feature [+Rel] to move to the specifier of CP. The subject and object RC are shown in configuration (22), repeated in (24).

(24) a. Subject RC

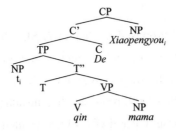

    b. Object RC

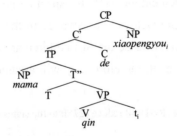

In (24a), there is no intervener between the target (specifier of CP) and the origin (place of extraction). In (24b), the subject is an intervener between the target and the origin. In the object RC example *Mama qin de xiaopengyou*, the lexical NP *xiaopengyou* is the target, *mama* the intervener, and *qin_* the origin. According to Friedmann *et al.* (2009), in the adult grammar, an intervener can block the establishment of a local A' relation only when the intervener and the attractor share the same featural specification, as in configuration (25).

$$(25) +A \ldots . +A \ldots . <+A> *$$

If the attractor is more richly specified in formal features than the intervener, there is no blocking effect, as in configuration (26).

$$(26) +A+B \ldots . +A \ldots . . <+A+B> \text{ ok}$$

The object RC is a case of (26), shown in (27). In this case, the attractor has a [+Rel] feature, which makes the attractor more richly specified. Thus, in adult system, (27) is ruled in.

$$(27) [+Rel, +NP] \ldots . . [+NP] \ldots . <+Rel, +NP>$$

According to EFUH proposed in chapter 2, SLI children's grammar cannot specify [Rel] feature of the moved element, which may give rise to blocking effect, and in turn causes the subject over object RCs advantage in production.[1] As discussed earlier, Grillo (2009) proposed that the aphasics are insensitive to the edge feature of strong phase (CP and vP), which resulted in the underspecification of the feature set of the element moved to the specifier position of strong phase.

We argue that this approach can be extended to the acquisition of Mandarin RCs by children with SLI. Because the SLI children are insensitive to the [+Rel] feature of the moved element, therefore they will assume that the target and the

---

[1]   The underspecification of [Rel] will reduce (27) into the status of (25)

intervener share a structural similarity. It is the existence of the intervener that makes the local relation cannot hold between the origin and the target for SLI children. Thus, we can give a satisfactory account of the subject / object RC asymmetry.

Now we turn to the performance of the TDY children. As for the TDY children, the scene is different. Although the two elements do not share the same feature set, they have one shared feature, namely, [+N]. Thus, the intervener has a subset of the features of the head. To interpret the object RC, one has to compute the subset–superset relation. Friedmann *et al.* (2009) proposed that limited computational resources sometimes prevent younger children from making this computation. Thus, a RM violation arises, which can account for subject over object RC advantage in production by TDY children.

In the performance of TDA children, no asymmetry exhibited, which possibly indicates that their grammar is adult-like, namely their grammar is mature enough to compute subset–superset relation. It is worthy of notice is that in Hu *et al.* (2015) the TD Mandarin children exhibited the subject-object RC asymmetry even at the age of eight, suggesting Mandarin children as old as eight cannot compute the subset–superset relation, which gives rise to the RM effect in RC production. We speculate that the disparities between Hu's study and the current study lie in the coding system. In Hu *et al.* (2015), they did not notice the fact that Mandarin RCs with demonstatives as relativizer are also acceptable. Thus we posit that the coding system in their study might underestimate the children's competence of RC production.

The avoidance strategies that the children adopted may lend plausibility to the existence of RM effect. As reported earlier, in the production of RCs, the headless RCs account for a large proportion by all the three groups. The headless RCs are also known as free RCs. Following Grosu's (2003) analysis of the Hebrew free RCs, we assume that Mandarin free RCs are construed with a null relative operator corresponding to the *Wh* element. In free RCs, what has been moved is a pure *Wh* operator, which does not contain a lexical NP, and does not have the feature [N]. Because in the object RC, the subject (intervener) has the feature [N], and the moved element has the feature [Q], they do not share a similar feature.

So the children did not need compute the subset–superset relation. Thus, the production of free RCs is relatively less demanding to the children.

Because Mandarin is an SVO language with head-final RCs, the intervention effect is a bit more complex. Structurally, the intervention happens in object RCs, and linearly there is blocking effect in subject RCs. A large proportion of free RCs were obtained in the subject RC task, which indicates that the linear intervention may also affect the production of RCs. The findings are in line with the proposal from Franck, Lassi, Frauenfelder, and Rizzi (2006). They found that linear intervention also gave rise to the production of agreement errors in a study investigating the production of structures involving subject–verb agreement.

A final point worthy of notice is that the TDA children opted for passive object RCs (14 sentences, 9.3%) instead of target object RCs, while the SLI and TDY groups nearly never produced such RCs. The possible reason is that the acquisition of passives was beyond the reach of the younger children (Hirsch & Wexler 2006) and the SLI children (van der Lely 1996). A question arising at this point is why the TDA children adopted passive object RCs instead of target object RCs. According to Belletti (2009), the reason also lies in the RM effect. As shown earlier, in the object RC there is blocking effect, as shown in the configuration (28). The presence of the subject DP blocks the establishment of local relationship.

(28) $[_{CP}...[_{TP} DP[_{vP}...V DP]]]$

However, Belletti (2009) proposed that the RM effect can be eliminated in passive object RCs based on Collins' 'smuggling approach' to the derivation of Passives. According to this approach, the verb and direct object in the passive construction move together first beyond the position of the subject and then the direct object becomes the head of the RC. Thus, the RM violation is avoided, as in (29).

(29) $[_{CP}...[_{TP} Pro ...[[V DP] by ...[vP ... <[V DP]>]]]]$

Here we cast doubt on this analysis, and we will address this question in the condition 2 of Experiment 1. In the condition we will require the children to produce passive object RCs with the aim to compare their performance with the production of object RCs.

3.4.3.2 The deficiency of the children with SLI in production of RCs

Next we will turn to the question what is the source of the impairment seen in children with SLI. As reported earlier, the children with SLI produced significantly less RCs than the TDA children, and even than the TDY children, who are one and a half years younger than them. In following paragraphs, we will examine what theories can account for the noticeable delay.

According to the Representational Deficit for Dependent Relationship theory (RDDR) (Novogrodsky and Friedmann 2006; van der Lely and Battell 2003), the deficit lies in SLI children's syntactic computational system dealing with A'-movement. The deficit makes them treat A'-movement as optional, rather than obligatory. As for production, the RDDR would predict that the children with SLI will have a chance performance, namely they will produce half of the target RCs. This prediction was not borne out by our findings, as the children with SLI had very low accuracy on RCs (subject RCs: 30%; object RCs: 18%).

Novogrodsky and Friedmann (2006) argue that SLI children have very low accuracy on RC production because they cannot assign thematic roles to heads that have replaced from their original positions. They predict that the inability to assign thematic roles will lead to errors related to thematic roles. This prediction is partly supported by our findings. The children with SLI have produced 6 subject RCs with thematic role reversals (4.6%) in the object RC elicitation task. However, what this theory fails to explain is why the children with SLI opt for the strategy of producing subject RCs with role reversal to take the place of the target object RCs. In addition, in our study both the TDA and TDY children are more likely to adopt the same strategy, which indicated that the inability to assign the thematic role was not unique to SLI children.[1]

---

[1] The TDA and TDY children produced 6% and 12.6% subject RCs in the object RC task respectively.

The difficulty in the production of RCs by children with SLI can be best captured by EFUH. According to EFUH, children with SLI cannot specify the EFs, and this underspecification will result in the error concerning the structural building-up. To be more specific, we attributed the deficit to the impaired knowledge of functional categories, including complementizers. The children with SLI will encounter difficulties in projecting a fully-fledged RC. This prediction is consistent with the theories assuming that the difficulty in children with SLI lies in in a structural deficit (Håkansson and Hansson 2000; Schuele and Tolberrt 2001). Previous studies of preschool children with SLI proved that the proposal is reasonable because the errors in production of RCs by them are related to the complementizer omission (Schuele and Nicholls 2000; Schuele and Tolberrt 2001).

The findings of the current study seem to corroborate this prediction. Firstly, the children with SLI did produce structural errors, and omitted the embedding marker in 7 of their responses (5.3%) in the object RC tasks. On the other hand, the TD children nearly never committed such errors. The fact that the SLI children committed errors concerning the complementizer directly indicated that there is a deficiency with the grammatical knowledge concerning the functional category Complementizer in children with SLI.

Secondly, EFUH can also help us to account for the fact that the SLI children's performance was even poorer than the TDY children. As mentioned earlier, the TDY children encounter difficulties in the production of object RCs because the intervener and the attractor share one feature, therefore the younger children cannot compute the subset–superset relation. If the knowledge of functional categories in children with SLI is impaired, they can not specify the [Rel] feature of the attractor, in turn the attractor and the intervener have exactly the same feature set. Consequently they will encounter greater difficulty in the production of object RCs.

Thirdly, the results of the current study suggested the declarative sentences and sentence fragments are the main avoidance strategies adopted by SLI children when they failed to produce target RCs. We proposed that the avoidance strategies can also lend support to the assumption that the

SLI children encountered severe difficulty in projecting the fully-fledged RCs, as predicted by EFUH. Stavrakaki (2002) assumed that syntactic knowledge in children with SLI is altogether impaired, and the production of simple declarative sentences in the RC elicitation task might be the results of controlled process. Following Paradis and Gopnik (1997) (cited from Stavrakaki 2002), Stavrakaki maintained that children with SLI follow a deviant pattern of linguistic development. Precisely, individuals with SLI use controlled processes to construct an utterance whereas children without language disorder employ an autonomous process to generate sentences. The simple sentence can be acquired by the application of explicit learning procedures whereas the complex structures (e.g. RCs), which require complex syntactic operations, are inaccessible through explicit learning processes. In a word, Stavrakaki assumed that the production of simple sentence in the RC elicitation task suggests the absence of knowledge of relativization. We are in disagreement with this assumption. As we have proposed in chapter 2, the underspecification of EFs does not mean the absence of such features and the knowledge concerning such features. As shown by the findings of the current research, children with SLI did produce some target RCs, although their ability is quite limited compared to their TD peers. There is no reason for us to assume that the knowledge of relativization in children with SLI is completely impaired.

In the following part, in line with EFUH, we will propose a more plausible explanation for the fact that children with SLI opted for the declarative sentences and sentence fragments instead of the target RCs, namely SLI children are insensitive to the semantic function of RCs, as predicted by EFUH. According to Quine (1960) (quoted in Heim and Kratzer 1998), restrictive RCs are traditionally considered as predicates. They are noun modifiers just as adjectival phrases and prepositional phrases. The restrictive RC functions to restrict the referent set given in the context. Kuno (1976) and MacWhinney (2005) also assumed that RCs must be about the referent of their head noun. The RC describes a property of the head of the relative clause. In other words, it attributes a particular property to the head noun. In our experiment, the children are required to response with a

RC to answer the question. However, the children with SLI produced declarative sentences and sentence fragments instead. We have good reason to assume that they possibly are insensitive to the semantic function of RC, and thus they adopt other strategies to replace the target RCs. We will continue to discuss this possibility in next chapters. What is crucial is the fact that such insensitivity is in agreement with the prediction of EFUH. According to EFUH, children with SLI cannot specify [Rel] on the head of CP, and it follows naturally they are insensitive to the semantic features of the whole CP.

To summarize the discussion, we have found that a subject-object RC asymmetry in production by children with SLI, which conforms to the prediction of RM and EFUH. The errors committed by SLI children seemingly indicate that there is a deficiency in the grammatical knowledge concerning the functional category, namely Complementizer, as predicted by EFUH.

3.5 Condition 2 of experiment 1: Reversible passive object RCs

3.5.1 Research questions

Base on the discussion in 3.4.3.1, we aim to answer the question whether Mandarin children differ in the production of object RCs and passive object RCs by analyzing the results of condition 2 of experiment 1. As discussed in 3.3.3.1, if the proposal given by Belletti (2009) is on the right track, we would predict that the performance on passive object RCs will be better than that on object RCs in the three groups, given that in passive object RCs there is no RM violation.

3.5.2 Method

3.5.2.1 Participants

The Participants are the same as those in condition 1[①].

3.5.2.2 Materials and Procedure

The task is the same as that in condition 1. The task consisted of ten trials. The

---

①   The reader may see descriptions on the participants on page 61-65.

NPs were always animate, therefore, the sentences are reversible, as in (30).

(30) Passive object RCs

Experimenter: You liang-ge xiaopengyou, yi-ge xiaopengyou bei baba
tui-zhe, yi-ge xiaopengyou bei mama tui-zhe. Ni xihuan
na-ge xiaopengyou?

'There are two children. one child is pushed by the father.
The other child is pushed by the mother. Which child do
you like?'

Target response: Wo xihuan bei baba\mama tui de xiaopengyou
'I like the child who is pushed by the father\mother'

All the nouns and verbs used in the task are the same as that in condition 1. The
procedure of the experiment is also the same as that of the condition 1.

3.5.2.3 Coding and Scoring

The coding system is the same as that in condition 1. The target response is
exemplified in (31).

(31) Target PSRC

Bei Mama tui   de xiaopengyou

BEI mother push DE child

'the child that is pushed by the mother'

3.5.3 Results

Table 3-13 provides target structures produced by the three groups in the passive
object RC task in condition 2 and the object RC task in condition 1. The latter has
been reported in 3.2.3. For the sake of convenience, we repeated it in the Table
3-13. Because non-target RCs and other responses are irrelevant to our discussion,
we will not report them here.

Table 3-13   Percentage (%), raw scores (N), means (M) and standard deviation
(SD) of target responses in the Passive object and object RCs tasks by each group

Groups	Passive object RCs				Object RCs			
	%	N	M	SD	%	N	M	SD
SLI	9	12/130	0.92	1.93	18	24/130	1.84	2.26
TDA	68	102/150	6.80	3.36	80	120/150	8.00	1.60
TDY	52	78/150	5.20	3.57	48	72/150	4.80	3.57

It seems that there is no apparent increase of the production of target structures in the passive object RC task compared to the object RC task (SLI children: passive object RCs: 9%; object RCs 18%; TDA children: passive object RCs: 68%; object RCs 80%; TDY children: passive object RCs: 52%; object RCs 48%;). The results of Wilcoxon Signed Ranks Test indicated that there is no significant difference in the production of object passive RCs and object RCs by SLI and TDY groups, as shown in Table 3-14 (SLI children $z=$ -1.291, $p=.197>.05$; TDY children $z=-.377$, $p=.706>.05$). The TDA children performed marginally significantly better on the object RC condition than the passive object RC condition ($z=-.667$, $p=.505>.05$).

Table 3-14   Wilcoxon Signed Ranks Test for production of the target
subject RC and object RC in the three groups

Groups	SLI	TDA	TDY
Z	-1.291	-.667	-.377
Asymp.Sig.	.197	.505	.706

The statistical analysis did not corroborate the prediction of the theory proposed by Belletti (2009) among many others. More informative is the avoidance strategies the children used when they failed to produce the target passive object RCs. Interestingly, in the passive object elicitation task, all the three groups produced the object RCs instead of the target passive object RCs, as shown in Table 3-15.

Table 3-15   **Numbers (N), percentage (%) of object RCs in**
each group in the passive object RC tasks

Groups	N	%
SLI	37/130	28.4%
TDA	31/150	20.6%
TDY	43/150	28.6%
Total	111/430	25.8%

3.5.4 Discussion

Our findings are in line with the results of a RC comprehension study of Mandarin TD children by Chang (1984). Chang (1984) used an act out task to examine the 48 preschool children's comprehension of SS, SO, OS and OO RCs. The stimuli are given in (32).

(32) a. SS RC

     yao   gou   de   mao   zhui   laoshu

     bite   dog   DE   cat   chase   rat

     'The cat that bit the dog chased the rat'

   b. SO RC

     bei   gou   yao   de   mao   zhui   laoshu

     Pass   dog   bite   DE   cat   chase   rat

     'the cat that was bitten by the dog chased the rat'

   c. OS RC

     laoshu   zhui   yao   gou   de   mao.

     rat   chase   bite   dog   DE   cat

     'the rat chased the cat that bit the dog'

   d. OO RC

     laoshu   zhui   bei   gou   yao   de   mao.

     rat   chase   Pass   dog   bite   DE   cat

     'the rat chased the cat that was bitten by the dog'

As indicated by the examples, the object RCs used in the studies should be categorized as passive object RCs. The results of Chang (1984) showed no significant difference in the accuracy between the subject passive RCs and the object RCs comprehension.

As mentioned earlier, the motivation for the proposal of Belletti (2009) is the fact that in the object RC production task, children opted for passive object RCs instead of object RCs. The finding of the current study remains unaccountable in the framework proposed by Belletti (2009). Taken together, we cannot arrive at the conclusion that the acquisition of passive object RCs is better than object RCs. Therefore the fact that the children opted for passive object RCs in the object RCs tasks cannot be regarded as evidence for the claim that the former is easier because of the absence of the RM violation.

At this point, we need to answer the question: which theory can account for the findings of the current study. In other words, we need to explain why there is no difference between the two tasks. Firstly, we proposed that the analysis in Belletti (2009) is problematic. According to the smuggling approach of Collins (2005), the derivation of passives involves a step-by-step 'smuggling' instead of long-distance movement. Thus, the derivation of passive object RCs involves more movements than that of object RCs, as shown in (33).

(33) a. object RC: [CP…[TP DP[vP …V DP]]]

b. passive object RC: [CP … [TP Pro …[[V DP] by …[vP … <[V DP]>]]]]

Jensen de López et al. (2014) claimed that the step-by-step movement is less costly because it may be less demanding in terms of processing. However, according to the Derivational Complexity Hypothesis (DCH) (Jakubowicz 2005, 2011), children prefer more economical derivations and young children tend to avoid using movement because it is costly. Young children are sensitive to the computational complexity of the derivation due to the developmental constraints. The computational complexity can be estimated by a metric whereby complexity is precisely defined, as in (34).

(34) Derivational Complexity Metric (DCM) (Jakubowicz 2005)

a. Merging α_i n times gives rise to a less complex derivation than merging α_i (n+1) times.

b. Internal Merge of α gives rise to a less complex derivation than Internal Merge of $\alpha+\beta$.

If the DCM is right, we can conclude that more movements are also costly to the children with SLI. Although passive object RCs do not involve the RM effect, they are costly for children with SLI to compute. In object RCs there is RM effect, and in passive object RCs more movements are involved. Thus, there is no significant difference in the accuracy of the two RC productions.

Secondly, whether the smuggling approach can hold water remains controversial. For example, Gehrke and Grillo (2008) proposed that though Collins' account seemingly solves the problems existing in the previous studies, it poses serious look-ahead problems. And if we adopt analysis of Mandarin long passive construction by Huang (1999), as shown in (35), the RM effect can also be avoided, because the patient of the verb (*Zhangsan*) is base-generated in the subject position. Thus, in the passive object RC, there is no RM violation involved.

(35) $[_{IP}$ Zhangsan$_{i\,V}$ bei $[_{IP}$ Op$_i$ Lisi dale t$_i$]].

Zhengsan   Bei   Lisi hit-Asp

'Zhangsan was beaten by Lisi.'

There is an alternative account for our findings. Xu and Yang (2008) find that the acquisition of long passives is also problematic for Mandarin TD children. Based on the Universal Phase Requirement (UPR) (Wexler 2004), they proposed that the movement of the operator in (35) is forbidden in the grammar of young children. Universal Phase Requirement assumes that immature children's difficulty with long passives stems from their definition of phase in their grammar. Chomsky (1995) proposed several phase categories, including vP. According to the Phase Impenetrable Condition (PIC) (Chomsky 2008: 143), once all the syntactic computations are complete within the lowest phase, that phase is transferred and becomes inaccessible to further syntactic computation. But the vP in the passives for adult is defective, hence movement of the operator within the vP is allowed. Yet according to the UPR, the immature children take the defective vP in passives as phase. Consequently, they will encounter difficulty in moving the operator out of the defective vP. If the above analysis is on the right track, we can also account for the fact that there is no difference in the accuracy of the production of object and passive object RCs, given the fact that the former involves the violation of RM, the latter involves the violation of PIC.

Interestingly, the fact that children with SLI will encounter difficulties in producing passive object RCs can also be accounted for by the hypothesis of this dissertation, namely EFUH. As mentioned above, children with SLI cannot specify the discourse-linked features, namely Edge Features. According to Gehrke and Grillo (2008), in passive constructions, a stative subevent of a structurally complex event is moved to a discourse-related position at the edge of the verb phrase. If we accept this analysis, it naturally follows that children with SLI will have troubles in producing passives, and this difficulty will in turn result in the attenuated performances in producing passive object RCs.

To summarize this section, we have not found a passive object-Object RC asymmetry in production by children with SLI and the TD children, which can be accounted for by EUFH.

3.6 Condition 3 of experiment 1: Irreversible subject and object RCs

3.6.1 Research questions

As discussed in 3.2.3, the animacy of the subject and object NPs involved in RCs can assist or hinder the production and processing of RCs. In condition 3, we will test the children's production of the irreversible RCs, in which one NP is animate and the other NP is inanimate. The specific questions that we will address are (1) whether or not there are differences in the production of reversible and irreversible RCs by SLI children? (2) whether or not there is asymmetry in the production of subject-object RCs in the irreversible condition by children with SLI.

3.6.2 Method

3.6.2.1 Participants

The Participants are the same as those in condition 1 of experiment 1[①].

3.6.2.2 Materials and Procedure

The task is the same as that in Condition 1. The task consisted of twenty trials: half eliciting subject RCs, the rest object RCs. In the RCs, the subject NP is animate, and the object NP is inanimate; and thus the sentences are irreversible, as in (36).

(36) a. Irreversible Subject RCs

　　　 Experimenter: You liang-ge xiaopengyou, yi-ge xiaopengyou zai tui xiaoqiche, yi-ge xiaopengyou zai tui xiaohuoche. Ni xihuan na-ge xiaopengyou?

　　　 'There are two children. One child is pushing the toy car. The other is pushing the toy train. Which child do you like?'

　　 Target response: Wo xihuan tui xiaoqiche\xiaohuoche de xiaopengyou 'I like the child who is pushing the toy car\toy train'

　　 b. Irreversible ORCs

　　　 Experimenter: You liang-ge xiaohuoche, Xiaogege zai tui yi-ge xiaohuoche, Xiaojiejie zai tui yi-gexiaohuoche. Ni xihuan na-ge xiaohuoche?

　　　 'There are two toy trains. The brother is pushing one toy train.

　　　 The sister is pushing the other toy train. Which toy train do you like?'

　　 Target response: Wo xihuan xiaogege\xiaojiejie tui de xiaohuoche

　　　 'I like the toy train which brother\sister is pushing'

---

① The reader may see description on the participants on page 61-65.

In addition to the verbs used in coodition1, three verbs are used in this condition, including *he* 'drink' , *xi* 'wash' and *chi* 'eat'. The nouns denoting animate NPs are the same as those in Condition 1. There are 17 nouns for inanimate objects, which consist of *xiaoqiche* 'toy car', *xiaohuoche* 'toy train' , *yinliao* 'drink' *gutou* 'bone', *putao* 'grape', *pingguo* 'apple', *qiaokeli* 'chocolate', *lanqiu* 'basketball', *zuqiu* 'football', *qiqiu* 'balloon', *piqiu* 'rubber ball', *shubao* 'schoolbag', *lüxingdai* 'travelling bag' , *pingzi* 'bottle' , *bangbangtang* 'candy' , *yu* 'fish', *niunai* 'milk'.

3.6.2.3 Coding and Scoring

The coding system is the same as that in the Condition 1.

3.6.3 Results

Table 3-16 provides the target structures produced by the three groups in the irreversible subject-object RC task.

In order to address question 1, we compared the performance of the SLI children in the reversible (we have reported in the experiment 1) and irreversible conditions, shown in Figure 3-2. For the convenience of discussion, we also compared the performances of the TDA and TDY children in the two conditions. The results were provided in Table 3-17.

**Table 3-16　Percentage (%), raw scores (N), means (M) and standard deviation
(SD) of target responses in the irreversible subject-object RC tasks by each group**

Groups	Irreversible Subject RCs				Irreversible Object RCs			
	%	N	M	SD	%	N	M	SD
SLI	30	39/130	3.00	2.94	33.8	44/130	3.38	3.57
TDA	93.3	140/150	9.33	1.17	80	120/150	8.00	2.57
TDY	83.3	125/150	8.33	3.24	72	108/150	7.20	3.85

The statistical analysis indicated that the TDY children produced significantly more target object RCs in the irreversible condition than in the reversible condition. Except for that, there was no significant difference in terms of the production of target RCs by the three groups between the reversible and

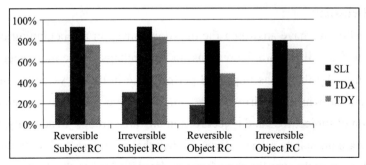

Figure 3-2 Production of subject RCs and object RCs by the typically developing age-matched children (TDA), the typically developing younger children (TDY), and the children with SLI in the reversible and irreversible conditions.

irreversible conditions. Although there was no significant difference in terms of the production of target object RCs by children with SLI, there was a considerable increase in the irreversible condition (reversible object RCs vs. the irreversible object RCs: 18% vs. 33.8%).

Table 3-17 Wilcoxon Signed Ranks Test for production of the target subject RCs and object RCs in the reversible and irreversible conditions by the three groups

Groups	SLI		TDA		TDY	
	Subject RC	Object RC	Subject RC	Object RC	Subject RC	Object RC
Z	0.000	-1.266	-3.45	-2.497	-1.053	-2.367
Asymp.Sig	1.000	.205	.730	.130	0.292	.018

The results of Wilcoxon Signed Ranks Test indicated that there was no asymmetry in production of subject RCs and object RCs in the three groups in the irreversible condition, as shown in Table 3-18.

Table 3-18 Wilcoxon Signed Ranks Test for production of the target subject RCs and object RCs in the three groups in irreversible condition

Groups	SLI	TDA	TDY
Z	-0.722	-1.610	-1.156
Asymp.Sig.	.470	.107	.249

3.6.4 Discussion

In last section we have answered the questions raised in the beginning of 3.5.1. In this part we will explore the reasons for our findings. To be more specific, we will discuss why there was improved performance in the irreversible object RC production and why in the irreversible condition there was no asymmetry in the production of subject RCs and object RCs in the three groups. In actuality, the two questions are intimately related, given the fact that the improvement on the object RC production will naturally, though not necessarily, lead to the disappearance of subject-object RC asymmetry in production.

There are two alternatives accounting for the relatively greater accuracy in production of irreversible object RCs. The first one is that children encountered less difficulty concerning the thematic role assignment in the production of irreversible object RCs. As discussed in section 3.4, such errors are rooted in the RM effect involved in object RCs. In the reversible condition, the TDY and SLI children both have committed errors concerning the thematic roles (SLI children: 4.6%; TDY children: 12.6%). The finding is in line with the previous studies. SLI children will encounter two difficulties in the production of RCs: projecting the fully-fledged CP (Håkansson and Hansson 2000) and the thematic role reversal (Novogrodsky and Friedmann 2006). The second difficulty manifested itself in the errors of thematic role assignment to moved constituents.

However, in the irreversible condition, nearly no such error has been detected. In the irreversible condition, the agents of the event are always animate, the patients (themes) are always inanimate. We proposed that the mismatch in terms of the animacy of the NPs involved in RCs will reduce the difficulty confronting the children when producing object RCs. According to Dowty (1991), typical features of proto-agent are volition, sentience, cause, movement and independent existence whereas the typical features of proto-patient are change of state, incremental theme, casually affected, relatively stationary and no independent existence. The animate entity is more likely to be assigned the agent role because it possibly has all the features of proto-agent. The inanimate entity is more likely to be assigned the patient role because it has all, at least most, of the features of Proto-patient. We have found that in the reversible condition, SLI children have difficulty in assigning the thematic roles to the entity in the event encoded by the RC. In the irreversible condition, the problem disappears. Thus, the performance of the RC production will be improved in the latter condition. This conclusion can also be supported by the fact that there is no improvement in terms of the production of subject RCs in the irreversible condition. As reported previously, in the reversible subject RC elicitation tasks, no children has committed errors concerning the thematic role reversal. We can conclude that the improvement of the performance of children with SLI is due to the reduction of the difficulties caused by RM effect in irreversible object RCs.

The second alternative is the Frequency Hypothesis, according to which, the higher frequency of a given structure in the input can facilitate the comprehension and production of that structure. Numerous studies have proved that in many languages, object RCs are more likely to occur with an inanimate head. In a corpus study of American English, Fox and Thompson (1990) found that English object RCs are more likely to have an inanimate head. Mak *et al.* (2002) had a similar observation that most of object RCs have an inanimate head and RC-internal animate NPs in Dutch and German corpora. Kidd *et al.* (2007) found that in the natural production of object RCs by the 3-and 4-year-old English-speaking children, the majority of RCs are that with inanimate head (75%). This suggests that the difficulty associated with object RCs is influenced by the frequency of different types of RCs in the input they receive.

Pu (2007) conducted a narrative study in which native Mandarin-speakers were required to recount a story in written and spoken language. The author calculated RCs produced and found that the head of subject RCs tends to be animate whereas the object RC tends to occur with an inanimate head. Similarly, Hsu (2014) found that subject RCs tend to occur with animate heads (12/14, 85.7%) while object RCs tend to occur with inanimate heads (28/30, 93.3%) in a corpus study of the spontaneous data from the Mandarin-speaking children in Taiwan. Thus we can safely arrive at the conclusion that the higher frequency of irreversible object RCs in the input facilitates the production of object RCs with inanimate head.

In other studies, the easiness of the production of the Mandarin object RCs with inanimate head has also been borne out. Yang (2013: 262-265) conducted a study of RC production by 180 Mandarin children (3;0-6;0). She found that there is no asymmetry between subject RC and object RC in terms of production, which is contrary to many other similar studies (Hsu *et al.* 2009; Hu *et al.* 2015). The stimuli used in the study are provided in (37).

(37) a. Subject RC

    xiang chi gutou de gou

    want eat bone De dog

    'the dog that wants to eat bone'

  b. Object RC

    houjiejie zhai de tao

    monkey pluck De peach

    'the peach that the monkey plucked'

We propose that the disappearance of the subject-object RCs asymmetry is owing to the easiness of the production of the Mandarin object RCs with inanimate head. In addition, the phenomenon is not unique to Mandarin RC acquisition. Kidd *et al.* (2007) examined sentence repetition by 57 English-speaking children (3; 1-4; 9) and found that there is no subject-object RC asymmetry when the object RCs occurred with inanimate head. The similar thing has been found in the language processing research. In a self-paced reading and eye-tracking experiment, Mak *et al.* (2002) found that Dutch adults read the subject RCs significantly faster than object RCs when both the head NP and RC internal NP are animate, while there is no asymmetry when the subject is animate and the object is inanimate.

There is no significant difference regarding the production of target object RCs by TDA children between the two conditions because the TDA children's performance in the reversible condition is at the ceiling level.

To conclude the discussion, we have found that children with SLI and TDY children encountered less difficulty in producing the object RCs with inanimate heads, which can be accounted for by the reduction of the thematic role errors or the Frequency Hypothesis.

3.7 Experiment 2: Priming production task

In 3.4 we presented the results of elicitation study, which indicated that there is a subject over object RCs advantage in production by SLI children and that the production of RCs by SLI children is severely impaired. We have arrived at the conclusion that children with SLI do not have an intact syntactic representation to project a RC. However, the afore-mentioned conclusion is in disagreement with the research in structural priming paradigm. According to Garraffa *et al.* (2015), the magnitude of priming effect in SLI children was the same as that in TD children, and SLI children possessed an abstract representation of subject RCs facilitating the production. Nevertheless, the above study only assessed the production of subject RC, which is often reported as less demanding. Thus in this experiment, we will test the production of subject RCs and object RCs by children with SLI using a priming production paradigm.

Syntactic priming paradigm appears to be very telling about syntactic representation of speakers. It is firmly established that speakers have a tendency to reuse the structure, which they have produced or comprehended, in the subsequent production. For example, when speakers are exposed to a double object structure (e.g., *The girl is sending her mother a bunch of flowers*), they are more likely to produce a double object sentence (*e.g., The girl is giving her mother a piece of cake*) than an equivalent prepositional object sentence (*e.g., The girl is sending a bunch of flowers to her mother.*) (Bock 1986,1989; Branigan, Pickering, and Cleland 2000).

The facilitation of particular structures in production through prior exposure has been labeled as syntactic priming effects (see Branigan 2007; Pickering and Ferreira 2008 for reviews). If there is priming effect in the production of a particular structure, the speakers can apply the abstract representation of the structure in both the prime and target sentences (Branigan, Pickering, Liversedge, Stewart, and Urbach, 1995). As such, the priming paradigm provides an implicit test of syntactic representation.

Extensive studies have used the syntactic priming effect to test the nature of adult syntactic representation (Bock and Loebell 1990; Branigan, Pickering,

McLean, and Stewart 2006; Cleland and Pickering 2003; Pickering and Branigan 1998). Recent studies have shown that young children may draw on abstract representation of syntactic structure during production and comprehension. The results indicated that children possessed a given syntactic representation at an earlier age than has been shown by using other tests of syntactic knowledge (Bencini and Valian 2008; Huttenlocher, Vasilyeva, and Shimpi 2004; Messenger, Branigan, and McLean 2011, 2012; Shimpi, Gámez, Huttenlocher, and Vasilyeva 2007).

3.7.1 Research questions

We will address the following specific questions by using the priming production task.

(1) Do Mandarin children with SLI differ in the production of subject RCs and object RCs in the structural priming paradigm?

(2) Do Mandarin children with SLI differ from their TDA and TDY peers in the priming production of subject RCs and object RCs?

(3) Do SLI children perform differently in the production of RCs in the baseline and priming conditions?

3.7.2 Method

3.7.2.1 Participants

The participants are the same as in the experiment 1[①].

3.7.2.2 Materials and Procedure

There were 10 pairs of experimental pictures. Prime pictures depict an animate entity carrying out an irreversible transitive action (e.g., *a boy is pushing a car*). The target pictures depicted a reversible transitive action (e.g., *a boy is pushing a girl*).

The examples of baseline, prime and target sentences are shown in (38). In order to fulfill the pragmatically felicitous requirement for the occurrence of RCs, in both the prime and target pictures, there are two NPs presented in the referent context. For example, for the subject RC (*this is the brother that is pushing the*

---

① The reader may see description on the participants on page 61-65.

car), there are two *boys* presented in the picture. The function of RC is to restrict the set of potential referents for the definite expression '*the brother*'.

(38) a. Subject RC

    Baseline sentence: Zhege shi qiche.

                This   is   car

                'This is a car'

    Prime sentence: Zhege shi tui   qiche de   xiaogege

              This   is push car   DE brother

              'this is the brother that is pushing the car'

    Target sentence: Zhege shi tui   xiaojiejie de   xiaogege

              This   is   push sister   DE brother

              'this is the brother that is pushing the sister'

  b. Object RC

    Baseline sentence: Zhege shi qiche.

                This   is   car

                'This is a car'

    Prime sentence: Zhege shi xiaogege tui   de qiche

              This   is brother   push DE car

              'this is the car that the brother is pushing'

    Target sentence: Zhege shi xiaogege tui   de xiaojiejie

              This   is brother   push DE sister

              'this is the sister that the brother is pushing'

Figure 3-3 Example prime picture

Figure 3-4 Example target picture

In order to ensure that the child understood the task, before the experiment, there was one practice trial. With a set of prearranged pictures placed in front of the participant and the experimenter, they took turns to describe pictures. The experimenter described the prime picture by using the prime RCs or the baseline sentences firstly, and then encouraged the participants to describe the corresponding target picture. All the participants' responses were audio-recorded, then transcribed and scored according to the criteria outlined below.

3.7.2.3 Coding and Scoring

The target structures are the same as the target RCs in experiment 1, which include the target RCs, the headless RCs. Word substitutions were also regarded as the target responses. The non-target RCs, the declaratives and the sentence fragments are excluded from the target structures.

3.7.3 Results

The experiment yielded a total of 520 responses from the SLI children, 600 responses from the TDA children and 600 responses from the TDY children. In all cases, half of the responses resulted from the subject RC elicitation task; the rest were obtained from the object RC elicitation task. In this dissertation, we only report the target responses obtained from our participants.

In the baseline condition, the children with SLI produced 17 (13%) target subject RCs and 4 (3%) target object RCs while in the priming condition, they produced 53 (40.7%) target subject RCs and 20 (9.2%) target object RCs. The TDA children yielded 59 target subject RCs, which accounted for 39.3% of the total responses and 62 target object RCs accounting for 41.3% of the total responses in the baseline condition; in the priming condition they produced 133 (88.6%) target subject RCs and 110 (73.3%) target object RCs. The TDY children produced 53 (35.3%) target subject RCs and 51 (34%) target object RCs in the baseline condition; in the priming condition they yielded 135 (90%) target subject RCs and 83 (50%) target object RCs. Table 3-19 and 3-20 provide the percentage, raw scores, means and standard deviation of the target subject-object RCs produced by the three groups in the baseline and the priming conditions respectively.

Table 3-19 Percentage (%), raw scores (N), means (M) and standard deviation (SD) of target responses in the baseline condition by each group baseline

Groups	Subject RCs					Object RCs			
	%	N	M	SD		%	N	M	SD
SLI	13	17/130	1.30	2.01		3	4/130	0.30	0.75
TDA	39.3	59/150	3.93	2.35		41.3	62/150	4.13	3.20
TDY	35.3	53/150	3.53	2.06		34	51/150	3.40	2.09

Table 3-20 Percentage (%), raw scores (N), means (M) and standard deviation (SD) of target responses in the Priming condition tasks by each group

Groups	Subject RCs					Object RCs			
	%	N	M	SD		%	N	M	SD
SLI	40.7	53/130	4.07	3.40		9.2	20/130	0.92	1.25
TDA	88.6	133/150	8.86	2.35		73.3	110/150	7.33	2.35
TDY	90	135/150	9.00	1.55		50	83/150	5.00	2.85

Firstly, we address the first question whether there is subject-object RC asymmetry in the priming condition in the three groups. The results of Wilcoxon Signed Ranks Test indicated that there was asymmetry in production of subject RCs and object RCs in the SLI children ($z=-2.60$, $p=0.009<.05$) and TDY children ($z=-2.98$, $p=0.003<.05$). As for the TDA children, there was no asymmetry detected ($z=-1.77$, $p=0.077>.05$). We found a pattern similar to that in the elicitation production tasks: the children with SLI and TDY children performed better on subject RCs than object RCs, while for the TDA children no asymmetry was detected in the production of the two types of RCs.

Secondly, we address the second question whether Mandarin children with SLI differ from their TDA and TDY peers in their production of RCs in the priming condition. As expected, there were significant differences in the production of target RCs between the SLI children and TDA children and between the SLI and TDY children. In the production of subject RCs, the accuracy of the children with SLI was significantly lower than that of the TDA (U=17.500, p<.01) and TDY (U=17.000, p<.01) children. In the production of object RCs, the children with SLI performed significantly poorer than both the TDA (U=3.000, p<.01) and TDY children (U=20.500, p<.01).

It seemed that in the priming condition all the three groups of children were more likely to produce the target structures. This observation was partly confirmed by the statistical analysis. The results of Wilcoxon Signed Ranks Test indicated that there was no significant difference detected in production of object RCs by children with SLI in the baseline and the priming condition (z=-1.380, p=0.168>.05) whereas in production of subject RCs, a significant difference was founded in the two conditions (z=-2.405, p=.016<.05), which suggested that the priming effect existed only in the production of subject RC in children with SLI. The TD children performed better on the priming condition than the baseline condition regardless of RC types (TDA subject RC z=-3.301, p=0.001<.05; TDA object RC z=-2.849, p=0.004<.05; TDY subject RC z=-3.309, p=0.001<.05; TDY object RC z=-2.056, p=0.04<.05), which reveals that the priming effect manifested itself in the production of subject and object RCs in TD children.

3.7.4 Discussion

We found that both the SLI children and TDY children performed significantly better in the production of subject RCs than object RCs by using the structural priming paradigm. The findings are in concordance with those in the elicitation production task. The theory capitalizing on the linear distance cannot account for the results in that the theory wrongly predicts that the opposite is true. As discussed earlier, we hold that the RM may provide a satisfactory explanation for the subject-object RC asymmetry in the production. To repeat, the object RC involves a blocking effect, which may pose severe challenge to the younger children and the children with language disorder, while in the subject RC, no such effect emerges. Thus the TDY children and the SLI children performed better on subject RCs. The similar performances of the TDA children in the two types of RCs suggest that their grammatical system is mature enough to overcome the intervention effect involved in the object RC.

Compared to the TDA and TDY children, the children with SLI were severely impaired in production of RCs, which reveals that the syntactic deficiency exhibited itself even in the priming paradigm. In the elicitation production tasks, we also detected the disparities between the children with SLI and the TD children. By analyzing the errors in their production, we attributed the difference to syntactic deficit in the grammar of children with SLI, which provides substantial evidence for EFUH.

The findings from the current study reconfirmed the assumption. As reported previously, when children with SLI and the TDA and TDY children were required to describe pictures, there was a greater likelihood of producing subject RCs in the priming condition, in which they had just a subject RC describing an unrelated picture than the baseline condition, in which they have heard a bare noun phrase describing an unrelated picture. The same pattern was also found in the production of object RCs for the TDA and TDY children. However, we failed to find such pattern in production of object RCs in children with SLI. To be more precise, the children with SLI did not produce more target object RCs in the priming condition than in the baseline condition.

The implication of the finding is that an intact abstract representation of subject RC probably can be retrieved by the children with SLI together with their TD peers when they heard the experimenter's sentence and be applied in the subsequent production as well[1]. In other words, the existence of structural

---

[1] One of the reviewers questioned the conclusion that SLI children have intact abstract representation of subject RCs, because he hold that the accuracy of 40.7% is not robust enough to make such claim. There are two points worthy of notice. Firstly, we posit that whether there is abstract representation of a given structure is based on the comparison between the performances in the baseline condition and the prime condition. Secondly, the poor performances on subject RC production are possibly owing to other non-syntactic factors, which will be discussed in detail in 6.3.3.

priming effects between unrelated subject RCs suggests that the abstract syntactic representation has a causal relationship with the better performance in the priming condition, in which the syntactic representation facilitated the production of target structures. If the above argumentation is on the right track, we can conclude that the TD children also have an intact representation of the object RCs and the children with SLI do not possess it, due to the fact that prior exposure to the target structure cannot facilitate the production of target RCs in children with SLI.[①] At this point, the answer to the third question has been given. We propose that the absence of syntactic representation is predicted by EFUH because the hypothesis assumes that children with SLI will have trouble to projecting full-fledged structure of CP.

Thus we can safely conclude that the disparities between the SLI children and their typically developing peers in the production of object RCs should be attributed to the decayed syntactic representation of the children with SLI, as predicted by EFUH. However, we also found that in the production of subject RCs, the accuracy of the children with SLI was significantly lower than that of the TDA and TDY children. Given the view that the three groups of children all possess the intact syntactic representation of subject RC, the difference between them possibly lies in their different processing capacities. This is because we have detected that compared to the TDA children, the SLI children performed worse on the tasks assessing the processing speed in the IQ test. We will discuss this point in detail in chapter 5 and chapter 6.

Some researchers have studied the production of RCs in children with SLI by adopting the priming task, but the results are mixed. By using the priming paradigm, Garraffa *et al.* (2015) examined the production of subject RC in Italian-speaking children with SLI, and found that the magnitude of priming effect is the same as the typically developing children, suggesting that children with SLI are equipped with an abstract representation of subject RCs. Our findings are in line

---

① A point worthy of notice is that the children with SLI have a representation of subject RCs instead of the object RCs may also be due to the fact that an intervention effect takes place in object RCs, as predicted by the RM and EFUH.

with their conclusion. However, they did not examine the production of object RCs, which is widely assumed to be harder for SLI children.

Our findings are at odds with Marinellie (2006). She found it is difficult to prime RC constructions even in 7–8-year-old children with SLI, regardless of RC types. Interestingly, the study also found that the priming effect did not exist even in the TD school children. She proposed that the lack of a prime effect may be related to the syntactic dependency involved in RCs and the low frequency of RCs. However, if we examine the stimuli used in the study more closely, a shortcoming in the experiment design can be detected. One example target picture for priming the target RC was designed as follows: there were two boys holding fishing poles and looking at a fish jumping from the water near a river. In this example, the target utterance that the child might be expected to produce is: '*The boys look at a fish that jumps high*'. As pointed out by Hamburger and Crain (1982), the use of RCs is pragmatically felicitous only when at least two fishes are presented in the referent context because the function of RCs is to restrict the set of potential referents for the definite expression 'the fish'. Hamburger and Crain (1982) showed that once the experimental setting was pragmatically felicitous, 3 and 4-year-old children's performance in comprehending RCs improved significantly. We suspect that it is the limitations of the experimental design that has a causal relationship with the absence of priming effect in RC production by children with SLI even by the typically developing children.

To summarize this section, we have found that the children with SLI do possess the syntactic representation of subject RCs but not that of the object RCs by using the priming paradigm. In the priming production, the children with SLI performed better on the subject RC than on the object RC, which can be accounted for by RM. According to EFUH, their inferior performance to their TD peers is due to the syntactic impairment.

3.8 Summary

Chapter 3 examined the production of RCs in children with SLI and two groups of control children by using the elicitation production and priming production tasks. In both the elicitation and priming production tasks, the children with SLI exhibited a clear subject-object reversible RC asymmetry, which is in line with RM. Moreover, we found that the children with SLI performed significantly more poorly on the production of object RCs than both the TDA and TDY children. The children with SLI committed errors related to thematic roles, produced structural errors by omitting the embedding marker, and opted for the declarative sentences and sentence fragments as the main avoidance strategies. We also found that children with SLI do not possess the syntactic representation of object RCs. Another finding is that the SLI children's accuracy on the irreversible RCs is higher than the reversible RCs and that there is no difference detected between object RCs and passive object RCs in elicitation production tasks.

Taken together, we posit that the disparities between the SLI children and the TD children in the production of RCs should be mainly attributed to their decayed grammar system. We further propose that SLI children have severe difficulty in projecting fully-fledged RCs and that they are insensitive to the semantic function of RCs, which are also the manifestations of the grammatical deficit in them. All the above findings are correctly predicted by EFUH.

Chapter 4
The Comprehension of Relative Clauses

This chapter assesses the comprehension of RCs by children with SLI by using two tasks: the sentence-picture matching task and the character-picture verification task. By exploring the comprehension of subject RCs, object RCs and passive object RCs in SLI children and their TD peers, we aim to explore the linguistic characteristics of the SLI children's comprehension of RCs. We compare the results from experiment 3 and experiment 4 with the purpose of showing the advantage of the character-picture verification task in assessing RC comprehension.

The chapter is structured as follows. In 4.1, we will review previous studies on TD children's comprehension of RCs, with the emphasis on the studies of the Mandarin-speaking children. In 4.2, previous studies on the comprehension of RCs in children with SLI will be presented. In 4.3 and 4.4 we report the sentence-picture matching task and the character-picture verification task respectively. Section 4.5 concludes this chapter.

4.1 Previous studies on the Relative Clause comprehension in TD children

RC comprehension has been widely investigated in a variety of languages in typically developing children. These studies found that object RCs are more problematic than subject RCs, such as in English (Booth, Mac Whinney, and Harasaki 2000; de Villiers, Tager Flusberg, Hakuta, and Cohen 1979; Goodluck and Tavakolian 1982; Kidd and Bavin 2002; Sheldon 1974; Tavakolian 1981);

in Italian (Adani 2011; Adani, van der Lely, Forgiarini, and Guasti 2010; Arosio, Adani, and Guasti 2009; Crain, McKee, and Emiliani, 1991); in Portuguese (Corrêa 1995); in Turkish (Özge, Marinis, and Zeyrek, 2009); in Hebrew (Arnon 2010; Friedmann et al. 2009); in German (Arosio, Yatsushiro, Forgiarini, and Guasti 2012) and in Mandarin (Hu et al. 2016).

In earlier studies assessing RC comprehension in children (de Villiers et al. 1979), the act out task has been employed widely. In the task, RCs are presented to children, and children are required to act out sentences by using a set of toys which map onto the NPs in the sentences. However, criticism has been levied at this methodology because the act out task may underestimate children's knowledge of RC due to the fact that children might pay more attention to playing with the toys than to following the instructions (McDaniel, McKee, and Cairns 1998). The second shortcoming of the task is that act out methodology has violated appropriate pragmatic conditions for the use of RCs. The function of RCs is to individuate the referent of the RC head, however, the act out task fail to provide a set of referents from which a subset can be picked out (Hamburger and Crain 1982).

To eliminate the limitations of the act out task, recently the picture-sentence matching task (Friedmann et al. 2009) has been adopted widely to assess the children's comprehension of RCs. In this task, children are asked to choose one of the two pictures: one picture matches the sentence that they hear; in the other picture the two arguments are reversed. For example, for the Hebrew object RC *Tare li et ha-pil she-ha-arie martiv.* (*'Show me the elephant that the lion is wetting.'*), the children are required to select one picture from those shown in Figure 4-1.

However, as noted by Adani (2011) and Arnon (2005), this method is not an appropriate task to individuate the referent of a RC head because the children are required to select a picture rather than a character in the picture. Thus, even when a correct picture was chosen, we are unclear whether the child is indeed pointing to the correct or incorrect referent. As noted by Hu et al. (2016), even if the children choose the correct picture matching the sentence *the elephant that the lion is wetting*, the correct choice does not necessarily reflect the knowledge of

Figure 4-1 A set of picture used in sentence-picture matching task
(Friedmann *et al.* 2009).

RC in children, given the fact that the child might merely rely on the embedded clause '*the lion is wetting*' to choose a picture depicting a lion is wetting.

Arnon (2005) and Hu *et al.* (2016) modified the sentence-picture matching task by asking children to point to a referent rather than a picture, which is named as character-picture verification task. By doing so, it is possible to pinpoint which character the children are choosing. In addition, the character-picture verification task might yield more fine-grained class of errors.

Several studies have been conducted on comprehension of Mandarin RCs in typically developing children by using the act out task and the character-picture verification task. Chang (1984) used the act-out task to test forty-eight school-aged Mandarin children's comprehension of SS, SO, OS and OO RCs. Results show that there is no significant difference on the accuracy between SS and SO RCs, and between OS and OO RCs, suggesting that there was neither the subject RC nor the object RC preference in comprehension. However, as Su (2006) noted, object RCs used in the experiment should be better categorized as subject RCs (object RC *bei gongche zhuang de qiche*, 'the car that was bumped into by the bus'). Given the problematic stimuli in the experiment, it is hard to interpret the results.

Lee (1992) tested sixty-one children's (age range 4;0-8;0) comprehension of

SS, SO, OS and OO, SIO and OIO RCs by using the act out task.[①] The findings pointed to a subject RC advantage across all age groups (e.g., at age four: SS 41.7%, SO 25%, OS 14.6%, OO 2.1%; at age six: SS 79.2%, SO 14.6%, OS 31.3%, OO 14.6%; at age eight: SS 93.8%, SO 72.9%, OS 93.8%, OO 45.8%). Cheng (1995) also used the act out task to test 36 preschool children on their comprehension of SS, SO, OS and OO RCs and found that subject RCs are easier to interpret than object RCs. Cao, Goodluck, and Shan (2005) (cited in Hu *et al.* 2016) tested thirty-four children (age range 4;1 to 6;1) and found that there was no subject-object asymmetry (e.g., 83% vs.78% for children aged 5;2; and under).

Hu *et al.* (2016) tested 120 Mandarin-speaking children (age range 3;0-8:11) on their interpretation of subject RCs and object RCs by adopting the character-picture verification tasks. The stimuli used in the experiment are illustrated in (1).

(1) a. Subject RC

       Na   yi-ge   shi da xiaogou de xiaomao?

       which one-CL is hit dog   DE cat

       'Which one is the cat that hits the dog?'

   b. Object RC

       Na   yi-ge   shi waipo   hua de xiaohai?

       which one-CL is grandma paint DE child

       'Which one is the child that the grandma paints?'

All the matrix sentences started with *na yi-ge* '*which one*' to ensure that the participants single out a character instead of a picture. Each experimental sentence was matched with a set of experimental pictures, consisting of two drawings, in which one is the target picture; the other is the one with opposite thematic roles. The results show that up to seven years of age, Chinese children showed a subject RC preference when asked to select a character (e.g. 3-year-old: Subject

---

① SIO indicates that the head noun functions as the subject of the main clause but the indirect object of the relative clause. OIO indicates that the head noun functions as the object of the main clause but the indirect object of the relative clause.

RC 47.8% , Object RC 24.8%; 5-year-old: Subject RC 72.5%, Object RC 20.6%; 7-year-old: Subject RC 99.4%, Object RC 45.6%). The observed subject over object RC primacy was attributed to the RM effect involved in the object RC.

Following Adani (2011), we hold that the experimental setting in Hu *et al.* (2016) does not satisfy Hamburger & Crain's felicity requirements, given the fact that within one picture no other possible referent to be chosen is presented (e.g. an extra-cat or child). We further assume that even if both pictures are to be taken into account at the same time, which can satisfy the felicity requirement, the design might underestimate the children's interpretation of RCs. Because when the children are required to select a single referent in two separate pictures, the children are considering four possible referents, which will impose more processing load than the tasks in which children are required to select one referent among three possible referents in one picture, which was adopted by Adani (2011).

4.2 Previous studies on the Relative Clause comprehension in children with SLI

Extensive studies have found that children with SLI across typologically different languages are impaired in the comprehension of RCs, for example, in English (Adams 1990), Greek (Stavrakaki 2001), Hebrew (Friedmann and Novogrodsky 2004), Swedish (Håkansson and Hansson 2000), Danish (Jensen de López *et al.* 2014) and Mandarin (He and Yu 2013). Studies of children with SLI speaking languages with head-initial RCs consistently report that there is a subject over object RC advantage in the comprehension, as the scene in the production. As in the English example in (2), the Subject RC (2a) is easier to be comprehended than Object RC (2b). Many hypotheses have been proposed to account for the language deficit exhibited in the RC comprehension and the subject RC over object RC asymmetry in comprehension. We will review them in the following subsections.

(2) a. Subject Relative Clause: the boy that is kissing the mother
    b. Object Relative Clause: the boy that the mother is kissing

4.2.1 Linear order analysis

The linear order analysis was first proposed to account for the syntactic deficits in agrammatism (Caplan 1983) (for a similar claim regarding SLI see Cromer 1978). This analysis is based on the assumption that SLI children do not have an intact representation of RC and that the assignment of thematic roles of arguments in RCs is solely dependent on their linear order. Namely, the first noun phrase is interpreted as the agent of the event and the second noun phrase as the theme.

This analysis predicts that the comprehension of subject relatives like (2a) is always without problem because in (2a) the first noun phrase happens to be the agent and the second is the theme. However, the comprehension of object relatives will encounter difficulties in that such a strategy of interpretation will always lead to a reversed interpretation of the sentence. For example, when SLI children are presented with the object relative '*the boy that the mother is kissing*', they will take *the boy* to be the agent and *the mother* to be the theme, according to their linear order. As such, they will constantly choose the picture depicting the boy is kissing the mother.

However, results of the previous studies seemingly do not endorse this analysis. For example, in Friedmann and Novogrodsky (2004), when the children are required to interpret an object RC, the SLI groups chose one of the pictures randomly and performed at a level not significantly different from chance. The analysis predicts that the SLI children will consistently commit thematic role reversal errors, namely, a below-chance performance in binary sentence-picture matching.

This analysis predicts that the Mandarin-speaking children with SLI will have greater accuracy in interpreting the object RC than the subject RC, which is contrary to the children with SLI speaking languages with head-initial RCs. Mandarin is a language with head-final RCs, as illustrated in (3), when children were asked to interpret the object RC (3b), they encountered no difficulty because the first noun phrase happens to be the agent and the second the theme. However, they will also choose the wrong picture when they are required to interpret the subject RC (3a), where the first noun phrase is the theme and the second is the agent.

(3) a. Subject RC

    qin mama de nühai

    kiss mother DE girl

    'the girl that the mother kissed'

  b. Object RC

    Mama qin de nühai

    mother kiss DE girl

    'the girl that the mother kissed'

This prediction has been borne out partially by He and Yu (2013). The authors found that the accuracy on the object RC comprehension (83.3%) in children with SLI is significantly greater than that on the subject RC (63.3%) by using a sentence-picture matching task. But this analysis cannot account for the fact that the children with SLI had a chance level performance in subject RC condition (63.3%). In addition, as discussed earlier, the sentence-picture matching task is problematic; therefore the results seem hard to be interpreted.

4.2.2 Representational deficit for dependent relationship theory

The Representational Deficit for Dependent Relationship theory (RDDR for short) was proposed first by van der Lely (1996), and developed by van der Lely and Battell (2003). They assumed that the deficit in SLI is located in the syntactic computational system. Specifically, the deficit is related to the children's impaired knowledge concerning syntactic movement, which makes them treat movement as optional, rather than obligatory.

The theory predicts that SLI children will be susceptible to errors, but it cannot predict the exact performance in comprehension of subject RCs and object RCs. Friedmann and Novogrodsky (2004) further proposed a detailed account by adopting the theory of Grodzinsky (1990). Precisely, the deficiency is due to inability to assign thematic roles to noun phrases (NPs) that have been replaced from their original sentential positions. When an NP lacks a thematic role because of movement, a non-syntactic strategy will be adopted to interpret this NP in terms of its thematic role. Namely the linear order will determine the thematic role. NPs that do not move retain their thematic roles.

In the subject RC condition (2a), the moved NP *the boy* cannot be assigned a thematic role by using the syntactic knowledge, but it is the first NP encountered by the SLI children. Thus it will be assigned an agent thematic role, which happens to be correct. Therefore, in such a condition, they will always choose the correct picture in the sentence-picture matching task. However, trouble arises when the NP without the thematic role is not an agent but rather, for example, a theme. In this case the theme receives an inappropriate agent role, as in the case of (2b). If the unmoved NP retains its thematic role, in (2b), the NP *the mother* will get an agent role also. In such case, the children with SLI will adopt a guessing strategy, which will give rise to the chance-level performance in object RC comprehension task.

This theory can also cover the data from Mandarin children with SLI. He and Yu (2013) reported an object over subject RC advantage in the comprehension task. RDDR predicts an object RC over subject RC advantage in Mandarin. In the object RC (3b), the moved NP *nühai* (the girl) cannot be assigned a thematic role by using the syntactic knowledge, but it is the second NP encountered by the SLI children. Thus, it will be assigned a theme role, which happens to be correct. Therefore, in such a condition, they will always choose the correct picture in the sentence-picture matching tasks. However, trouble arises when the NP without the thematic role is an agent. In this case the agent receives an inappropriate theme role, as in the case of (3b), where the moved NP *nühai* (the girl) is the second NP. If the unmoved NP retains its thematic role, in (3b), the NP *mama* (the mother) will get a theme role also. In such a case, the children with SLI will adopt a guessing strategy, which will give rise to the chance-level performance in object RC experiment.

However, the picture is not so simple. In last chapter, we have concluded that the RDDR cannot account for the performance of SLI children in production. An ideal theory should explain the performance in both modalities.

4.2.3 Relativized minimality

Many researchers converge at the view that the widely-observed subject RC preference in comprehension of children with SLI is attributable to RM effect. As discussed in last chapter, the object RC involves RM violation, but the subject RC does not.

Jensen de López *et al.* (2014) explored the comprehension of subject and object RCs in 18 Danish-speaking children with SLI (aged from 5;0 to 8;4), 18 age-matched controls (aged from 5;0 to 8;2) and 9 language-matched controls (aged from 4;0 to 6;5) by adopting the picture-sentence match task following Friedmann and Novogrodsky (2004). The results showed that the three groups did not differ in terms of subject RCs, whereas the accuracy of the children with SLI in comprehension of the object RC was significantly lower than both the aged-matched and language-matched children. All the three groups performed significantly better on the subject RC than the object RC, which corroborates the prediction of RM.

Arosio, Panzeri, Molteni, Magazù, and Guasti (2017) tested the comprehension of Italian RC in 12 children with SLI (age range 6;1–10;2 years) and children with Developmental Dyslexia (DD) and 2 groups of typically developing children (age matched and language matched children). By using a sentence-picture matching task, they tested the comprehension of subject RCs, object RCs and passive object RCs. The results indicated accuracy in passive object RC comprehension is significantly better than in object RC comprehension for all groups (SLI children: object RC 47%, passive object RC 72%; age-matched TD children: object RC 73%; passive object RC 97%; language-matched TD children: object RC 64%; passive object RC 77%). The comprehension of subject RC in the three groups is unproblematic (SLI children: 96%; age-matched children: 94%; language-matched children: 89%). They accounted for intervention effects using RM and further held that children with SLI have a deficit in transferring thematic roles to moved elements.

But RM seems unable to account for the data from Mandarin-speaking SLI children. According to RM, Mandarin children with SLI will have more difficulties in comprehension of object RC than that of subject RC. He and Yu (2013) studied the comprehension of RCs in Mandarin children with SLI aged from 4;0-6;1 by adopting a sentence-picture matching task following Friedmann and Novogrodsky

(2004). They found that the accuracy on the object RC comprehension (83.3%) in children with SLI is significantly better than that on the subject RC (63.3%). For TDA and TDY children, there was no significant difference in the accuracy between the two RCs. They attributed the impaired performance on the subject RC to the inability to identify the thematic role of the head in subject RCs. The findings are inconsistent with the prediction of RM.

The results obtained from the studies of the population with aphasics speaking Mandarin also indicate that there is an object RC preference in comprehension. Zhou *et al.* (2010) found a similar object RC primacy in the comprehension in 2 aphasic adults. By using the sentence-picture matching task similar to that in He and Yu (2013), they found that subject RCs are harder to comprehend than object RCs (aphasic one: subject RC 60%, object RC 70%; aphasic two: subject RC 40%, object RC 90%). They proposed Argument Crossing Hypothesis to explain the object RC advantage in comprehension. The core assumption of the Hypothesis is that the structures involving the displacement of an element across the verb are harder to process. In Mandarin Chinese, the movement of the head in object RC crosses the verb, whereas in subject RC, the movement does not cross the verb, as shown in (4).

(4) a. Subject RC: __qin   mama   de nühai

                 V   O   S

             kiss the mother DE girl

             'the girl that kissed the mother'

      b. Object RC: Mama   qin __   de nühai

                S   V   O

             the mother kiss   DE girl

             'the girl that the mother kissed'

The findings from the Mandarin RC comprehension seemingly do not corroborate the prediction of RM approach, pointing to the object RC preference. In fact, we propose that the object RC advantage found in the above-mentioned two studies is caused by the limitations of the research design, as discussed previously. To repeat, the picture-sentence matching task may permit the participants to use alternative strategy to fulfill the task, and thus does not necessarily reflect the knowledge of RC of the participants.

4.2.4 Impaired processing mechanisms

All the theories discussed previously reach the consensus that the deficit seen in the RC comprehension lies in the impaired syntactic representation. Other scholars hold that the deficit is due to the impaired processing mechanisms instead of the decayed grammar.

Hestvik *et al.* (2010) showed that perception difficulties with RCs seen in children with SLI are due to the limitations in processing mechanisms but not the impairment in the grammatical knowledge. By using a cross-modal picture naming task, they examined whether English-speaking SLI (age range: 8–13 years) and TD (age range: 8–12 years) children performed differently in their real-time construction of filler-gap dependencies in RCs. The results indicated that the mean naming accuracy for TD children (89%) was higher than for SLI children (84%), which is consistent with both the grammatical knowledge impairment account and the processing mechanism impairment account. However, on the off-line measure of comprehension of the same stimuli sentences, SLI children (mean accuracy 76%) and TD children (mean accuracy 78%) did not differ qualitatively, which does not corroborate the prediction of the grammar impairment theories. Thus they arrived at the conclusion that the core deficit in SLI is impairment in language processing functions, rather than in grammatical knowledge.

Rakhlin, Kornilov, Kornilova, and Grigorenko (2016) investigated RC comprehension in Russian-speaking TD children (age range: 7; 08–15; 25) and children with developmental language disorder (DLD) (age range: 5; 08–15; 83) and adults. Russian is a language characterized by flexible word order and rich morphological case, which allows them to identify sources of syntactic complexity and evaluate their roles in RC comprehension by children with DLD. They administered a working memory task modeled after the analogous subtest of Wechsler Intelligence Scale for Children and an RC comprehension task, in which the stimuli consisted of subject and object-gap center-embedded and right-branching RCs.

The DLD group (subject center-embedded RC: 42%; object center-embedded RC: 26%; subject right-branching RC 42%; object right-branching RC: 45%) exhibited lower overall mean accuracy than TD children (subject center-embedded RC: 65%; object center-embedded RC: 40%; subject right-branching RC 43%; object right-branching RC: 56%), which is attributed to the limited working memory scores. And the lower accuracy on the object RC relative to the subject RC is caused by the non-canonical word order in object RCs or the greater representational complexity measured by the depth of gap. The greater accuracy on the center-embedded RCs relative to right-branching RCs is attributed to the different working memory resources needed in comprehension of the two RC types. The significantly lower overall accuracy in RC comprehension in the DLD group compared to their TD peers has a causal relation with the limited working memory in children with DLD. In addition, children with DLD exhibited a less effect of case relative to the TD children, suggesting reduced sensitivity to morphological case markers as processing cues. They arrived at the conclusion that the key deficit in children with DLD is not attributable to syntactic component but to limitations in working memory resources.

This chapter seeks to explore the linguistic characteristics of the Mandarin-speaking SLI children's comprehension of RCs. Based on previous studies reviewed above, we will address the following specific research questions by using the character-picture verification tasks in Experiment 4: (1) Do Mandarin children with SLI differ in the comprehension of subject RCs, object RCs and passive object RCs; (2) Do Mandarin children with SLI differ from TDA and TDY children in their comprehension of RCs? (3) Do children with SLI commit the same errors as TDA and TDY children? By using the sentence-picture matching task in Experiment 3, we seek to examine whether or not the Mandarin children have similar performance in the sentence-picture matching task and the character-picture verification task.

To our best knowledge, no other studies have examined the comprehension of RCs in Mandarin children with SLI by using sentence-picture matching task and character-picture verification task at the same time, by which we might ascertain the nature of the deficit seen in children with SLI more deeply by teasing apart the factors affecting results of the experiment. We also compare the comprehension of the object RC and passive object RC by using the character-picture verification task for the first time in the studies on Mandarin children with SLI. In addition, by comparing the data of the current study and those in previous studies, we might have a deeper understanding of the impairment in those children because Mandarin is a language with head-final RCs, which is typologically different from the languages, which have been examined extensively.

4.3 Experiment 3: Sentence-picture matching task

4.3.1 Method

4.3.1.1 Participants

The participants are 17 children with SLI; 15 TDA children and 15 TDY children. The procedure of identification of the children with SLI is the same as that reported in Experiment 1[①]. The language proficiency was assessed by using the *Peabody Picture Vocabulary Test– Revised Chinese Version 1990* (PPVT-R for short), and *Diagnostic Receptive and Expressive Assessment of Mandarin* (DREAM for short) (Ning *et al.*, 2014).The children's performance IQ was assessed with *Wechsler Preschool and Primary Scale of Intelligence--Fourth Edition* (WPPSI-IV (CN) for short). All the children with SLI have fulfilled all the tasks. The TDA and TDY children are the same as those participating in Experiment 1 and 2.

4.3.1.2 Materials and Procedure

The stimuli consisted of 10 subject RCs, 10 object RCs, as exemplified in (5).

(5) a. Subject RC

Zheli you sange   xiaogege, zhiyixia qin xiaojiejie de xiaogege

here exist three-Cl broter   point to kiss sister   DE brother

---

① The reader may see the procedure of identification on page 61-65.

'There are 3 brothers, point to the brother that kissed the sister.'

b. Object RC

Zheli you   sange   xiaogege, zhiyixia xiaojiejie qin de xiaogege

here exist three-Cl brother   point to sister   kiss DE brother

'There are 3 brothers, point to the brother that the sister kissed.'

To build up our stimuli, we used the same transitive verbs for all the two sentence types, which include *tui* 'push', *ti* 'kick' , *qin* 'kiss', *zhuang* 'bump', *pai* 'beat', *yao* 'bite' , *mo* 'touch', *bao* 'hug', *bei* 'carry on back', *zhui* 'chase'. A total of eight nouns were employed to depict the animate characters (*gege* 'brother', *jiejie* 'sister', *xiaomao* 'cat', *xiaogou* 'dog' , *xiaoyang* 'sheep', *xiaoniu* 'calf' , *laohu* 'tiger' , *shizi* 'lion'). Experimental items were randomized and presented in the same order to all participants. All the test sentences were between nine and eleven words.

All sentences were semantically reversible. Each sentence was matched with a set of cultured pictures, consisting of three pictures. One picture matched the sentence whereas the second picture depicted the reverse action, and the third picture functioned as a distraction. An example was provided in Figure 4-2.

Figure 4-2 A set of pictures used in Experiment 3

The participants were tested individually in a quiet room of the kindergarten. The children were instructed to listen carefully to the experimenter and to point to the picture that best illustrated what they heard. Before each experimental sentence was presented, the experimenter asked children to select one picture after hearing a simple declarative sentence (e.g. *Zheli you sanfutu, Zhiyixia xiaogege qin xiaojiejie* '*There are three pictures, show me the brother is kissing the sister*'). If children can choose the correct picture, the experiment will continue. Through this procedure we made sure that children comprehended simple declarative sentences. All the participants chose the correct pictures after hearing the simple declarative sentences.

4.3.1.3 Scoring and error coding

We coded a response as correct when the participant accurately identified the correct picture (out of three). Otherwise, we coded the response as Error. Errors were labeled as Reversal error and Other error. A Reversal error was coded when the children pointed to the picture depicting the reverse action, namely, they refer to the picture where *the boy is kissing the girl*, when they were asked to point to *the brother that the sister is kissing*. Other error was coded when children pointed to the distraction picture.

4.3.2 Results

We calculated children's accuracy on the comprehension of subject and object RCs, which is provided in Table 4-1. The experiment yielded 940 responses in total, half of which were obtained from the subject RC comprehension task and the other half from the object RC comprehension task. The descriptive results indicate that in all the three groups no clear subject or object RC primacy was displayed. The observation was confirmed by the statistical analysis.

Table 4-1   Numbers (N), percentage (%), means (M), and standard deviations (SD) of correct responses in each group in the sentence-picture matching task

Groups	Subject RCs					Object RCs			
	N	%	M	SD		N	%	M	SD
SLI	137	80.5	8.05	1.81		134	78.8	7.88	2.31
TDA	150	100	10	0.00		150	100	10	0.00
TDY	141	94	9.4	1.45		125	83.3	8.33	2.05

Firstly, we examine whether there is subject-object RC asymmetry in the comprehension of RCs. Wilcoxon Signed Ranks Test shows that in all the three groups, there was no significant difference in the accuracy on the subject RC and object RC comprehension (children with SLI z=-.040, p=.968>.05; TDA children z=0.000, p=1.000>.05; TDY children z=-1.703, p=0.089>.05).

Secondly, we compare the performance of RC comprehension in the three groups. Kruskal-Wallis Test indicates that there is significant difference among the three groups in comprehending the subject RC (χ^2=18.085, p<.01). The Mann-Whitney tests show that significant difference was detected between the children with SLI and the TDA children (U=37.500, z=-3.927, p<.01), and between the children with SLI and the TDY children (U=65.000, z=-2.572, p=.01<.05). There was no significant difference between the two groups of typically developing children (U=90.000, z=-1.792, p=.073>.05). Kruskal-Wallis Test indicates that there is significant difference among the three groups in comprehending the object RC (χ^2=14.288, p=.001<.05). The Mann-Whitney tests show that a significant difference was detected between the children with SLI and the TDA children (U=37.500, z=-3.915, p<.01), and between the TDA and the TDY children (U=60.000, z=-2.940, p=.003<.05). There was no significant difference between the children with SLI and the TDY children (U=110.500, z=-0.668, p=.504>.05).

When children failed to choose the correct picture, they consistently pointed to the picture depicting the reverse action. No participant in the current study committed other errors, suggesting that all the children have a sound knowledge of the semantic meaning of the verbs used in the stimuli.

To conclude, by testing the comprehension of RCs in the picture-sentence task, we observed that (I) Mandarin SLI children experienced more difficulties in comprehension of subject RC and object RC than both the TDA and TDY children. (II) No asymmetry of the subject-object RC in comprehension in the three groups has been detected. The first finding conforms to the previous studies, whereas the second result does not. All previous studies showed that SLI children had more difficulties with object RCs, compared with subject RCs (eg. Friedmann and Novogrodsky 2004; Jensen de López *et al.*, 2014).

4.3.3 Discussion

As reported in 4.3.2, no subject-object RCs asymmetry has been detected in the comprehension by the three groups. The findings are at odds with that of most studies on TD Mandarin-speaking children's comprehension of RCs and the SLI children's comprehension of RCs in other languages. More crucial is the fact that the comprehension results are in contradiction to the production results in this dissertation, which indicate that the children with SLI produced significantly more subject RCs than object RCs. In chapter 3, we arrived at the conclusion that RM might account for the asymmetry, given that in the object RC there is an intervening element blocking the establishment of the local relationship between the head and the gap. In fact no theory mentioned in 4.2 can provide satisfactory explanation for the absence of subject-object RCs asymmetry in comprehension.

We propose that the Surface Account (Leonard 2014a: 288-292) might give a satisfactory explanation. Leonard (1989) first proposed the theory to explain the serious difficulties with grammatical morphology in children with SLI and then in subsequent works more details were added to it (Leonard 2014b). The account was termed as the 'surface' account because of its emphasis on the physical properties of grammatical morphology. This account ascribed the difficulties with grammatical morphemes in SLI children to the short duration of the morphemes. According to the account, because of limited processing capacity, children with SLI are severely taxed when they encounter the morphemes, with brief duration, playing important grammatical roles. In other words, when the morphemes play separate grammatical roles, the children must perform additional operations, such as discovering the grammatical functions of them. This is done in the press of perceiving the rest of sentence being heard. It is assumed that the additional operation plus the brevity of the morphemes will give rise to incomplete processing of the morphemes. As a result, the children with SLI will need more encounters with the morphemes before they are established in the children's grammar.

If we extend this analysis to the case of Mandarin RCs, the results of sentence-picture matching task can be accounted for satisfactorily. In Mandarin RCs, the function word 'de' plays an important grammatical function, at the same time, it is brief in duration. We propose that Mandarin children with SLI have incomplete processing capacity of the function word, when perceiving RCs. As a result, when they process the object RC (e.g. *xiaojiejie qin de xiaogege 'the brother that sister kissed'*) they will mistakenly reckon that the sentence is a SVO sentence (*Xiaojiejie qin de xiaogege* 'The sister kissed the brother'). In the picture-sentence matching tasks, they will happen to make the correct choice. Whereas in the subject RC condition, when they heard the experimental sentence (e.g. *qin xiaogege de xiaojiejie 'the sister that kissed brother'*), the sentence will be regarded as an illicit sentence (*Qin xiaogege de xiaojiejie*). Hu (2014: 64-65) proposed that in this case the young children may parse the subject RCs as a declarative clause with a dropped topic, as shown in (6).

    (6) a. qin xiaojiejie de xiaogege

          kiss sister   DE brother

          'the brother that kissed the sister'

       b. *pro* qin xiaojiejie

             kiss sister

        ' (the brother) kissed the sister'

We adopt this propose and hold that in the subject RC condition the children with SLI happened to have the correct choice by only processing the embedded part of RCs.

    More crucial is the fact that the Surface Account can also explain the data from other topologically different languages. For example, when English SLI children encounter a subject RC as in (2a), they might omit the complementizer *that*, and get a SVO sentence (*the boy that is kissing the mother*). In the sentence-picture experiment, they will choose the correct picture. In the case of object RCs (2b), they will get an illicit sentence (*the boy that the mother is kissing*). If they adopt a guessing strategy, they will have a chance-level performance in the task of object RC comprehension. If the above analysis is on the right track, the sentence-picture matching task might overestimate the subject RC comprehension in languages with head-initial RCs, given the fact that the children might parse the subject RC as a simple sentence. The Surface Account can also be supported by the findings obtained from the sentence repetition studies in chapter 5. We will turn to this question in detail in that chapter.

In summary, the findings from experiment 3 indicate that Mandarin-speaking children with SLI have similar accuracy in comprehension of subject and object RCs, which is contrary to the results of previous studies and the production studies. We assume that the outcome is owing to a non-syntactic strategy employed to interpret RCs by our participants. Therefore, this experiment cannot assess the children's syntactic knowledge of RCs. In Experiment 4, we will adopt a different method, which ensures that the children cannot use this strategy to interpret RCs.

4.4 Experiment 4: Character-picture verification task

4.4.1 Motivation for Experiment 4

We assume that Experiment 3 is far from being ideal to test the SLI children's comprehension of RCs. The reasons are two-fold. The first reason is that the choices presented to the children should not be whole pictures. Experiment 3 is labeled as sentence-picture matching task, which cannot be used as a technique to test the children's knowledge of RCs. As pointed by Quine (1960) (quoted in Heim and Kratzer 1998), restrictive RCs are noun modifiers, and they have the same function as adjectival phrases and prepositional phrases. For instance, in order to interpret RCs in (7), the listener must understand that the embedded clause is a noun modifier and that the noun that is being modified is the NP '*the boy*'. So the choices presented to children must be some characters in the picture, not the whole picture. As discussed in 4.3.4, even if the children happen to choose the correct picture, we cannot surely conclude that they have the necessary syntactic knowledge to interpret the RC.

(7) the boy that is kissing the mother

The second reason is that the design of Experiment 3 is not pragmatically felicitous (Adani 2011). Restrictive RCs are to restrict the referent set given in the context. Hence, in order for the RC in (7) to be pragmatically felicitous it is presupposed that at least two or more *boys* are presented in the context. The design of Experiment 3 follows Friedmann and Novogrodsky (2004). Friedmann and Novogrodsky explicitly stated that the experimental setting satisfies Hamburger and Crain's felicity requirement. Adani (2011) suggested that this is not the case given that within one picture no other possible referents to restrict the set are presented. In other words, the choice between two pictures as in experiment 3 is not the correct task to individuate the referent of a RC head. In order to overcome the weakness in experimental design, we conduct Experiment 4 to test the comprehension of RCs by children with SLI. The experiment design follows Adani (2011).

By conducting Experiment 4, we seek to answer the following specific questions: (1) Is there any difference between the comprehension of subject RCs, object RCs and passive object RCs by SLI children? (2) Compared to TDA and TDY children, do Mandarin SLI children have more difficulties in their comprehension of RCs?

4.4.2 Method

4.4.2.1 Participants

The participants are the same as those in Experiment 3, which consisted of 17 children with SLI, 15 TDA children and 15 TDY children[1].

4.4.2.2 Material and Procedure

The stimuli under investigation are given in (8), which consisted of 10 subject RCs, 10 object RCs and 10 passive object RCs. To build up our stimuli, we used the same transitive verbs for all three sentences types, which include *tui* 'push', *ti* 'kick' , *qin* 'kiss', *zhuang* 'bump', *pai* 'beat', *yao* 'bite' , *mo* 'touch', *ca* 'wipe', *shi* 'wet', *zhui* 'chase'. A total of eight nouns were employed to depict the animate characters (*gege* 'brother', *jiejie* 'sister', *xiaomao* 'cat', *xiaogou* 'dog', *xiaoyang* 'sheep', *xiaoniu* 'calf', *laohu* 'tiger', *shizi* 'lion'). Experimental items were randomized and presented in the same order to all participants. All the test

---

[1] The reader may see descriptions on the participants on page 116.

sentences were between nine and eleven words.

    (8) a. Subject RC

        Zheli you liang ge xiaogege, zhiyixia qin xiaojiejie de xiaogege

        here exist two CL brother point to kiss sister DE brother

        'there are two brothers, show me the brother that is kissing the sister'

    b. Object RC

        Zheli you liang ge xiaogege, zhiyixia xiaojiejie qin de xiaogege

        here exist two CL brother point to sister kiss DE brother

        'there are two brothers, show me the brother that the sister is kissing'

    c. Passive object RC

        Zheli you liang ge xiaogege, zhiyixia bei xiaojiejie qin de xiaogege

        here exist two Cl brother point to Pass sister kiss DE brother

        'there are two brothers, show me the brother that is kissed by the sister'

All sentences were semantically reversible. Each sentence was matched with one cultured picture, which had the same structure: person (animal) X on the left, person (animal) Y in the middle and person (animal) X on the right. For example, a boy that is kissing a girl and the girl is kissing another boy, as shown in Figure 4-3. The direction of the action in the experimental trial pictures was towards the left in 5 pictures and towards the right in 5 pictures.

Figure 4-3 A sample of the experimental pictures

The experimental sentences were presented to the participants in pseudo-random order. Participants were tested individually in a quiet room of the kindergarten. The children were instructed to listen carefully to the experimenter and to point to the character that best matched what they heard. When the experimenter gave the directions, he or she pointed to the two X persons or animals in order to ensure that the children will point to the character in the picture, instead of the whole picture. For example, the experimenter pointed to the two boys in figure 4-3 one after another, when she or he said: *zheli you liang ge xiaogege, zhiyixia qin xiaojiejie de xiaogege* (*There are two brothers, show me the brother that the sister is kissing.*).

4.4.2.3 Scoring and error coding

We coded a response as correct when the participant accurately identified the correct character (out of two). Otherwise, we coded the responses as Errors. Errors were labeled as Reversed error or Middle error respectively. When the children chose the other character corresponding to the head NP, we coded the response as Reversed error. For example, when children heard an object RC (*Zhiyixia xiaojiejie qin de xiaogege*, '*Point to the boy that the sister kissed.*'), they pointed to the boy on the right rather than the boy on the left in Figure 4-3. Therefore, it seems that the children misinterpreted theta-roles of the NP head, namely in the object RC, the head NP is the Patient, but the child interprets it as an Agent. When children pointed to the character in the middle, we coded this response as Middle error. For instance, the child pointed to the sister in the middle after hearing the object RC (*Zhiyixia xiaojiejie qin de xiaogege,* '*Point to the boy that the sister kissed.*').

4.4.3 Results

We calculated children's accuracy on the comprehension of subject, object and passive object RCs, which is provided in Table 4-2. The experiment yielded 1410 responses in total, one third of which were obtained from the subject RC comprehension and one third from the object RC comprehension, the rest from the passive object RC task. Percentages of different response types by each group are provided in Table 4-2.

Firstly we will investigate the question whether there is any difference in the comprehension of subject RCs, object RCs and passive object RCs. The results of Wilcoxon Signed Ranks Test indicated that SLI children performed significantly better in the subject RC condition than in object RC condition ($z=-2.22$, $p=.026 <$ .05). However, there was no significant difference between the object and passive object RC conditions ($z = -.74$, $p=.458 > .05$). For the TDA children, they reached at the ceiling level in all the three conditions, and thus there is no difference in the comprehension of the three RCs. For the TDY children, there is no significant difference either between the subject RC and object RC ($z = -1.59$, $p=.113 >$ .05) or between the object RC and the passive object RC ($z = -.30$, $p=.763 >$ .05). Thus, we can answer the first specific research question of this chapter: for children with SLI, they performed better on the subject RC condition than the object RC condition, whereas for the two groups of typically developing children, no difference was detected among the three RCs. The results of the target response analysis confirmed the prediction that the children with SLI had greater accuracy in the subject RC than in the object RC, and that no difference existed between the object RC and passive object RC.

Table 4-2   Percentage (%) of responses in the comprehension of subject RCs, object RCs and passive object RCs in each group

Group	Subject RCs			Object RCs			Passive object RCs		
	T	R	M	T	R	M	T	R	M
SLI	75.8%	10.5%	13.5%	48.2%	30.5%	21.1%	56.4%	28.2%	15.2%
TDA	100%	0	0	98.6	1.3%	0	100%	0	0
TDY	92%	4.6%	3.3%	86.7%	8.6%	4.7%	88%	12%	0

Note: T= Target; R= Reversed error; M=Middle error

Secondly we will examine whether there is any difference among the three groups in the comprehension task, to answer the second specific question of this chapter. For the comprehension of subject RCs, the Mann-Whitney Test indicated that there is significant difference between the SLI and TDA children ($U= 60.00$, $z = -3.215$, $p < .01$), but no significant difference was detected between the SLI and TDY children ($U = 91.00$, $z = -1.523$, $p=.128 > .05$). In the object condition, there is significant difference between the TDA and SLI children ($U = 34.00$, $z = -3.833$, $p = < .01$) and between the SLI and TDY children ($U = 51.50$, $z = -2.980$, $p < .01$). For the performance in the passive object task, significant difference was also detected both between the children with SLI and the TDA children ($U = 37.50$, $z = -3.910$, $p = < .01$) and between the children with SLI and the TDY children ($U = 70.50$, $z = -2.215$, $p = .027 < .05$). Therefore, we can provide answer to the second research question: compared to their typically developing peers, the children with SLI were severely impaired in the comprehension of the RCs, especially in the case of the object RC comprehension task.

To sum up, in the character-picture verification tasks the subject RC preference manifested itself, which was contrary to the results of the experiment 3, but consistent with the results of the production studies of this dissertation and the studies on the TD Mandarin-speaking children's comprehension of RCs. Compared to the results of Experiment 3, the children with SLI had lower accuracy in the RC comprehension, which is due to the fact that in Experiment 3, children with SLI may interpret RCs as simple sentences by ignoring the complementizer, whereas in Experiment 4, such strategy is unavailable to the children with SLI.[1]

We turn to the non-target responses, which are also very informative to the nature of deficiency in processing the RC in children with SLI. We can see that Middle Errors are nearly restricted only to the children with SLI and Reversed Errors were more common than Middle Errors in TDY children.

In comprehension of three types of RCs by children with SLI, no significant difference was found between the Reversed Errors and the Middle Errors (subject RC condition: $z = -.418$, $p = .676 > .05$); (object RC condition: $z = -1.054$, $p = .292 > .05$); (passive object RC condition: $z = -1.072$, $p = .284 > .05$).

Because no error was committed by the TDA children, we will only

---

[1] One of the reviewers raised the question why the children with SLI cannot interpret the RCs as simple sentences by ignoring the complementizer in Experiment 4. Our answer to this question is that in Experiment 4, when children with SLI want to interpret the RCs as simple sentences, they will find that the intended SVO sentences does not match the given picture, because in the picture there are three characters, which cannot be depicted by an SVO sentence.

compare the performances of the children with the SLI and TDY children. For the comprehension of subject RCs, there is no significant difference between the children with SLI and the TDY children in terms of the two errors (the reversed Error: U=99.50, z=-1.221, p=.222>.05; the Middle Error: U=96.50, z=-1.429, p=.153>.05). For the comprehension of object RCs, the SLI children committed significantly more Reversed Errors (U= 63.00, z= -2.530, p=.011< .05) and Middle Errors (U= 65.50, z= -2.527, p=.018<.05) compared to TDY children. For the comprehension of passive object RCs, there is no significant difference between the children with SLI and the TDY children in terms of the Reversed Errors (U=95.50, z=-1.256, p=.209<.05). In the comprehension of passive object RCs, the percentage of Middle Errors is 15.2%, whereas TDY children never committed such errors. In the comprehension of object RC, there was no significant difference between the target response and the Reversed errors by the children with SLI (z=−1.822, p=.069>.05). To conclude, when the children with SLI failed to choose the correct response, they will commit the Reversed and Middle errors evenly. In the comprehension of object RCs, they made more Reversed and Middle errors even than the TDY children.

4.4.4 Discussion

To begin with, we will address the question why the children with SLI had greater accuracy in the subject RC task than the object RC task. Both the linear order analysis and the Representational Deficit for Dependent Relationship theory cannot account for the results of the current study.[①] According to such theories, the comprehension of object RCs in Mandarin Chinese will be better than that of subject RCs, which is in contrary to our findings.

As discussed in Chapter 3, the RM and EFUH can provide a satisfactory explanation for the findings of the current study. According to RM, in the configuration of object RCs, the dependency between the relative head and the trace is hard to establish for children with SLI because there is a qualified element intervening between them. Due to a temporary computation overload

---

① For detailed analysis, the reader may refer to the discussion in 4.3.3.

of the impaired language system, the children with SLI will encounter difficulty in establishing a dependency when the head and its origin are separated by an intervening element in the object RC condition. In subject RCs, there is no such qualified element intervening between the relative head and the origin, and thus no RM violation arises.

RM effect does not manifest itself in the TDA children and TDY children's comprehension of the RCs. Just as discussed in last chapter, the TDA children's grammar is nearly adult-like, given the fact that they have reached the ceiling level in processing the two types of RCs. The RM effect manifested itself in the TDY children's production of RCs but does not in the comprehension tasks, possibly due to the fact that the comprehension task was less taxing than the production task.

The results of the current study are different from Hu *et al.* (2016), which reported that even seven-year-old Mandarin-speaking children cannot interpret object RCs correctly (accuracy percentage: 45.6%). We propose that the discrepancy between their results and the findings of the current study might be attributable to the different research design. Hu *et al.* (2016) conducted a character-picture verification task by using two pictures, in which there were four characters. Children's responses were categorized as correct response, the Embedded NP Error, Reversal Error, and Other Error. However, in the current study, there are three characters to be chosen. The children were considering four possible referents in their study, which imposed more processing load than the tasks in which children are required to select one referent among three possible referents in one picture, as in current study. Tentatively, we assume that the study using two pictures might underestimate the RC knowledge of the children.

Interestingly, in the comprehension task we observed that there is no significant difference between object RCs and passive object RCs. The findings are consistent with that in the production studies in this dissertation reported in last chapter. Although according to Belletti (2009), in passive object RCs, the RM may not arise, there are many other constraints restricting the processing of them, such as EFUH, as discussed in Chapter 3. However, the results are inconsistent with that reported in Arosio *et al.* (2017), in which the Italian-speaking children with SLI had a greater accuracy in the comprehension of passive object RC (72%) than the object RC (47%) in a sentence-picture matching task. They ascribed the improved performance in the passive object RC to the absence of RM effect in that structure following Contemori and Belletti (2014). We propose that the reasons for the differences in the two studies are two-fold. The first reason is that in their study, the children with SLI aged from 6;1–10;2, who probably have a better mastery of the passive sentence. The children in our study are much younger (age range: 4;5 to 6;0), and thus they might encounter greater difficulty in the interpretation of passive sentence (e.g. Li 2015). The second reason is that Arosio *et al.* (2017) adopted the sentence-picture matching task to assess the comprehension of RCs, which might overestimate the children's knowledge of RCs, as discussed previously.

Now we turn to discuss the nature of the syntactic deficiency of children with SLI shown in the comprehension data. The performance of children with SLI in this task also corroborates EFUH. Firstly, our results show that children with SLI already performed 75.8% correct in the subject RC condition and no significant difference was detected between the SLI and TDY children in the subject RC comprehension. We tentatively conclude that the children with SLI understand the structure, although not in a consistent way. The scene in the object RC comprehension is different. Although the children with SLI can perform 48.2% correct, there is significant difference even between them. Hence we cannot hastily arrive at the conclusion that the representation of object RC is available to children with SLI. Considering the findings in the priming production Experiment, we maintain that the poorer performances of the children with SLI in the object RC tasks are the repercussions of a more severely impaired syntactic representation of object RCs.[①] As discussed in Chapter 2, EFUH correctly predict that children with SLI will exhibit an impaired syntactic representation of structures involving EFs.

[①] In the priming production task reported in Chapter 3, children with SLI does not exhibit priming effect in the object RC task, which indicates that the syntactic representation of object RCs are absent in their grammar.

Secondly, the non-target responses may be more informative to the nature of the syntactic deficit. According to Adani (2011), the occurrence of the Middle error is an indication of a genuine problem in deriving the correct representation of a RC. In other words, the Middle error consists of interpreting only the embedded TP. In the comprehension of object RCs, the children with SLI committed more Middle errors than the TDY children, which may lend additional plausibility to the conclusion that there is a serious problem for the SLI children to project the representation of object RCs in their grammar.

Thirdly, the presence of the Middle errors may provide further evidence for the proposal we raised in last chapter. In the production study, we found that the children with SLI opted for the declarative sentences and sentence fragments instead of the target RCs. We proposed that the SLI children may be insensitive to the semantic function of RCs. When the children with SLI encountered an object RC (e.g. *qin xiaojiejie de xiaogege* '*the brother that kissed the sister*'), they cannot recognize that the RC is about the referent of the head noun (*xiaojiejie* '*the sister*'). In such a situation, they may just process the embedded part of the RC, which in turn resulted in the Middle errors.

Fourthly, according to the RDDR, the Reversed error is caused by the fact that the children with SLI are unable to assign thematic roles to noun phrases (NPs) that replaced from their original sentential position. The RM states that the reason for this deficiency is that in the object RC the local dependency is blocked by an intervener. Friedmann and Novogrodsky (2004) proposed that when the moved NP cannot be assigned a thematic role by using the syntactic knowledge, the children with SLI will adopt a non-syntactic strategy to solve the problem. The moved NP is the second NP in the object RC; and thus the SLI children will reckon that it has the theme role according to the linear order. If this argument is on the right track, the children with SLI will choose the correct character. But this prediction was not collaborated by our findings.[1] We proposed another explanation for our findings. When children with SLI found that the local relationship between the head and

---

[1] Our findings indicate that children with SLI had poor performance in the object RC task, which is inconsistent with the prediction of RDDR.

the copy is hard to be established, they probably treat the object RC (*xiaojieie qin de xiaogege* 'the brother that the sister kissed') as a subject RC (*qin xiaojiejie de xiaogege* 'the brother that kissed the sister'). In such situation, they will commit the Reversed errors.

The findings in the elicitation production can support this proposal. In the production task, the intended object RCs (e.g. *xiaojieie qin de xiaogege* 'the brother that the sister kissed') are occasionally replaced with subject RCs with thematic role reversal (e.g. *qin xiaojiejie de xiaogege* 'the brother that kissed the sister') by the children with SLI because subject RCs are less demanding to the impaired grammar system. The cross-linguistic studies can provide further evidence to our proposal. In a study of 55 typically developing (aged 5;0-9:0) Italian children's comprehension of object RCs, Adani *et al.* (2010) found that the majority of the non-target responses that children adopt at all ages results from interpreting an object RC as a subject RC. They attributed the results to the intervention by the intervener DP, along the lines proposed by Friedmann *et al.* (2009). However, we found that in the subject RC condition, there were also Reversed errors. We proposed that the reason is that the linear blocking effect manifested itself in Mandarin subject RCs.

In last section, we have mentioned that the Surface Account (Leonard 2014a: 288-292) can give a satisfactory explanation for the absence of the subject-object asymmetry in the first comprehension task. Now we will explore the question whether the surface Account can explain the findings of the current study. According to the Surface Account, if children with SLI omit the relativizer '*de*' in the object RC condition, they will get a declarative sentence (*xiaojieie qin de xiaogege* 'the sister kissed the brother'), in subject RC condition, they will get an illicit sentence (*qin xiaojieie de xiaogege* '*kissed the sister the brother'). Unlike the experiment 3, there is only one picture to choose; therefore the children with SLI cannot select one picture to match the sentences they perceived. We predict that they will select the characters in the given picture randomly. Therefore, there is no difference between the two conditions, which is contrary to our findings. The conclusion is that the Surface Account cannot explain the findings of this experiment.

4.5 Summary

In summary, this chapter has found that in Experiment 3 there is no subject over object RC advantage in comprehension by children with SLI, which is interpreted as a result of badly-designed experiment. The results of the current study indicate that the methodology issues exert great influence on outcomes of the research, as shown by the discrepancy of Experiment 3 and Experiment 4. The character-picture verification task used in Experiment 4 might assess the genuine competence of children in the comprehension of RCs, in that it prevents children from using alternative strategy to interpret RCs. We observed a subject RC primacy in the comprehension of RCs by children with SLI, which corroborates the prediction of RM. The errors in children with SLI suggest that the there is a genuine problem in deriving the correct representation of object RC in children with SLI. In a word, the results obtained from the comprehension task also lent support to EFUH.

In next chapter we assess the repetition of RCs in children with SLI, with the aim to further examine the nature of deficiency in children with SLI exhibited in the acquisition of RCs.

Chapter 5
The Repetition of Relative Clauses

Sentence repetition is considered a reliable measure of children's grammatical knowledge. This chapter assesses the repetition of RCs by children with SLI by using Experiment 5, in which children were required to repeat subject RCs and object RCs with the adjective placed in the main clause or the embedded clause. We aim to investigate linguistic characteristics of SLI children's repetition of RCs in this chapter. This chapter is organized as follows. In 5.1, we will introduce the sentence imitation task briefly, in which two different views will be discussed. In 5.2, we will review previous studies on repetition of RCs in the TD children. In 5.3, previous studies on the RC repetition by children with SLI will be presented. In 5.4, we report experiment 5. Section 5.5 is a conclusion.

5.1 The elicitation imitation

Clay (1971) is one of the first scholars who proposed that sentence repetition can be used as an important paradigm to test the syntactic representation of children. The argumentation goes like this: the repetition of an utterance longer than the children's word span, which is the number of random words they can repeat, is not only dependent on the short-term memory (STM) but also long-term memory (LTM). The syntactic representation in LTM can facilitate the long sentence recall, which is impossible relying solely on the STM.

Lust, Flynn, and Foley (1996) also assumed that sentence repetition permits researchers to investigate children's grammatical competence. The assumption is that if the child can successfully repeat the full sentence, that they hear, then it can be inferred that the child can retrieve the syntactic representation of the sentence and reuse it in reproduction. The child could not repeat the sentence correctly, if they are not equipped with the grammatical competence, which is indispensable for analyzing and reconstructing the stimulus sentence. Given its sensitivity to syntax, many researchers use it to test typically developing children's syntactic competence (Frizelle, O'Neill, and Bishop 2017; Kidd *et al.* 2007).

However, other researchers claimed that in addition to the syntactic representation, the sentence repetition also involves numerous cognitive processes: phonological STM to keep short-term phonological information (Rummer 2004; Willis and Gathercole 2001), the Central Executive to deal with the exchange of information between STM and LTM (Jefferies, Ralph, and Baddeley 2004), and phonological output processes (Riches *et al.* 2010). Because we do not have a clear knowledge about cognitive processes involved, we usually encounter difficulties when deciding root causes of poor performance in sentence repetition. However, because the results of sentence repetition are open-ended, children can make a wide variety of errors. Given variation in error patterns across different populations, many scholars proposed that sentence repetition data can be used to investigate underlying language difficulties (Riches *et al.* 2010).

It should be noted that recent studies have found that sentence repetition is capable of distinguishing between children with SLI and the non-affected individuals with high degrees of sensitivity and specificity (Conti-Ramsden, Botting, and Faragher 2001; Everitt, Hannaford, and Conti-Ramsden 2013; Seeff-Gabriel, Chiat, and Dodd 2010; Smolík and Vávrů 2014; Stokes, Wong, Fletcher, and Leonard 2006). Therefore in this chapter we will adopt sentence repetition as a testing technique to assess the SLI children's competence in RC. It may give further evidence to the assumption that sentence repetition is a highly discriminating diagnostic marker of SLI.

Lust *et al.* (1996) proposed that sentence repetition can be readily applied cross-culturally and cross-linguistically, with only minimal variation in conducting results analysis. In this chapter, we will adopt the sentence imitation task to investigate the RC knowledge in Mandarin children with SLI. This continuity in methodology is critical to the attempt to investigate whether or not the difficulty reported for children in other languages manifests itself in Mandarin-speaking children with SLI. In addition, sentence repetition is accessible to children with limited language resources, even to children as young as 1 to 2 years of age. Thus, it is easier to test children with SLI using elicited imitation than other experimental methods (e.g. the truth value judgment task), which are often too complicated for the children with SLI, because it is widely assumed that the language development in children with SLI is severely delayed.

5.2 The repetition of RCs in TD children

Diessel and Tomasello (2005) examined the 4-year-old English and German-speaking children's imitation of RCs. The stimuli used in the experiment were the Subject-, Object-, Indirect Object-, and Genitive-RCs. They found that both the two groups of children had a similar pattern of responding: the best performance was on subject RCs, which is followed by object RCs, indirect object RCs, oblique RCs and genitive RCs. They claimed that the results of the study challenged the analysis capitalizing on the varying distance between filler and gap (Gibson 2000) and proposed a multifactorial analysis.

Firstly, they proposed that children's good performance on subject RCs can be accounted for by the greater easiness with which subject RCs are activated than other types of RCs because of the higher frequency in the input received by the children. It is commonly acknowledged that the more frequently occurred construction will be more deeply entrenched in mental grammar, which is in line with the spirit of the Frequency Hypothesis. Secondly they claimed that variances in the acquisition of different RCs is primarily dependent on the similarity of various types of RCs to simple sentences. To be more precise, children performed best on subject RCs than on all other RCs because subject RCs resemble simple non-embedded sentences.[1] While the similar performance on the object-, indirect object-, and oblique -RCs were attributed to the fact that these RCs involve the same sequence of nouns and verbs (NP [NP V . . .] REL), which distinguishes

---

[1] For example, the word order of English subject-RCs resembles that of SVO sentences.

them from all other RCs.

Interestingly, Diessel and Tomasello (2005) claimed that their proposal can also account for the results from the Mandarin RC processing studies. Hsiao and Gibson (2003) showed that in Mandarin, object RCs cause fewer difficulties than subject RCs. As discussed previously, Mandarin uses RCs before the head noun, in turn it is object RCs (NP VP DE NP) that are more similar to simple sentences (NP VP NP) instead of subject RCs (VP DE NP NP). They claimed that the results can be accounted for by the filler-gap Hypotheses (Gibson 2000) and a word-order theory raised by themselves and the latter provided a more straightforward account for their findings. However, whether there is a subject RC preference or object RC preference in Mandarin RC processing is quite controversial. For example, Lin and Bever (2006) argued that Hsiao and Gibson's (2003) assumption of an object RC preference in Mandarin did not hold water, as their experiment was confounded by a crucial factor. They conducted a self-paced reading study of regular RCs and that of possessor RCs and showed a preference for subject-extracted RCs in Mandarin. Bearing this in mind, we should be very cautious to claim that the word-order theory can explain the results of the Mandarin RC processing studies, as well as the results of the acquisition study, which shows that the subject RCs are acquired earlier and better (Hsu *et al.* 2009; Hu *et al.* 2016; Hu *et al.* 2015).

Kidd *et al.* (2007) examined RC repetition in English- and German-speaking children (3;1-4;9 years) by employing the stimuli, which are used most frequently in their natural speech. In corpora studies, they found that the input may exert significant influences on the children's production of object relatives. Specifically, children often produce object relatives with an inanimate head noun, and a pronominal relative clause subject, which is in conformity to the distributional and discourse regularities of the ambient language.

The repetition results indicated that when children were required to imitate the object relatives with inanimate head noun, no subject-object RC asymmetry was detected and that children performed better at repeating RCs with pronominal subjects than those with lexical NP subject. They proposed that the better performance on the object RC with inanimate head is due to the fact that an inanimate head is not topic-worthy enough and makes no good candidate for an agent (Mak, Vonk, & Schriefers 2006) and therefore primes the use of object RCs. Taken together, they proposed that children are sensitive to the same constraints on RC processing as adults, which suggested a large degree of continuity between the child and adult processing and production systems. And the subject-object RC asymmetry derives from the violation of constraints on processing rather than constraints on syntactic derivation. The argumentation is open to criticism because the study has not teased apart the syntactic factors, which are widely assumed to be critical to the successful reproduction of a sentence.

Frizelle *et al.* (2017) compared TD children's performance on multiple choice picture-matching sentence comprehension task and sentence repetition task. Thirty-three typically developing children (age range: 5;0 to 6;6) were recruited to complete both tasks, in which the subject, object, indirect object, oblique, genitive subject and genitive object RCs were assessed. They found that repetition was easier than the comprehension because children showed the ability to repeat sentences which they did not understand, which is primarily ascribed to the fact that the sentence-picture matching task require skills beyond those of linguistic competence, and thus increasing the processing load.

Modeled on Kidd *et al.* (2007), Hsu (2014) investigated the RC acquisition in Mandarin-speaking TD children (3-year-olds, 4-year-olds, and 5-year-olds) using the sentence repetition task. By analyzing the database of the Taiwan Corpus of Child Mandarin (TCCM for short) (Cheung, Chang, Ko, and Tsay 2011), she found that in the spontaneous production of the eight children, subject RCs are usually with animate heads (12/14, 85.7%) while object RCs with more inanimate heads (28/30, 93.3%). She created test materials that matched distributional and discourse regularities found in the corpus study. The stimuli used in this study are provided in (1).

(1) a. Short Subject-gap RC

     ___ Dakai nahe   liwu   de nühai yijing huijia   le

        Open   that-CL   present   DE   girl   already go home Asp

        'The girl that opened the gift has gone home already'

b. Short Object-gap RC

Nawei   nühai dakai___de liwu   yijing bujian le

That-CL girl open   DE present already gone Asp

'The gift that the girl opened has disappeared already'

c. Long Subject-gap RC

___ Dakai nahe   shengri liwu   de nühai yijing huijia   le

    Open that-CL birthday present DE girl   already go home Asp

'The girl that opened the birthday gift has gone home already'

d. Long Object-gap RC

Nawei   duanfa   nühai dakai___de liwu   yijing bujian le

That-CL short-haired girl   open   DE present already gone Asp

'The gift that the short-haired girl opened has disappeared already'

As shown in (1), the study also manipulated the length of RCs. In long RCs, an adjective is positioned in the RC; while in the short RCs, an adjective in the main clause.[1] The results showed that while inconsistent patterns in subject RC and object RC manifested themselves in the younger children, the 5-year-olds consistently exhibited a clear subject over object RCs advantage.[2] Children of all groups scored higher in the short RC condition than in the long RC condition. She concluded that children under age four rely more on the surface word order in their production of RCs; while children above age four rely more on the syntactic representation in production, given the fact that they performed better on subject RCs than object RCs consistently because object gaps are more deeply embedded in the hierarchical structure than subject gaps.

It should be noted the research design in Hsu (2014) is not flawless. The stimuli in the study mimicked the features found in the child corpus, as a consequence, the study did not control the animacy of the NPs involved in RCs.

---

[1] In long subject RCs, the distance between the head and the trace is greater than that in short subject RCs. However, the position of adjectives in object RCs does not affect the length between the head and its trace.

[2] The younger children refers to those aged from 3-4.

Thus, all the RCs in the study are not irreversible, namely, the agents are animate NPs, while the patients are inanimate NPs. Processing such RCs does not require full syntactic knowledge, which has been proved in chapter 3. Therefore, the RCs employed in the sentence repetition task cannot be used to assess the children's competence of RCs.

5.3 The sentence repetition in population with SLI

Most researchers hold that the limitations in RC repetition by children with SLI suggest that the decayed knowledge lies in the limited working memory or processing capacities, instead of an impaired syntactic knowledge.

Riches *et al.* (2010) used the sentence repetition to assess the competence of RCs in three groups: adolescents with SLI, autism spectrum disorders plus language impairment and typically developing adolescents. They were required to repeat sentences containing RCs that varied in syntactic complexity, as in (2)

(2) a. SRCM: The policeman who chased the thief wore a **big black** hat.

b. SRCR: The policeman who chased the **tall thin** thief wore a hat.

c. ORCM: The thief who the policeman chased wore a **big black** hat.

d. ORCR: The thief who the **tall thin** policeman chased wore a hat.

They manipulated both the gap position and the length of RCs. As a result, there are four conditions, namely, subject RC with adjectives in the main clause (SRCM), or in the relative clause (SRCR) and object RC with adjectives in the main clause (ORCM) or in the relative clause (ORCR). The linear distance between the filler and the gap may be altered by different positions of adjectives. To be more specific, the distance between the filler and the gap in ORCR is greater than that in ORCM.

The results show that the adolescents with SLI are more severely impaired than the other two groups. They are more likely to commit errors on object RCs, and to make syntactic changes during repetition. Errors with particular syntactic structures may provide an insight into an individual's syntactic competence, and their linguistic representations in LTM. The SLI groups' performance was significantly affected by the adjectives positions in the two ORC, because the adjectives placed within ORCR increase the length of the head and the gap, and thus placing a greater burden on working memory. This may result in poor comprehension, which in turn affects repetition. They ascribed the severe syntactic difficulties in SLI to their STM limitations.

By using a sentence-recall task, Frizelle and Fletcher (2014) investigated RCs in English-speaking school-aged children with SLI. The head of the RC represented a range of syntactic roles, namely subject, object, indirect object, oblique, genitive subject and genitive object. The results show that the limitations in the repetition of RCs in children with SLI were starkly revealed, compared to their age-matched and younger TD children. In addition, the results indicate that the children with SLI had the best performance on subject RCs, followed by object relatives. Interestingly, compared to object RCs with an inanimate head noun, and a personal pronoun as the subject, the advantage for subject RCs did not hold. They concluded that children with SLI who are close to 7 years of age have significantly greater difficulty with RCs than their age peers and typically developing children who are on average 2 years younger. They imputed the limitations of SLI children to both the processing of grammatical structure and the frequency of specific structural types.

Coco, Garraffa, and Branigan (2012) examined the production of subject RCs in Italian Children with SLI (mean age=5;4) by comparing the performance in the structural priming paradigm and sentence repetition task. The results indicated that children with SLI were much more likely to produce subject RCs during priming (24%) than in sentence repetition (16%). They assumed that children with SLI can spontaneously produce subject RCs in the structural priming paradigm, suggesting their decayed performance in repetition is possibly related to working memory, instead of a deficit in syntactic representation.

Garraffa *et al.* (2015) investigated the production of subject RCs in Italian pre-school children (51-75 months) with SLI and age-matched typically-developing children controls. In a sentence repetition task, children were required to imitate subject RCs. In the priming task, children with SLI were required to produce subject RCs after hearing the experimenter use subject RCs with the same lexical content. In effect, the children in the second task also repeated the heard subject RC, which may be termed as repetition in the priming paradigm. The results show that the children with SLI performed markedly better in the latter (77%) than in the former task (16%). They proposed that the wide disparity of the performance in children with SLI between the two tasks may lie in the demands placed upon working memory. To be more precise, the repetition task requires children to maintain a representation of the whole sentences in working memory during the reproduction in order to reproduce the sentences in entirety; while in the repetition in the priming paradigm, the children can comprehend priming sentences and subsequently reproduce their own responses incrementally. They summarized that the poor performance in the repetition tasks may not always provide a reliable reflection of children's underlying grammatical knowledge, although it has been claimed to be a clinical marker of SLI.

The above mentioned studies are in line with an influential hypothesis suggesting that sentence repetition measures a distinct memory system (Alloway & Gathercole 2005). To be more precise, sentence repetition tasks are to tap primarily the capacity of the episodic buffer, and to a lesser extent of the phonological loop (Alloway, Gathercole, Willis, and Adams 2004).

However, many other scholars challenged the assumption. Klem *et al.* (2015) proposed that sentence repetition should be seen as a valuable tool to assess comprehensive language capacities because it draws upon a wide range of language processing skills rather than only a distinct memory system. Thus, the performance in the sentence repetition tasks is a reflection of the underlying language ability because the morphological, grammatical and phonological knowledge are involved during sentence repetition. Archibald and Joanisse (2009) also proposed that a variety of linguistic and memory skills are necessarily involved in sentence repetition, and thus children with SLI may perform poorly on the task for linguistic or processing limitations. Especially, they suggested that sentence recall was a relatively better marker of the language impairment than the working memory impairments possibly owing to its greater linguistic demands. Seeff-Gabriel *et al.* (2010) also suggested that the sentence imitation test is informative about the morpho-syntactic abilities of children with speech disorders.

Based on the previous studies reviewed in 6.2 and 6.3, we will address the following specific research questions by using experiment 5: (1) Is there subject-object RC asymmetry in sentence repetition by SLI children? (2) Do children with SLI differ from the TDA and TDY children in sentence repetition? (3) Will the repetition of RCs by children with SLI be affected by variance of the linear distance between the filler and the gap? (4) What is the nature of the possible limitations exhibited in the repetition of RCs in children with SLI?

To date, no study has examined the repetition of RCs in Mandarin children with SLI. Thus, the current study allows us to probe deeply the performance of the children with SLI in repeating RCs, by which we might ascertain the nature of the deficit seen in the children with SLI. In addition, by comparing the findings in the current study and those in the elicitation production and the comprehension tasks, we might obtain a more comprehensive understanding of the competence of RCs in children with SLI.

5.4 Experiment 5: The sentence repetition task

5.4.1 Method
In this subsection we will illustrate the method of Experiment 5, which consists of the participants, the material and procedure and the data coding.

5.4.1.1 Participants
The participants are the same as those participating in the elicitation production task in Experiment 1 and 2[①].

5.4.1.2 Material and Procedure
There were twenty-four left-branching RCs used as the stimuli in the task, half of which were subject RCs, and half of which were object RCs, which allows

----

① The reader may see descriptions on the participants on page 61-65.

us to examine whether there was asymmetry of subject-object RC in repetition. To overcome the weakness in Hsu (2014), we conduct an experiment, in which the materials are all designed as reversible sentences. Following Riches *et al.* (2010), we put some adjectives in main clauses or RCs to increase the linear distance between the gap and filler in subject RCs. Thus, we have four types of RCs: namely subject RCs with adjectives in the main clauses (SRCM) or in RCs (SRCR); object RCs with adjectives in the main clauses (ORCM) or in RCs (ORCR). Please note that only in subject RC condition, the position of the adjectives will change the linear distance between the filler and the gap. For example, in the SRCM (3a), there are three words intervening between the filler and the gap, whereas in the SRCR (3c) four words occur between the filler and the gap. However, in the object RC condition, the place of the adjectives does not affect the linear distance between the filler and the gap, where in both conditions only one word intervenes between the filler and the gap. To compare the performance on the SRCM and SRCR, we seek to answer the question whether or not the repetition of RCs by children with SLI will be affected by variance of the linear distance between the filler and the gap.

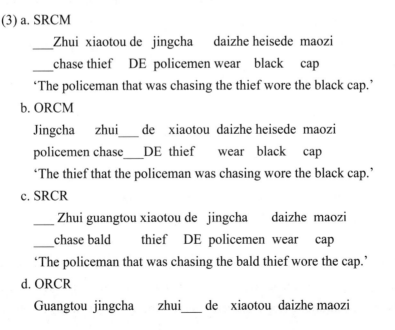

(3) a. SRCM

    ___Zhui xiaotou de jingcha   daizhe heisede maozi

    ___chase thief   DE policemen wear   black   cap

    'The policeman that was chasing the thief wore the black cap.'

  b. ORCM

    Jingcha   zhui___ de   xiaotou daizhe heisede maozi

    policemen chase___DE thief   wear   black   cap

    'The thief that the policeman was chasing wore the black cap.'

  c. SRCR

    ___ Zhui guangtou xiaotou de jingcha   daizhe maozi

    ___chase bald   thief   DE policemen wear   cap

    'The policeman that was chasing the bald thief wore the cap.'

  d. ORCR

    Guangtou jingcha   zhui___ de xiaotou daizhe maozi

    bald   policemen chase___DE thief   wear   cap

    'The thief that the bald policeman was chasing wore cap.'

To build up our stimuli, we used the same transitive verbs for all four sentences types. The verbs used in the RCs include *tui* 'push', *yao* 'bite', *qin* 'kiss' , *bao* 'hug', *la* 'drag', *zhui* 'chase'. The verbs used in the main clauses include *dai* 'wear a hat', *you* 'have', *chuan* 'wear a dress'. A total of nine nouns were employed to depict the animate characters involved in the RCs (*gege* 'elder brother', *jiejie* 'elder sister', *xiaomao* 'kitten', *xiaogou* 'puppy' , *xiaoji* 'chicken', *xiaoya* 'duckling' , *ayi* 'aunt' , *meimei* 'younger sister', *didi* 'younger brother'). The adjectives used in the stimuli consist of *heise* 'black', *baise* 'white', *huangse* 'yellow', *hongse* 'red', *duanfa* 'short-haired', *piaoliang* 'beautiful', *keai* 'cute', *changfa* 'long-haired', *datou* 'big-headed'. All the test sentences were between eleven and twelve words.

Participants were tested individually in a quiet room of the kindergarten. Experimental items were randomized and presented in the same order to all participants. The experimenter read the sentences slowly to the participants and then asked them to reproduce what they heard verbatim. If a child did not respond to a test sentence, the experimenter repeated the sentence once, and then moved on. The whole experiment was audio-taped and then transcribed by the experimenter.

5.4.1.3 Data Scoring

Following Diessel and Tomasello (2005); Hsu (2014) and Kidd *et al.* (2007), a score of 1, 0.5, or 0 was assigned to the children's responses. We assigned the score of 1 for the exact repetition. The minor modifications of the sentence, which did not change the structure or the meaning of the target sentence, were permitted. For example, the omission, addition or modification of the aspect markers, determiners and classifiers (e.g. *dai-zhe* 'wear-Progressive' for *dai-le* 'wear-PAST') was assigned a score of 1. We assigned a score of 0.5 to the response containing minor deviations from the target sentence. Such deviations included (1) lexical substitutions (e.g. *xiaojiejie* 'sister' for *ayi* 'aunt'.); (2) addition and

omissions of adjectives or adverbs (e.g. *heise maozi* 'black cap' for *maozi* 'cap');
(3) the headless RCs (e.g. *zhui xiaotou de* 'the one that is chasing the thief' for
zhui xiaotou de jingcha 'the policeman that is chasing the thief').

We assigned a score of 0 to the response which is ungrammatical or alters the
structure or the meaning of the target sentence. The simple declarative sentences, the
sentence fragments and the uninterpretable sentences were all given a score of 0.

5.4.2 Results

The experiment yielded a total of 1032 responses, with 258 responses under each
condition. The frequency of each score under each condition for all the three
groups is provided in Table 5-1.

Table 5-1   Frequency of Score "0, 0.5, 1" under each condition for each group

	SRCM			ORCM			SRCR			ORCR		
	0	0.5	1	0	0.5	1	0	0.5	1	0	0.5	1
SLI	58	12	8	53	8	17	61	14	3	66	6	6
TDA	13	3	74	20	1	69	27	16	47	32	11	47
TDY	20	10	60	20	8	52	34	22	34	39	10	41

As shown in Table 5-1, in terms of the exact repetition of the sentences, the TDA
children ranked first, and the SLI children the last in all conditions. While in terms
of the completely incorrect repetition, the opposite is true. For all conditions,
the children with SLI produced more incorrect responses than exact responses
suggesting that they produced many non-target responses in imitating RCs. While
the TDA and TDY children produced more exact responses than the incorrect
responses across all conditions. Taken together, such patterns indicate that the
repetition of RCs by children with SLI is severely impaired compared to the TDA
and TDY children.

The sum scores and the average scores are summarized in Table 5-2 and 5-3.
The TDA children obtained highest scores and the SLI children got the lowest.
For all groups of children, when the adjectives are in the main clause, they
obtained higher scores regardless of the RC gap position. Unlike the findings in

the previous studies reported in last two chapters, all groups did not gain higher scores for subject RCs than for object RCs.

Table 5-2   Sum score (S), percentage (%), means (M) and standard deviation (SD) of each group in RCs with adjective in the main clause

	SRCM				ORCM			
Groups	S	%	M	SD	S	%	M	SD
SLI	14	18	1.07	1.15	21	27	1.61	1.78
TDA	75.5	84	5.03	1.90	69.5	77	4.63	3.5
TDY	65	72	4.33	1.79	56	62	3.73	2.06

The above observation was confirmed by a statistical analysis with a three-way mixed model ANOVA based on the raw scores: group (3) x gap position (2) x Adjective position (2). The analysis revealed significant main effects of group (F (2, 172) = 54.526, $p < .001$) and adjective position (F (1, 172) = 14.169, $p < .001$). There was no main effect of the gap position (F (1, 172) =.215, p =.644>.05). There were no interactions among the three factors or between any of the two factors *(ps > .05)*. The statistical analysis confirmed that the three groups have significant differences in imitating the RCs. The Turkey HSD post-hoc comparison revealed that the children with SLI performed significantly more poorly than both the TDA (*MD=-3.189, P<.001*) and TDY children (*MD=-2.514, P<.001*). There is no subject over object RCs advantage in all the three groups of children in sentence repetition.

Table 5-3   Sum score (S), percentage (%), means (M) and standard deviation (SD) of each group in in RCs with the adjective in the embedded clause

	SRCR				ORCR			
Groups	S	%	M	SD	S	%	M	SD
SLI	10	13	0.76	0.85	8	10	0.61	1.24
TDA	55	61	3.66	1.55	52.5	58	3.5	1.33
TDY	45	50	3.00	1.76	46	51	3.06	1.99

The three groups of children had better performance in RC with the adjective in the main clause than the RC with adjective in the relative clause. Given the fact that only in the case of subject RC condition, the position of the adjective can alter the linear distance between the head and the gap, we will further examine whether there is difference between the SRCM and SRCR and between the ORCM and ORCR. Firstly, we will explore whether there is difference between the repetition of SRCM and SRCR. We conducted a two-way mixed model ANOVA based on the raw scores of the subject RC imitation: group (3) x Adjective position (2). The analysis revealed significant main effects of group (F (2, 86) = 36.273, p < .001) and adjective position (F (1, 86) = 8.686, p =.004< .005). The results indicated that the three groups of children performed significantly better in imitating subject RCs with the adjective in the main clause than the subject RCs with adjective in the relative clause.

The same scene happened in the condition of object RC imitation tasks. We conducted another two-way mixed model ANOVA based on the raw scores of the imitation of object RCs: group (3) x Adjective position (2). The analysis revealed significant main effects of group (F (2, 86) = 20.567, p < .001) and adjective position (F (1, 86) = 5.855, p =.068<.005). The results indicated the three groups of children performed significantly better in imitating object RCs with the adjective in the main clause than the object RCs with adjective in the relative clause.

Now we turn to the non-target responses produced by our participants when they failed to produce the intended RCs. The definitions for these non-target responses are listed in (4).

(4) Seven types of non-target responses and their definitions
    a. The omission of the relativizer
        *zhui xiaoji   xiaoya daizhe heise maozi
        chase chichen duck   wear   black cap
        '*chasing chicken, the duck wore black cap'
        Intended: zhui xiaoji de xiaoya daizhe heise maozi
        (' The duck that is chasing the chicken wore black cap').
    b. The substitution of the relativizer for a verb
        *zhui xiaoji   zhui xiaoya daizhe heise maozi

chase chichen chase duck   wear   black cap

'*chasing chicken, chasing the duck, wore black cap'

Intended: zhui xiaoji de xiaoya daizhe heise maozi

(' The duck that is chasing the chicken wore black cap').

c. The substitution of the relativizer for a coordination marker *he*

*zhui xiaoji   he   xiaoya daizhe heise maozi

  chase chichen and duck   wear   black cap

'*chasing chicken and the duck, wore black cap'

Intended: zhui xiaoji de xiaoya daizhe heise maozi

(' The duck that is chasing the chicken wore black cap').

d. Responses transforming an object relative into a subject relative and vice versa

bao didi   de jiejie dai   hongse weijin

hug broter DE sister wear red   scarf

'the sister that hugged the brother wore red scarf'

The intended sentence

didi bao de jieji daizhe hongse weijin

'the sister that hugged the brother wore the red scarf'

e. Fragments:

yao xiaomao…heise you bandian

bite cat   black have spot

intended sentence:

yao xiaomao de xiaogou you heise bandian

bite cat   DE dog   have black spot

'The dog that bit the cat has black spot'

f. Uninterpretable utterances

xiaogou xiaomao daizhe weijin de   maozi

dog   cat   wear   scarf POSS hat

Intended sentence

Zhui heise xiaoya de   xiaoji   daizhe maozi

chase black duck   DE chichen wear   hat

'the chicken that was chasing the duck wore hat'

g.Non-RC responses

duanfa   jiejie chuan zhe chenshan

short-haired sister wear ASP shirt

'the short-haired sister was wearing a shirt'

Intended sentences

duanfa   jiejie tui   de ayi chuan zhe chenshan

short-haired sister push DE aunt wear ASP shirt

'the aunt that the short-haired sister was wearing a shirt'

The counts for these non-target types under each gap condition and for each age group are summarized in Table 5-4 and Table 5-5. Some interesting observations can be obtained from the analysis of the non-target responses. Firstly, the major difference between the children with SLI and the TD children is the errors concerning the relativizer DE, i.e. the omission of the relativizer, the substitution of the DE for a verb and the substitution of DE for a coordination marker *he* (*and*). This type of errors in the imitation task by children with SLI outnumbered that by the TDA children by two to one. The TDA and TDY children committed nearly equal such errors (TDA 37 vs. TDY 35).

Table 5-4   Frequency of each non-target type under each gap condition for each group in the RC with the adjectives in the main clause

Category	SLI		TDA		TDY	
	SRCM	ORCM	SRCM	ORCM	SRCM	ORCM
The omission of the relativizer	15	17	2	12	10	8
The substitution of the DE for a verb	9	7	4	0	3	0
The substitution of DE for a coordination marker *he*	3	0	0	0	0	0
RC transformation	0	4	5	7	0	3
Fragments	13	13	0	0	1	0
Uninterpretable utterances	8	6	1	0	4	11
Non-RC responses	13	11	0	1	2	8

Table 5-5 Frequency of each non-target type under each gap condition for each group in the RC with the adjectives in the relative clause

Category	SLI		TDA		TDY	
	SRCR	ORCR	SRCR	ORCR	SRCR	ORCR
The omission of the relativizer	6	5	5	14	7	7
The substitution of the DE for a verb	8	7	0	0	0	0
The substitution of DE for a coordination marker *he*	0	0	0	0	0	0
RC transformation	0	2	3	8	1	0
Fragments	16	12	3	3	3	4
Uninterpretable utterances	20	2	13	2	18	8
Non-RC responses	11	32	1	5	4	18

Secondly, the secondly-ranked errors for children with SLI in the repetition of RCs are Fragments and Non-RC responses. While for the TDA children, they usually transformed the RC structures. Thirdly, all three groups of children produced more uninterpretable sentences and fragments in the condition imitating the subject RCs with adjectives in the RC than the condition imitating the subject RCs with adjectives in the main clause.

Now we will explore for the children with SLI and TDA children whether a correlation exists between the imitation performance with the working memory and the processing speed using Pearson correlation parameters. For both groups combined, Processing Speed positively correlated significantly with the overall repetition score (r=.417, p=.027) and the Working memory did not correlate significantly with the overall repetition score (r=.173, p=.378).

5.4.3 Discussion

5.4.3.1 The subject-object RCs symmetry in the repetition task

The results of sentence imitation task indicate that all the three groups of children exhibit no subject-object RC asymmetry, unlike the results from the production study and the comprehension study in this dissertation. The results obtained from the current study are in disagreement with the proposals solely based on canonical word order, in that these proposals incorrectly predict that there is object over subject RC advantage. This is because in Mandarin object RCs (S V DE O, omission of the relativizer) have similar word order to the canonical sentences (SVO), while the subject RCs (V O DE S) has the word order of VOS.

The Linear Distance Hypothesis (Gibson 2000) also predicts that there is object over subject RC advantage. This is because the distance between the head and the gap in Mandarin object RCs is shorter than the distance between the head and the gap in subject RCs. The Frequency Hypothesis cannot explain the data either. The theory assumes that the easiness of acquisition of a particular structure is in proportion to the frequency of that structure in the input received by the children. As mentioned in chapter 3, the corpus studies on the input frequency of Mandarin children have yielded mixed results. Thus, we cannot determine whether our findings can corroborate the prediction of Frequency Hypothesis.

The theories based on the structural complexity cannot explain the results either. According to the analysis in last two chapters, we have firmly hold that in the comprehension and production of Mandarin RCs, there is clear subject-object RC asymmetry in all the three groups. The asymmetry was attributed to the blocking effect in object RCs, given the fact that in object RCs, the subject functions as a qualified intervener blocking the establishment of the local dependency between the relative head and its copy. It seems that the data obtained from the current imitation study are beyond the reach of RM and EFUH.

Some researchers claimed that no movement is involved in the derivation of Mandarin RCs (Yang 2013: 145). If we adopt such analysis, the data can be accounted for, because if no movement involved in the derivation of RC, there is no intervention effect in the object RC. In a priming production task, Yang (2013) found that there was no significant difference between the production of Mandarin subject RC (86%) and object RC (90%) by the young children (aged 3;0-6;0). She concluded that the symmetrical performance in the two conditions by the young children can provide further evidence to the non-movement analysis of RC derivation. However, as we discussed in chapter 2, the non-movement analysis cannot cover the syntactic features of Mandarin RCs. More crucial is the fact that the data from her priming production tasks are not reliable, because the animacy of the NPs in RCs was not controlled.

Therefore we cannot adopt the non-movement analysis, and thus the data from the current study remains unexplained.

We propose another explanation for the findings. The symmetric performance of our participants in the subject RC and object RC condition is due to the fact that in the object RC the structural intervention arises, but in the subject RC the linear intervention counts more. As discussed previously, in object RCs, the subject NP can function as an intervening element, which gives rise to the intervention effect. In the subject RC, although structurally there is no intervention effect, linearly the gap and the head of the RCs are intervened by the object NP (e.g.__zhui xiaomao de xiaogou. 'the dog that is chasing the cat'). We tentatively speculate that in the imitation of subject RCs, the linear intervention is also detrimental to the successful repetition.

As mentioned above, the success of repetition of an utterance longer than the children's word span is not only dependent on the STM but also LTM, in which the syntactic representation is included. In other words, the participant's accuracy rate depends heavily on memory and processing capacities and the syntactic representation. For children with SLI, when they are required to repeat object RCs, they have poor performance owing to the decayed syntactic representation, which has been proved by the production and comprehension studies of this dissertation. When it comes to the subject RC, the children with SLI will encounter difficulty due to their limited processing capacity because in the subject RC, the linear distance between the head and the gap is greater, which causes the processing cost (Gibson 1998). The TDA and TDY children's performances can also be explained in the same fashion: in the object RC there is structural intervention but in the subject RC the greater distance between the head and the gap causes difficulty.

Here we need to address the question why the linear intervention does not manifest itself in the production and the comprehension task. In other words, we need to answer the question why there is subject-object RC asymmetry in the production and comprehension task. We speculate that the key difference between the production, comprehension and imitation task lies in the fact that the imitation task is more dependent on the memory and processing factors, whereas the former two tasks mainly assess syntactic factors.[①] Garraffa *et al.* (2015) proposed that the imitation task require children to reproduce the target sentence while concurrently maintaining a representation of the entire heard sentence in working memory in order to reproduce it exactly. While in the comprehension and production tasks, children can mainly resort to the syntactic representation of the RC to fulfill the given tasks, which is less dependent on the processing and memory factors. The results from the production and comprehension experiment of the dissertation have manifested that the structural intervention can override the processing cost, given the fact that in the object RC there is structural intervention but processing the subject RC is more costly.

In a study of the RC imitation in Mandarin typically developing children (3;0-6;0), Hsu (2014) found that no asymmetry of the subject-object RCs manifested itself in the performance of the 3-year-olds (subject RC: 0.233 vs. object RC: 0.203) and 4-year-olds (subject RC: 0.402 vs. object RC: 0.375), while a clear subject over object RC advantage was detected in the 5-year-olds (subject RC: 0.612 vs. object RC: 0.456). Based on the observation that the word order of Mandarin object RC is similar to canonical word order, Hsu (2014) claimed that younger children (under 4) are more dependent on the surface word order in their imitation of RCs, whereas the more mature children (5 years old) gradually begin to resort to the abstract syntactic representation of RCs because abstract syntactic representations are usually developed gradually in childhood.

This explanation is far from being satisfactory. Firstly, if children under 4 rely more on the surface word order in their imitation, we would predict that the children will perform better in the object RC than in the subject RC, which has not been borne out by both the findings of Hsu (2014) and the current study. Secondly, Hsu (2014) conducted a three-way mixed model ANOVA: age (3) x gap position (2) x RC length (2) and found that there was a main effect of gap position. She speculated that it is the clear subject-object asymmetry of the 5-year-old group that contributed most to the overall significant main effect of gap

---

① In the previous chapters, we have proved that the syntactic factors outweigh the processing factors in production and comprehension tasks.

position. But this speculation was not confirmed by the statistical analysis directly. Thirdly, in the design of the study, the animacy of the NPs in the RCs is not controlled. As presented in chapter 3, the children performed better in producing the object RC with an inanimate head and animate RC-internal NP than the object RC with two animate NPs, whereas the animacy of NPs exerted less influence on the production of subject RCs. Thus it is difficult to interpret the finding from Hsu (2014) because the absence of the asymmetry of the two RCs may partly be owing to the mismatch of animacy of the NPs in the RCs. Fourthly, the proposal raised in Hsu (2014) fails to explain the data from the current study. As reported earlier, we did not find a clear subject-object asymmetry of the imitation in all the three groups. We have demonstrated in Chapter 4 that the TDY and TDA children have the intact syntactic representation of both the subject and object RCs. Therefore it is not plausible to claim that in the priming task they resort to the syntactic representation, while in the imitation task they mainly rely on the word order.

To summarize, we conclude that the absence of the subject-object asymmetry of the imitation in all the three groups should be attributed to the extra memory and processing overload required by the imitation task. Following Garraffa *et al.* (2015), we speculate that the performance of the children in sentence repetition may be not always the accurate reflection of children's underlying grammatical competence.

5.4.3.2 The asymmetry of RCs with adjective in main clauses or in the RCs
As reported earlier, adjective position affected performance of the sentence recall in the three groups. To be more precise, the results indicated the three groups of children performed significantly better in imitating RCs with the adjective in the relative clause than RCs with adjective in the main clause. The length of the dependency between the head and the gap is greater in subject RC with adjectives placed within the RC (SRCR) (e.g. ___ *Zhui guangtou xiaotou de jingcha daizhe maozi 'The policeman that is chasing the bold thief wore a hat.'*), than in subject RC with adjectives placed in the main clause (SRCM) (e.g. ___ *Zhui xiaotou de jingcha daizhe heise maozi 'The policeman that is chasing the thief wore a black hat'*). The fact that children had better performance in the SRCM than in

the SRCR is in agreement with the prediction of the Linear Distance Hypothesis (Hawkins 1989 among many others).[①] This is because in the SRCR the filler must be maintained longer in working memory, which may give rise to poorer comprehension, therefore it is harder to process SRCR compared to SRCM.

However, the results of the current study can only be partially accounted for by this hypothesis. The ORCM (e.g. *Jincha zhui __ de xiaotou daizhe heise maozi* '*The thief that the policeman was chasing wore black cap.*') and ORCR (e.g. *Guangtou jincha zhui__ de xiaotou daizhe maozi* '*The thief that the bald policeman was chasing wore cap.*') do not differ in the dependency length between the head and the gap. However, the results show that the children performed significantly better on the latter than on the former.

A similar finding was reported in Riches *et al.* (2010). They found that the English children performed better on the SRCM (e.g. *The policeman who__ chased the thief wore a big black hat.*) than on the SRCR (e.g. *The policeman who__ chased the tall thin thief wore a hat.*), although the position of the adjectives do not alter dependency length. They proposed that the different performance on the two RCs lies in the fact that the adjectives placed in the SRCRs increase the distance between the subject and the verb in the main clause. The greater distance means more demand of the working memory because the thematic role of subject is unspecified until we encounter the main verb. Thus, Working Memory may be more taxed by this kind of structure because a representation of the subject must be actively maintained before it can be integrated with the main verb.

However, this account failed to explain our data given the fact that in Mandarin, ORCM and ORCR do not differ in the length between the subject and the main verb. We propose an alternative account for this phenomenon. Mandarin ORCR (e.g. *Guangtou jincha zhui__ de xiaotou daizhe maozi* '*The thief that the bald policeman was chasing wore cap.*') is ambiguous to some degree, in

---

① It should be noted that the Linear Distance Hypothesis only holds water in the repetition task. We have proved in previous chapters that such hypothesis cannot explain the results of the comprehension and production tasks.

that the adjectives can be reckoned as a modifier of the subject NP in the RC ($[_{REL}[_{DP}$ *Guangtou jincha] zhui__ de xiaotou] daizhe maozi 'the thief that the bald policeman was chasing wore cap.*') or a modifier of the head of the RC ($[_{DP}$ *Guangtou* $[_{REL}$ *jincha zhui__ de xiaotou]] daizhe maozi 'The bald thief that the policeman was chasing wore cap.*'), whereas the Mandarin ORCM does not have two readings. We assume that it is the ambiguity in the ORCR that taxed more on the Working Memory, and thus leading to the poorer comprehension and the repetition.

The ambiguity of Mandarin object RCs with a modifier occurring before the RC was also reported in Wu and Sheng (2014). They found that object RCs with demonstrative-calssifier occurring before the RC are ambiguous and those with demonstrative-calssifier occurring after the RC are not ambiguous as shown in (5), whereas in the subject RC, the position of the demonstrative-calssifier does not affect the meaning of the sentence (e.g. *Nage yujian xingtan de nühai hen piaoliang. 'That girl who met the talent spotter is very beautiful.'*); *Yujian xingtan de nage nühai hen piaoliang. 'That girl who met the talent spotter is very beautiful.'*).

    (5) a. object RC with demonstrative-calssifier occurring before the RC

        Na-ge   xingtan   yujian de   nühai hen piaoliang.

        Demontrative-classifier talent spotter meet DE girl very beautiful

        First reading: 'That girl who the talent spotter met is very beautiful.'

        Second reading: 'The girl who that talent spotter met is very beautiful.'

      b. object RC with demonstrative-calssifier occurring after the RC

        Xingtan   yujian de na-ge   nühai hen piaoliang.

        talent spotter meet DE Demontrative-classifier girl very beautiful

        'That girl who the talent spotter met is very beautiful.'

In the production of object RCs, the participants were more likely to produce the unambiguous RCs with demonstrative-classifier occurring after the RC (51%). In the production of subject RCs, subject RCs with demonstrative-classifier occurring after the RC (22.5%) less frequently occurred. The findings were accounted for by the Audience Design Hypothesis (Temperley 2003): in production the speakers tend to avoid the ambiguous expression to the benefit of the hearers.

To summarize, we propose that position of the adjectives in the RCs affects the accuracy of the repetition because the adjectives placed in the RC taxed more on the Working Memory. In the SRCR, the adjective increases the length of dependency; whereas in the ORCR, the adjective causes the ambiguity. In consequence, our participants performed equally worse on the subject-object RCs with adjectives placed in the RC (e.g. SLI children SRCR: 13%; ORCR: 10%). We speculate further that this fact may contribute to the absence of the main effect of RC type in the overall accuracy of repetition.

5.4.3.3 The nature of the impairment in children with SLI in imitating RC

Frizelle *et al.* (2017) hold that researchers are now in agreement with the view that sentence repetition not only reflects grammatical representations in long-term memory (Klem *et al.* 2015) but also the phonological short-term memory processes (Alloway and Gathercole 2005). Thus, it is natural to infer that both the grammatical and the processing limitations can be revealed by analyzing the performance in the sentence repetition by children with SLI.

The syntactic impairment may possibly be revealed by comparing the performance of the children with SLI and two other control groups. As reported previously, the RC type did not affect the children's overall performance in sentence repetition, possibly due to the fact when the adjective are placed in the RCs, the performances on both the subject and object RCs were equally poor because such RCs caused extra processing cost. When we examined the performances of the three groups of children on the RC with adjectives in the main clause, namely SRCM and ORCM, the syntactic impairment of the children with SLI manifested itself. Both the TDA and TDY children performed better on the subject RC than the object RC (TDA: Subject RC 84%; object RC 77%; TDY: subject RC 72%; object RC 62%), whereas for the children with SLI the opposite is true (subject RC 18%; object RC 27%). The performance of the typically developing children was in conformity with the prediction of the RM, according to which the object RC involves the intervention effect, and thus poses greater difficulty to the young children. The performance of the children with SLI was in disagreement with the RM approach, possibly suggesting a severe syntactic deficit in the representation because the very prerequisite for the RM effect is an intact syntactic representation of subject RCs.

The analysis of the errors committed by the three groups of children may be informative to the nature of deficiency in children with SLI. The errors concerning the complementizer including the omission of the relativizer, substitution of the DE for a verb, substitution of DE for a coordination marker in SLI children (77; 24%) outnumbered the same errors in the TDA (37; 10.2%) and TDY (35; 9.7%) children, which may be accounted for by the Surface Account (Leonard 2014a: 288-292).[①] This account attributed the difficulties with grammatical morphemes in SLI children to the short duration of the morphemes. According to the account, because of limited processing capacity, the children with SLI are severely taxed when they encounter the morphemes, with brief duration, playing grammatical roles. In other words, when the morphemes play separate grammatical roles, the children must perform additional operations, such as discovering the grammatical functions of them. This is done under the pressure of perceiving the rest of the sentence being heard. It is assumed that the additional operation plus the brevity of the morphemes will give rise to incomplete processing of the morphemes. As a result, the children with SLI will need more encounters with the morphemes before they are established in the children's grammar.

In the sentence repetition task, the children with SLI were more likely to omit the comprelmetizer *De*, which plays a crucial grammatical role in the structure and at the same time is brief in duration. We propose that the Mandarin children with SLI have incomplete processing capacity of the function word, when perceiving the RCs they heard. In consequence, they tended to omit it or substitute it for other content words, such as verbs. In conclusion, more errors concerning the complementizer may suggest that there is a severe processing limitation in

---

① Note that this account can only account for the results of the repetition task in that in such task, processing factors count more than the syntactic factors. In Chapter 4, we have proved that this account cannot explain the findings of the comprehension task.

children with SLI.

Additionally, the children with SLI produced a lot more fragmental responses and uninterpretable sentences (90; 29%) than their typically developing peers (TDA: 22; 6.1%; TDY: 49; 13.6%). Frankly speaking, to discern the origin of such errors remains difficult to us, given the converging view that the sentence repetition involves both the grammatical representation in LTM and the processing capacities in STM. Possibly, both the syntactic and processing limitations contributed to the poorer performance in children with SLI.

There is clear evidence suggesting that the children with SLI in the current study suffered from the processing limitations. In the IQ test, the children with SLI scored significantly poorer than the TDA children in terms of the processing speed. As reported earlier, for the TDA and SLI children combined, Processing Speed positively correlated significantly with the overall repetition score. Taken together, the findings of the current study may ascribe the limitations exhibiting in sentence repetition in children with SLI to the impaired processing capacities.

5.5 Summary

To summarize the chapter, the results of the RC imitation tasks suggest that the difficulty encountered by the children with SLI can be partially accounted for by their syntactic deficit, partially by their processing limitation. The conclusion is in line with the previous studies. Some researchers proposed that the impairment of children with SLI lies in linguistic competence (Friedmann and Novogrodsky 2004; van der Lely and Battell 2003); while others address the question from the perspective of processing limitations, which cause the difficulties in acquiring complex sentences (Montgomery, Magimairaj, and Finney 2010). More crucial is the fact the very findings in this chapter provide substantial evidence for the hypothesis of this dissertation: the deficits in children with SLI lie in both the representational and processing aspects.

Chapter 6
General Discussion

The preceding chapters have presented five experiments aimed at exploring the production, comprehension and repetition of RCs in Mandarin-speaking children with SLI and two groups of TD children. In this chapter by summarizing the findings of the experiments, we try to answer the following two questions, namely whether there is subject-object RC asymmetry in children with SLI and what is the nature of the deficit exhibited in children with SLI. In 6.1 we discuss the first question, and in 6.2 the answers to the second question will be provided. In 6.3 we will present the comparison among the results obtained from the production, and comprehension and repetition tasks. In 6.4 we will discuss the implications of this dissertation.

6.1 The sequence of acquisition of Relative Clauses

One of the overarching goals of this dissertation is to probe the sequence of RC acquisition in children with SLI, namely whether there is subject or object RC advantage in Mandarin-speaking children with SLI. We explored this question by using five experiments including the elicitation production experiment, the priming production experiment, the sentence-picture matching experiment, the character-picture verification experiment and the sentence repetition experiment. Being similar to the results of previous studies on the acquisition of RCs in Mandarin-speaking children, the findings of the studies in this dissertation are inconsistent.

6.1.1 The subject over object Relative Clause advantage

In the elicitation and priming production tasks and the character-picture verification task, we found a subject over object RC primacy, which is consistent with the prediction of RM and EFUH. According to RM, it is the object RC that involves a structural intervention because the embedded subject occurs between the head and its copy. The children with SLI had problems in specifying the [Rel] feature of the head according to EFUH, therefore the object RCs are hard to be acquired. In subject RCs, no structural intervention occurs because the embedded object does not c-command the copy of the RC head, and thus the subject RCs are acquired with less difficulty. Other theories, including the Linear Distance Hypothesis, the Canonical Word Order Hypothesis, the Structural Distance Hypothesis[①], the Frequency Hypothesis and the Semantic Prominence Hypothesis cannot account for the subject over object RC advantage in Mandarin satisfactorily.

Moreover, the intervention effect also manifested itself in the responses from children with SLI when they failed to produce target object RCs in elicitation tasks. In the object RC elicitation task, children with SLI opted for subject RCs with thematic role reversal instead of target object RCs, which is in line with the RM approach, according to which, the subject RC does not involve the RM effect. Also crucial is the fact that a substantial proportion of object RCs produced by the children with SLI are headless RCs. In the headless RCs, what has been moved is a pure *Wh* operator, which does not contain a lexical NP, and thus does not have the feature [N]. Because in the object RC, the subject (intervener) has the feature [N], and the moved element has the feature [Rel], they do not share a similar feature. Thus, the production of headless RCs is relatively less demanding to children with SLI.

In addition to subject RCs and object RCs, we also explored the acquisition of passive object RCs in the elicitation production task and the character-picture verification task. To our surprise, the children with SLI did not perform better on

---

① This theory can account for the subject over object RC advantage. However, it cannot explain other findings of the experiment in chapter 3, which we have discussed in detail.

passive object RCs than object RCs, which is seemingly contrary to the prediction of RM approach. Belletti (2009) adopted the smuggling approach of Collins (2005), and proposed that the derivation of passives involves a step-by-step 'smuggling' instead of long-distance movement. Thus, the derivation of passive object RCs does not involve RM effect. If so, the acquisition of passive object RC will be acquired more easily than object RCs. We proposed that although passive object RCs do not involve RM effect, they are costly for the young children to compute, which can be accounted for by EFUH.[①] Thus, there is no significant difference on the accuracy of the two RCs in the production and comprehension tasks. In previous studies and the present study, the children opted for the passive object RC on the condition of object RC in the elicitation task. Many researchers (e.g. Jensen de López *et al.* 2014) claimed that the fact constitutes the evidence supporting the assumption that passive object RCs are easier to be produced than object RCs because passive object RCs do not involve RM effect. Based on the findings of the current study, we propose that the fact cannot be regarded as evidence for the claim that the former is easier.

6.1.2 The absence of the subject-object RC asymmetry

However, in the elicitation production of irreversible RC task, sentence-picture matching task and sentence repetition task, we did not detect any significant difference between subject RCs and object RCs, which is contrary to the prediction of RM. We posit that the absence of the subject-object RC asymmetry is not due to the invalidity of RM, but to other non-syntactic factors.

In the elicitation of irreversible RCs, in which one of the NPs is an animate entity, the other is inanimate, the children with SLI did not exhibit the subject-object RC asymmetry. Moreover compared to the reversible RC condition, their performance was improved significantly. We maintain that there are two reasons for the disappearance of subject-object RC asymmetry. Firstly, children will encounter less difficulty concerning the thematic role assignment in the

---

① According to EFUH, passive construction will pose challenges for children with SLI. The natural consequence is that the passive object RCs will also be problematic for such children.

production of irreversible object RCs, which is supported by the fact that in the irreversible condition, nearly no thematic role assignment error has been detected. We propose that the mismatch in terms of the animacy of the NPs involved in RCs reduces the difficulty confronting the children when producing object RCs. Secondly, numerous studies have proved that in many languages, object RCs are more likely to occur with an inanimate head. We maintain that the higher frequency of irreversible object RCs in the input might facilitate the production of that structure.

In the sentence-picture matching task, we also found that the children with SLI did not perform differently on the comprehension of subject and object RCs. In line with the Surface Account (Leonard 2014a: 288-292), we posit that children with SLI may interpret object RCs as declarative sentences by ignoring the relativizer '*de*', whereas they will parse subject RCs as declarative clauses with a dropped topic. In a word, we posit that the symmetric performances are results of a non-syntactic strategy employed by children to interpret RCs in the sentence-picture matching tasks. However, the same strategy cannot be applied in the character-picture verification task, and thus in that task, the subject-object RC asymmetry manifested itself.

The results of sentence imitation experiment indicate that children with SLI exhibit no subject-object RC asymmetry, unlike the results from other production tasks and the character-picture verification comprehension task in this dissertation. We maintain that the symmetric performance of our participants in the subject RC and object RC condition is due to the fact that in the object RC, the structural intervention arises according to the RM approach, but in the subject RC, the linear intervention counts more, given the fact that in mandarin subject RCs, the object in RCs intervenes linearly between the relative head and its trace. We further speculate that the imitation task diverge from the production, comprehension tasks because the imitation task is heavily dependent on the memory and processing factors. Following Garraffa *et al.* (2015), we posit that the performance of the children in sentence repetition may not be always the accurate reflection of children's underlying grammatical competence.

To summarize this section, the results of the present study indicate that there is subject-object RC asymmetry in the production and comprehension of reversible RCs, which is imputed to the structural intervention in object RCs, as predicted by RM and EFUH, whereas in the repetition task, no such asymmetry is detected, which is due to the fact that the extra memory and processing overload are required in the imitation task.

6.2 The nature of the deficit in children with SLI

The second overarching goal of this dissertation is to explore the nature of deficit in children with SLI, which manifests itself in the RC acquisition. As discussed previously, two broad competing theoretical perspectives have attempted to explain SLI. One perspective posits that the disorder is specific to the domain of language, specifically to the impaired grammatical knowledge. The second perspective assumes that the deficit in children with SLI is caused by the limitation in information-processing capacity. Based on previous studies, in this dissertation we propose that the disorder in children with SLI is caused by both the linguistic and processing limitations.

The findings of the present study indicate that compared to TDA children, the SLI children performed poorly on all tasks and compared to the TDY children, the children with SLI are inferior in most tasks. In this section, we will summarize the findings concerning the deficits in children with SLI in the present study, and propose that the attenuated performances in children with SLI are caused by both the grammatical and processing deficits, which is consistent with the prediction of the hypothesis of this dissertation.

6.2.1 The grammatical deficit

To begin with, we will summarize the findings from the production tasks. Firstly, in both the elicitation and priming production tasks, the children with SLI exhibited a clear subject-object reversible RC asymmetry, whereas the TDA children performed equally well on both the subject and object reversible RCs. We proposed that the SLI children's grammar cannot specify [Rel] feature of the moved element, which may give rise to blocking effect, and in turn cause the subject over object RCs advantage in production. However, the TD children of the same age have surmounted the difficulty in specifying the feature set of the moved element, and thus no intervention effect arises.

Moreover, children with SLI performed significantly more poorly on the production of object RCs than both the TDA and TDY children. According to RM, TDY children had problems in computing the subset relation, therefore the object RCs are hard to acquire, whereas according to EFUH, in the grammar of the children with SLI, the moved element and the intervener share the exactly same feature, given the inability to specify [Rel] feature of the moved element, therefore the intervention effect will be enlarged, which in turn gives rise to the poorer performance than the TDY children in the object RC production task. In a word, the first piece of evidence for the grammatical deficit is that children with SLI are insensitive to the formal feature of the moved element.[1]

Secondly, the children with SLI committed errors related to thematic roles in the elicitation production task, which are repercussions of their inability to assign thematic roles. Although this error is not restricted to the children with SLI, we assert that the assignment of thematic role in children with SLI is vulnerable.[2]

Thirdly, the children with SLI produced structural errors by omitting the embedding marker in the elicitation production tasks. On the other hand, the TD children nearly never committed such errors. The fact that the SLI children committed errors concerning the complementizer directly indicates that there is a deficiency in the grammatical knowledge concerning the functional category Complementizer in children with SLI, which is also predicted by EFUH.

Fourthly, the results of the current study indicate that the declarative sentences and sentence fragments are the main avoidance strategies adopted by SLI children when they failed to produce target RCs in the elicitation production task. We propose that the avoidance strategies can also lend support to the assumption that

---

[1]　Precisely, the formal feature refers to [Rel].

[2]　As discussed earlier, the inability to assign thematic roles in children with SLI is caused by RM effect.

SLI children encountered severe difficulty in projecting the fully-fledged RCs. As predicted by EFUH, we assume that the SLI children are insensitive to the semantic function of RCs, which might also account for the fact that the children with SLI opted for the declarative sentences and sentence fragments instead of target RCs.

Fifthly, we find that when children with SLI and the TDA and TDY children were required to describe pictures, there was a greater likelihood of producing subject RC sentences in the priming condition than in the baseline condition. The same pattern was also found in the production of object RC for the TDA and TDY children. However, we failed to find such a pattern in the production of object RCs in children with SLI. The implication of the finding is that the typically developing children have an intact representation of the subject and object RCs and the children with SLI do possess an intact representation of the subject RCs but not of the object RCs. Thus we can safely conclude that the disparities between the SLI children and their TD children in the production of object RCs should be imputed to the decayed syntactic representation, which corroborates EFUH.

Now we turn to the grammatical deficit, which manifests itself in the comprehension task in children with SLI. To begin with, in the character-picture verification tasks, there was a subject-object RC asymmetry in children with SLI, whereas in the two groups of TD children, no such asymmetry was detected, suggesting that the structural intervention in children with SLI takes effect, but for TD children, RM effect does not arise in the comprehension task. Moreover, in the object RC comprehension task, there is significant difference even between the SLI and TDY children. We maintain that the poorer performances of the children with SLI in the object RC task are the repercussions of a more severely impaired representation of the object RC.

Secondly, the non-target responses may be more informative to the nature of the syntactic deficit. In the comprehension of object RCs, the children with SLI committed more Middle errors than the TDY children, which may lend support to the finding that there is a serious problem for the SLI children to represent object RCs in their grammar. An alternative explanation for Middle Errors may be that the SLI children may be insensitive to the semantic function of RCs.[1] The reversed errors might result from their inability to assign the thematic roles to the moved elements in RCs.

The children with SLI also evinced grammatical deficit in the repetition task. When we examined performances of the three groups of children on the RC with adjectives in the main clause, namely SRCM and ORCM, the syntactic impairment of the children with SLI manifests itself. Both the TDA and TDY children performed better on the subject RC than the object RC, whereas for the children with SLI the opposite is true. The performance of the typically developing children was in conformity with the prediction of RM, according to which the object RC involves the intervention effect, and thus poses greater difficulty to the young children. The performance of the children with SLI was in disagreement with the RM approach, possibly suggesting a severe syntactic deficit in the syntactic representation because the very prerequisite for the RM effect is an intact syntactic representation of subject RCs. Probably the syntactic representation of subject RC in children with SLI is not in a stable state, and thus under the pressure of other factors, they cannot retrieve it in the repetition task.

6.2.2 The processing deficit

In the production and comprehension tasks, there is also evidence supporting the processing deficit account. We found that in the production of subject RCs, the accuracy of the children with SLI was significantly lower than that of the TDA and TDY children, and in the comprehension of subject RCs, the children with SLI performed worse than the TDA children. Given the conclusion that the three groups of children possess the intact syntactic representation of subject RCs,[2] the disparities in the production and comprehension between them possibly lies in their different processing capacities.

---

[1] Both the middle errors in the comprehension task and the fact that children with SLI opted for declarative sentences in the elicitation task are the repercussions of their insensitivity to the semantic function of RCs.

[2] We arrived at the conclusion in the priming production task in 3.7.

The processing deficit in children with SLI mainly manifests itself in the repetition task. Firstly, the analysis of the errors committed by the three groups of children in the repetition task may be informative to the nature of deficiency in children with SLI. The errors concerning the omission of the relativizer '*de*', substitution of the '*de*' for a verb, substitution of '*de*' for a coordination marker in SLI children outnumbered the same error in TDA and TDY children, which may be accounted for by Surface Account (Leonard 2014a: 288-292).[①] This account attributed the difficulties with grammatical morphemes in SLI children to the short duration of the morphemes. According to the account, because of limited processing capacity, the children with SLI are severely taxed when they encounter the morphemes, which are with brief duration and at the same time playing important grammatical roles. More errors conerning the complementizer might suggest that there is a severe processing limitation in children with SLI.

Secondly, the children with SLI produced a lot more fragmental responses and uninterpretable sentences (90; 29%) than their typically developing peers (TDA: 22; 6.1%; TDY: 49; 13.6%) in repetition task. Frankly speaking, to discern the origin of such errors remains difficult to us, given the converging view that the sentence repetition involves both the grammatical representation in LTM and the processing capacities in STM. Possibly, both the syntactic and processing limitations contributed to the poor performance in children with SLI.

Thirdly, results indicated that the children with SLI performed significantly better in imitating subject RCs with the adjective in the relative clause than subject RCs with adjective in the main clause. The length of the dependency between the head and the gap is greater in subject RCs with adjectives placed within the RC (SRCR), than in subject RCs with adjectives placed in the main clause (SRCM). The fact that children had better performance in the SRCM than in the SRCR suggests that when the processing burden increased, their performance was more likely negatively affected.

In the end, in the IQ test, the children with SLI scored significantly poorer

---

① In this dissertation, the relativizer and the complementizer are used interchangeably, both of which refer to 'de' in Mandarin RCs.

than the TDA children in terms of the processing speed, which constitutes the direct evidence that the children with SLI in the current study suffered from the processing limitations.

6.2.3 The nature of deficit

To summarize, the results of our research suggest that children with SLI manifest poor performance in the production, comprehension and repetition of RCs and demonstrate impaired syntactic representation and processing capacity. The findings corroborate the hypothesis of this research. This conclusion is consistent with some influential studies attempting to explain SLI. For example, Leonard (2014a: 272) proposed the assumption that the deficit in children with SLI is caused by multiple factors. He posited that children with SLI might lack knowledge of some aspects of language and at the same time show inconsistency in making use of those aspects they do know, due to limitations in processing capacity.

Our conclusion is also in agreement with PDH, which posits that a substantial number of individuals with SLI are afflicted with the abnormalities of brain structures which compose the brain system called the procedural memory system. The abnormalities of the related brain structures can lead to deficits in implicit sequence learning, grammar learning, and functions dependent on the procedural memory and additionally, some non-procedural functions correlated with these brain areas tend to be problematic, involving working memory, temporal processing and lexical retrieval (Ullman and Pierpont, 2005). This account has received accumulating empirical supports (Gabriel, Maillart, Guillaume, Stefaniak, and Meulemans 2011; Lum, Conti-Ramsden, Page, and Ullman 2012; Tomblin, Mainela-Arnold, and Zhang 2007).

Acquisition of the skills involved in procedural system is gradual because the learning is based on multiple trials. In contrast, the learned skills generally apply quickly and automatically. The contrast of the profiles of the children with SLI and TD children corroborates this prediction. The grammatical deficits in children with SLI include the inability to assign thematic roles, the insensitivity to the formal feature of the moved element, the deficiency concerning the functional category, and insensitivity to the semantic function of RCs. All the above-mentioned mental knowledge is stored in the procedural memory system, which underlies the capacity to produce and comprehend complex forms. Because of the impaired procedural memory system, all the aspects of grammar that involve rule-governed operations should be impaired, which leads to the poor performance in RC acquisition by children with SLI. On the other hand, the TD children, who are not affected by the procedural memory system impairment, can apply the rules quickly and automatically.

The impairment in processing capacity is also predicted by PDH because evidence indicates that the brain structures that underlie the procedural system are also responsible for important aspects of timing and rapid temporal processing (Ullman and Pierpont 2005). Some researchers claimed that the deficit in children with SLI is a non-linguistic processing deficit in nature (Bishop 1992; Leonard, McGregor, and Allen 1992; Norbury, Bishop, and Briscoe 2001), or the dysfunction of phonological working memory (Archibald and Gathercole 2007; Montgomery 1995). These accounts can capture the processing deficits of the empirical studies, but none of them can account for the disparate impaired functions of SLI easily. The PDH can account for several aspects of the abnormalities of SLI: language, mental imaginary, working memory and temporal processing.

In terms of language, a categorical distinction was made between lexicon and grammar in the hypothesis. Namely, the idiosyncratic mappings are stored in a mental lexicon, which involves the declarative memory, whereas the learning and use of rule-governed computations depends on mental grammar in procedural memory. According to PDH, the declarative memory system in children with SLI remains intact. The findings of the present study provide evidence for this prediction. In the elicitation production tasks, the children with SLI performed significantly better on the irreversible RCs than the reversible RCs, suggesting that the children with SLI are sensitive to the animacy feature of the NPs in the RCs. We have asserted that it is the mismatch of the animacy feature of the two NPs involved in the irreversible RCs that facilitates the production of the irreversible RCs. The animacy feature of the NPs is idiosyncratic linguistic knowledge and is normally stored in the lexicon, which may develop normally, as predicted by the PDH.

In a word, the findings of this research demonstrate that the deficiency in children with SLI is reducible to both the representational and the processing limitations. According to PDH, the limitations in this population are possibly rooted in the abnormalities of brain structures which compose the brain system called the procedural memory system.

6.3 The comparison among comprehension, elicitation production and repetition tasks

6.3.1 The descriptive comparison

We first present a descriptive comparison among the results from the production, comprehension and repetition tasks, with the purpose to determine which task best reveals the innate knowledge of RCs in children with SLI. Table 6-1 shows the percentages of the correct responses for each sentence type in all the experiments.

The performances of the TDY children varied in the production, comprehension. In the production of reversible RCs, including the elicitation and priming production tasks, the TDY children exhibited a clear subject-object RC asymmetry, which has been attributed to RM effect. Moreover the TDY children's accuracy in production is lower than that in the TDA children, who have nearly reached the ceiling level. It seems that we might arrive at the conclusion that the TDY children's grammar is not mature enough. However, the results from the comprehension tasks deny such an assumption. In the character-picture verification task, no subject-object RC asymmetry was found, and there was no significant difference between the TDA and TDY children. Actually, the TDY children's accuracy in the comprehension task nearly reached the ceiling level (subject RCs: 90%; object RCs: 88%).

For TDA children, their performances are at the ceiling level on the subject and object RCs in both the production and comprehension tasks and no subject-object RC asymmetry was detected in all tasks. In production of passive object RCs, their accuracy was lower than the adult-like level, whereas in the comprehension of passive object RCs, they reached the ceiling level. For both two groups of TD children, their accuracy in imitating subject RCs and object RCs was much lower than that in the production tasks, especially lower than that in the comprehension task.

For the children with SLI, they performed significantly more poorly than both the TDA and TDY children in nearly all tasks. Except for the imitation task, they exhibited clear subject over object RC advantage in all other tasks. Crucially, their performances in the comprehension tasks are in stark contrast to that of the TD children. Both the TDA and TDY children are at the ceiling level on the subject, object and passive object RCs, whereas the performances of children with SLI are severely compromised.

**Table 6-1   Percentages of the correct responses for each sentence
type in all the experiments in all groups**[1]

Groups	Elicitation production			Priming production	
	Subject RC	Object RC	Passive object RC	Subject RC	Object RC
	%	%	%	%	%
SLI	30	18	9	40.7	9.2
TDA	93	80	68	88.6	73.3[2]
TDY	76	48	52	90	50

---

[1]   The scores on the irreversible RC elicitation tasks are not included in this table, because it is irrelevant to the discussion in this section. The scores of the comprehension are from the character-picture verification tasks.

[2]   One of the reviewers raised the question why TDA children performed poorer in priming production task than in elicitation tasks, given the widely-accepted assumption that the priming production task is easier than the elicitation task. We propose that the results cannot be compared directly because of the different design in the two experiments. The possible reason for the disparity is that TDA children's knowledge of RCs is mature enough, therefore the direct assessing method (elicitation task) is more efficient than the priming task to make them produce the target structures.

Continued

Groups	Comprehension			Repetition			
	Subject RC	Object RC	Passive object RC	SRCM	ORCM	SRCR	ORCR
	%	%	%	%	%	%	%
SLI	75.8	48.2	56.4	18	27	13	10
TDA	100	98.6	100	84	77	61	58
TDY	92	86.7	88	72	62	50	51

6.3.2 Comparison of TD and SLI children

The TD (both TDA and TDY) children's ceiling-level symmetric performances on the comprehension task indicate that their grammatical knowledge of RCs are adult-like, which is consistent with the Modularity Matching Model proposed by Crain and Thornton (1998: 29-30). The first core assumption of this model is that the human language-processing apparatus is modular. In other words, the language faculty is independent from other cognitive systems, and the operation of language apparatus is subject to principles that are specific to it. Consequently, the construction of syntactic and semantic representations does not depend on the general cognitive mechanisms, which are used to represent and process real world knowledge.

The second core assumption is that there is no essential difference between child's language-processing system and that of adults. If the faculty of language in adults is sealed off from other cognitive systems, which is responsible for the real world knowledge, the same is expected to happen in children. The model posits that both adults and children have similar processing capacity and memory limitations. The model allows some possible mismatches between child and adult grammars, but there is a limit to them. According to the Continuity Hypothesis, children's developing grammars can differ from the adult grammar, only in ways in which adult grammars can differ from each other (Crain 1991; Pinker 1984 cited from Crain and Thornton 1998: 31). The TD children performed at the ceiling level in the character-picture verification task, which suggests that their syntactic knowledge of RCs is the same as that of adults, which corroborates the prediction of the Modularity Matching Model.

However, the SLI children exhibited severe deficiency in all the tasks conducted in this dissertation, which indicates that their linguistic ability is deviant from that of normal individuals. According to the Modularity Matching Model, all of the linguistic abilities of a normal child are the same as an adult's. The model posits that children have access to Universal Grammar, just as adults do, and that children are equivalent to adults in the mechanisms they use to process language; in other words, they have access to a universal parsing strategy. The prediction of this model was not borne out by the attenuated performance of the children with SLI in all the tasks. As such, the possible explanation is that the grammar of the children with SLI is not the same as that of adults, unlike their typically developing peers. This conclusion may provide further support for the hypothesis of this dissertation, which posits that the deficit in children with SLI partly lies in representational level.

At this point, we need to discuss the question whether the language of children with SLI is merely delayed or deviant from the normal development. There are two main competing hypotheses for the development of SLI children's grammar in previous studies. Firstly, Rice *et al.* (1995) posit that children with SLI follow a normal developmental path but with some delay. In other words, there is a maturational process of SLI children's grammar. Secondly, Paradis and Gopnik (1997) postulate that what the SLI children follow is not the normal developmental path, and they must make use of non-grammatical communicative cues and metalinguistic knowledge. From the above discussion, it is plausible to conclude that the second hypothesis is on the right track because the SLI children's grammar is qualitatively different form the normal development. Even the grammar of the TDY children, who are one and half years younger than them, resembles the adult's grammar system; whereas SLI children have not reached that level. There are other manifestations of the qualitative difference. For example, in the elicitation task, the SLI children tended to omit the complementizer, and in the character-picture verification task, children with SLI committed Middle Errors, both of which can lend more support to the existence of a deviant grammar system in children with SLI.

To wrap up, the stark contrast between TD and SLI children found in the current study lend plausibility to the assumption that the grammar of children with SLI is qualitatively different form the normal development.

6.3.3 Comparison of different tasks

Here a question arises. We are obliged to account for the disparities of the performances of our participants in different tasks, given the fact that the TD children performed much better on the comprehension task than the elicitation production and sentence repetition tasks. We proposed that only the character-picture verification comprehension task used in this dissertation is a reliable measure to assess the syntactic knowledge of children, whereas other tasks adopted in this dissertation might obscure the grammatical knowledge of children because they involve non-linguistic factors.

To begin with, the repetition task might underestimate the children's knowledge of RCs in that RCs in the task occur in null context, which does not satisfy the pragmatic felicity conditions associated with this construction (Crain and Thornton 1998: 92).[①] The task is highly unnatural, in that the sentences

---

① One of the reviewers pointed out that the RCs tested in repetition tasks in (i) are different from those in the production and comprehension tasks in (ii) and (iii) in terms of embedding. In (i), the RC is center-embedded, whereas in (ii) and (iii), the RC is left-branching. He expressed doubts about whether the difference in embedding will affect results of the research. However, Center-embedded RCs have been repeatedly shown to be more difficult to process than right-branching head-initial RCs in adults (Warren & Gibson, 2002, among many others). It naturally follows that in Mandarin left-branching head-final RCs (there is no right-branching RCs in Mandarin) will be easier to be processed than center-embedded RCs. The conclusion is that the RCs in repetition tasks are easier than the RCs in the other two tasks. Thus, the poorer performances of children with SLI in repetition tasks should not be reducible to the embedding.

(i) **Zhui xiaotou de** jingcha   daizhe heisede maozi
    chase thief   DE policemen wear   black   cap
    'the policeman that was chasing the thief wore the black cap.'

(ii) Wo xihuan **tui   baba de**   xiaopengyou
     I   like   push father DE   child
     'I like the child who is pushing father\mother'

(iii) Zheli you liang ge xiaogege, zhiyixia **qin xiaojiejie de** xiaogege
      here exist two CL brother point to kiss sister   DE brother
      'there are two brothers, show me the brother that is kissing the sister'

are presented in the so-called null context, where the sentences fail to satisfy presuppositions of RCs. Hamburger and Crain (1982) posited that restrictive RCs have two presuppositions. For instance, the restrictive RCs in (1) might be used pragmatically felicitous, only if there are at least two '*policemen*' presented in the context because the semantic contribution of a restrictive relative clause is to identify one particular policeman in a set of policemen presented in the context. The second presupposition is that the action involved in the RC happened before the sentence was produced. In other words, the information contained in the RC is conceptually prior to the information described in the main clause. Because in the RC repetition tasks, no context is presented before the use of RCs, the RCs are used unnaturally, which might do detriment to the successful reproduction of the target sentences.

(1) Zhui xiaotou de jingcha   daizhe heisede maozi.
    chase thief   DE policemen wear   black   cap
    '*The policeman that was chasing the thief wore the black cap.*'

Crain and Thornton (1998: 151) maintained that adults are usually insensitive to the contexts necessary for a particular structure to be used felicitously in that they have the ability to compensate for the absence of context. However, young children (3-5 years old) do not have the same capacity to interpret sentences occurring in infelicitous circumstances. In other words, they might not fill in the missing inferential steps in response to the sentences without the necessary conditions, which underlie the proper use of the sentences. Presumably, this is because they do not share adults' general knowledge of the world.

Following the above arguments, we propose that the poor performance of our participants in sentence repetition has little to do with children's linguistic knowledge because the accommodation of presuppositional failures is an ability that develops in children over time. We posit that in order to successfully reproduce a structure for a child, the pragmatics must be exactly appropriate. Children tend to encounter difficulties in imitating the target sentences, if an experimental context does not satisfy the presuppositions for an utterance. In that case, they probably will not understand what is being required to do, and in turn will quickly become frustrated with the experiment.

Secondly, the RCs in elicitation production tasks are natural because there is context where the two presuppositions of RCs are satisfied. In consequence, the performances of our participants are much better compared to their performance in the sentence repetition tasks. However, we propose that the elicitation production is quite dull to the participants, which may be responsible for the attenuated performance compared to the character-picture verification task. The elicitation production task are presented to the participants in a question-answer fashion, where the experimenter presented the context and subsequently raised a question, and the children were required to answer the question. This procedure might render the children uncomfortable because they might feel that they are being examined.

Crain and Thornton (1998: 131) posited that a key factor of successful data collection is to make sure that children enjoy the experiment. We posit that the relatively worsened performances of the children in this task are possibly due to the fact that child does not enjoy the time spent in the experiment because the fun factor is especially important in elicited production studies, since children are required to produce constructions that are not always totally familiar to them. It is worthy of notice that although their performances are attenuated, the variances of performances are compatible with the RM approach of Universal Grammar, which predicts that object RCs are more difficult to be produced.

Finally, in the character-picture verification task, RCs meet the two presuppositions of RCs. Moreover, the participants are more interested in the experiment because it resembles a familiar daily game, in which they are asked to point to the picture after hearing the directions. In consequence, in the comprehension task, the children are highly involved in the experiment, and therefore they complied with the experimenters' requests. The second reason for the better performance in comprehension task is that the comprehension task was less taxing than the production task. In the production task, in order to produce the target structure, the children must retrieve the grammatical knowledge and at the same time recall the information presented by the experimenter, whereas in the comprehension task, the children only are required to apply the syntactic representation to the heard sentences in order to successfully interpret RCs. Our findings are also in consistent with the almost unanimous assumption that language comprehension precedes the production. The performances in the comprehension task are compatible with the Modularity Matching Model because in such task all the extra non-linguistic factors are sealed off.

To sum up, we posit that the character-picture verification comprehension task used in this dissertation is a reliable measure to assess the syntactic knowledge of children. The disparities of the performances of our participants in different tasks lie in the fact that other tasks involve non-linguistic factors.

6.4 Implications

The findings of the current study have implications for both the assessment of RC knowledge in children with SLI and the intervention of children with SLI.

6.4.1 Implications for the RC assessment in children

The implications for the assessment of RC in children are two-fold. Firstly, based on the comparison between Experiment 3 and Experiment 4, we found that the character-picture verification task is more reliable to be used in assessment of RC comprehension because in the sentence-picture matching task used in Experiment 3 the children might adopt other strategies to interpret RCs, which may overestimate their comprehension of RCs. There are some studies, in which the sentence-picture matching task was used to explore the comprehension in Mandarin-speaking TD individuals, finding that object RCs are easier to be comprehended than subject RCs, which is opposite to the findings of the current study. We postulate that the disparities arise because in those studies the individuals resorted to other cues to comprehend the RCs. Studies on other languages with the head-final RCs also found that the subject RCs are harder than object RCs in comprehension, such as Basque (Gutierrez-Mangado 2011) and Japanese (Suzuki 2011). The tasks employed in those studies are sentence-picture matching tasks, which are subject to criticisms leveled at the task in Experiment 3.

Moreover, the sentence-picture matching task used in studies of children with SLI speaking a language with head-initial RCs might enlarge the subject RC advantage in comprehension. Unanimously, those studies found that there is a subject RC primacy in comprehension in children with SLI. However, as discussed previously, if the children with SLI ignore the complementizer, they will interpret subject RCs as simple SVO sentences. Thus, in the task, they might have the correct response even if they do not have the intact knowledge of subject RCs.

Secondly, the comparison of the findings from different tasks assessing the production, comprehension and repetition of children revealed that different tasks yielded different results. The implication is that to have a better understanding of the grammatical knowledge of children, it is advisable to employ multiple measures to probe the competence of RCs in children. Comparison of data from different tasks can disambiguate the result obtained from one task, which might provide misleading conclusion, if used alone. For example, we found that both the children with SLI and TD children exhibited no subject-object RC asymmetry by using imitation tasks, which cannot be accounted for by the available theories. Also we have found the TD children's capacity of RC repetition is also very limited, which might lead us to the conclusion that TD children's representation of RCs may differ significantly from what the adult has assumed. However, in the comprehension task used in Experiment 4, we found that the TD children's performances are at the ceiling level, suggesting that the intact syntactic representation of RCs are accessible to those children. Moreover, unlike the findings in repetition task, we found that the children with SLI exhibited a clear subject-object RC asymmetry in the comprehension tasks, which is consistent with the prediction of RM. Therefore, the discoveries from different tasks have been particularly important in cases where the data form one task alone might lead to incorrect conclusion on children's grammatical knowledge.

6.4.2 Clinical implications

The findings of the current study also have implications for the intervention and identification of children with SLI. Firstly, speech and language therapists working with these individuals should take cognizance of the significant deviance, which these children experience in their development of RCs. Secondly, the comparative easiness of irreversible RCs, as opposed to the reversible ones, suggests that the irreversible RCs should serve as the priority of any intervention approach for RCs. The superior performance of children with SLI in RCs, where the subject is relativized, indicates the subject RCs should function as the spearhead in the RC intervention program. Thirdly, many errors were found to be restricted only to children with SLI, including the complementizer omission in production, the Middle errors in the comprehension, which suggests that special measures should be adopted to cope with such weaknesses in children with SLI.

Now we turn to the implications for identification of children with SLI. Measures of finite-verb morphology (e.g. the tense composite of Rice *et al.* 1998) have been proved to be useful to discriminate between the children with SLI and their age-matched TD peers and the younger TD children in languages with rich verb inflections, such as English. Mandarin is a language with no inflection on verbs, and thus such measures are invalid. The results of this study suggest that RC constructions may distinguish children with SLI from TDA children and the TDY children (who are on average one and half years younger). The results of the current study further indicate that the character-picture verification task has discriminative value in comparing the grammatical knowledge of RCs in children with SLI and their typically developing age peers, given the fact that such task is most reliable in assessing children's competence of RCs, whereas the sentence repetition tasks may distinguish the children with SLI from those unaffected in terms of processing capacities.

6.5 Summary

To summarize, we found that an advantage of subject RCs holds for children with SLI in comprehension and production of reversible RCs. However, the distinction is not so crisp in all cases. We have identified the fact that the performances in the tasks are attenuated in children with SLI compared to TD children. The contrast between the language profiles of the children with SLI and that of the TD children reveals that the children with SLI exhibit severe deficiency in the acquisition of RCs, which is attributable to both grammatical and processing deficits. By comparing the results from different type of experiments used in the current study, we have arrived at the conclusion that the character-picture verification task is more reliable to be used in the assessment of the RC comprehension. Lastly, we have discussed the implications of this dissertation for the diagnosis and intervention of children with SLI.

Conclusion

The preceding chapters have presented the five experiments to explore the acquisition of RCs in Mandarin-speaking children with SLI. In the concluding chapter, we first summarize the main findings of this dissertation; subsequently we proceed to discuss the contributions and limitations of the current study.

1 Summary of the main findings

The two overarching goals of the current study are to explore the sequence of RC acquisition in Mandarin-speaking children with SLI and to locate the nature the deficiency of children with SLI in acquiring RCs.

In chapter 2, we first discussed the syntax of Mandarin RCs and arrived at the conclusion that the derivation of Mandarin RCs involves head movement. Subsequently, we presented various theories on the deficits of children with SLI. We reviewed two broad competing theoretical perspectives attempting to explain SLI. The grammatical deficit account posits that the disorder is specific to the domain of language, specifically to the impaired knowledge of particular rules, which underlie the combination of the words into complex structures. The processing deficit account assumes that the deficit in children with SLI is caused by the limitation in information-processing capacity, which has been proved to be able to account for both the linguistic and non-linguistic impairments prevalent in SLI. The previous studies have proved that both of the two perspectives can successfully account for some findings, but they both have shortcomings. At last we presented the research hypothesis of this dissertation, which both overlaps with and differs from the grammatical deficit account and the processing deficit account. In addition, we proposed EFUH to account for the grammatical deficits seen in children with SLI.

Chapter 3 examined the production of RCs in children with SLI and two groups of control children by using the elicitation production and priming production tasks. We first reviewed previous studies on the RC production in TD and SLI children both at home and abroad. In both the elicitation and priming production tasks, the children with SLI exhibited a clear subject-object reversible RC asymmetry, which is in line with RM and EFUH. Moreover, we found that children with SLI performed significantly more poorly on the production of object RCs than both the TDA and TDY children. The children with SLI committed errors related to thematic roles, produced structural errors by omitting the embedding marker, and opted for the declarative sentences and sentence fragments as the main avoidance strategies. We found that children with SLI do not possess the syntactic representation of the object RCs. We also found that the SLI children's accuracy on irreversible RCs is higher than reversible RCs and that there is no difference detected between object RCs and passive object RCs in elicitation production task.

Taken together, we posit that the disparities between SLI children and TD children in the production of RCs should be attributed to the decayed syntactic representation, which is correctly predicted by EFUH. We further proposed that the SLI children encountered severe difficulty in projecting the fully-fledged RCs and that they are insensitive to the semantic function of RCs, which are also the manifestations of the grammatical deficit in them.

Chapter 4 explored the comprehension of RCs in children with SLI. In the character-picture verification tasks, there was a subject-object RC asymmetry in children with SLI, whereas in the two groups of TD children, no such asymmetry was detected, which suggests that the structural intervention in children with SLI takes effect, but for the TD children, the RM effect does not arise in the comprehension task. In the comprehension of object RCs, the children with SLI committed more Middle errors[1] than the TDY children. This kind of error may lend support to the conclusion that there is a serious problem for the SLI children

---

[1]   They sometimes pointed to the character in the middle.

to project the object RC in their grammar. The Reversed errors might result from their inability to assign the thematic roles to the moved element in the RC. We maintain that the poorer performances of the children with SLI in the object RC task are the repercussions of a more severely impaired representation of the object RC. We also compared the findings from the sentence-picture matching task and those from the character-picture verification task, which indicates that the latter is a more reliable measure to assess the comprehension of RCs in children with SLI.

Chapter 5 investigated the repetition of RCs in children with SLI, which indicated that the children with SLI performed significantly more poorly than both the two groups of TD children. On the one hand, the grammatical deficit exhibited in the repetition tasks. The syntactic representation of subject RC in children with SLI is not in a stable state, and thus under the pressure of other factors, they cannot retrieve the representation in the repetition task. On the other hand, the processing deficit in children with SLI was also detected in the repetition task. More errors concerning the complementizer may suggest that there is a severe processing limitation in children with SLI. The fact that children had better performance in the SRCM than in the SRCR suggests that when the processing burden increased, their performance was likely to be negatively affected.

In chapter 6, we presented the general discussion with the aim to answer the two questions of the dissertation. The answer to the first question is complex: there is subject-object RC asymmetry in the production and comprehension of RCs, as predicted by RM and EFUH, whereas in the repetition task, no such asymmetry is detected. The answer to second question is that the deficits in children with SLI are two-fold: the grammatical deficit and the processing deficit, which is covered by the hypothesis of this dissertation. We posit that children with SLI might lack knowledge of some aspects of language and at the same time show inconsistency in making use of those aspects they do know, due to limitations in processing capacity. We also compared the results from different tasks and found that the comprehension tasks can function as a reliable measure to assess children's grammatical knowledge of RCs. The TD (both TDA and TDY) children's ceiling-level symmetric performances on the comprehension task indicate that their grammatical knowledge of RCs is adult-like, which is consistent with the Modularity Matching Model proposed by Crain and Thornton (1998: 29-30). However, the SLI children's linguistic ability is deviant from that of normal individuals. We also discussed the implications of the findings of this dissertation for the RC assessment and the intervention and identification of children with SLI.

2 Contributions of the book

Firstly, the book is the first study examining RC production, comprehension and repetition in the same group of SLI children. In both production and comprehension parts, we assessed the children's performance by using two different tasks. As discussed in the previous chapters, results from the experiments testing different modalities might be in conflict. Therefore, this study can provide a more comprehensive description of the characteristics of Mandarin-speaking SLI children's acquisition of RCs. In the comprehension study, we found that the sentence-picture matching task cannot function as a reliable measure to assess the innate knowledge of children, which is instructive to the RC assessment in the future studies.

Secondly, we proved that RM is a universal constraint. The RM, which was initially proposed based on the data from the languages with head-initial RCs, can account for the subject over object RC advantage in Mandarin-speaking children with SLI, who speak a language with head-final RCs. In addition, we also found that in the repetition task, the linear intervention also negatively affects the accuracy of sentence imitation. This result also has some implications for the RC acquisition studies in languages with head-initial RCs.

Thirdly, the assumption that there is subject over object RC advantage can provide evidence to settle the controversy: whether syntactic movement is involved in Mandarin RC. This dissertation has provided substantial evidence for the movement analysis. This dissertation imputes the language delay in SLI children to both the grammatical deficiency and the processing limitations, which provides empirical evidence for the hypothesis of this research.

Fourthly, we presented evidence that the performances of children with SLI corroborate the prediction of PDH. Most of the previous studies assessed the acquisition of RCs in children with SLI by using one or two tasks, and their results comply with either the grammatical deficit account or the processing deficit account. The current study adopted different measures to assess the RC knowledge in children with SLI, thereby the results are more comprehensive and closer to the nature of language deficits of children with SLI.

Fifthly, we proposed the EFUH to account for the representational deficits exhibited in children with SLI. Compared to previous studies, the breadth of the coverage of EFUH is more impressive in that it can capture nearly all the linguistic characteristics of children with SLI in acquiring RCs.

Lastly, we have presented suggestions for assessing and remedying the Mandarin-speaking children with SLI, which might be useful in defining new rehabilitation strategies. We have proved that thesentence-picture matching task cannot be used to assess the children's performance in comprehension of RCs and the elicitation production task may underestimate children's ability to produce RCs. The irreversible RCs should serve as the priority of any intervention approach for RCs. The superior performance of children with SLI in RCs, where the subject is relativized, indicates subject RCs should function as the spearhead in the RC intervention program.

3 Limitations and implications for future studies

There are some potential problems in the current study, which need to be addressed in future studies.

Firstly, the sample of the children with SLI in the current study is not large enough because of the limited time and resources. Secondly, in the present study we only manipulate the animacy of the NPs in RCs in the production tasks, but we have not examined the possible effect of the animacy on the comprehension and repetition of RCs because it is difficult to assess the effect of animacy by only using the picture-pointing task. Some studies have suggested that the animacy might facilitate the adults' processing of RCs (Mak *et al.* 2006). In future studies, closer examination on the animacy effect will be of necessity. Thirdly, in this study we mainly examined the acquisition of subject, object and passive object RCs in children with SLI. There are many other types of RCs, in which a range of roles (indirect object, oblique, Genitive subject, Genitive object) might be relativized, remaining unaddressed. Fourthly, we maintain that the PDH might provide satisfactory account of the results of the current study. However, some scholars have questioned the plausibility of PDH. In the future the cross-disciplinary studies are needed to verify the predictions of the PDH.

References

陈宗利：《限定性关系结构生成语法研究》，北京大学出版社 2007 年版。

何晓炜、于浩鹏：《汉语特殊型语言障碍儿童关系从句理解研究》，《现代外语》2013 年第 4 期。

刘丹青：《汉语关系从句标记类型初探》，《中国语文》2005 年第 1 期。

桑标、缪小春：《皮博迪图片词汇测验修订版（PPVT—R）上海市区试用常模的修订》，《心理科学通讯》1990 年第 5 期。

吴芙芸、盛亚南：《关系从句中指量词的位序选择及其对言语产生理论的启示》，《外国语》2014 年第 3 期。

熊仲儒：《以"的"为核心的 DP 结构》，《当代语言学》2005 年第 2 期。

杨彩梅：《英，汉语中的关系化都是移动的结果吗？》，《外语教学与研究》2008 年第 1 期。

杨彩梅：《生成语法框架下关系结构的句法与一语习得研究》，商务印书馆 2013 年版。

于浩鹏、何晓炜、王海燕：《普通话特殊型语言障碍儿童关系从句产出研究》，《现代外语》2017 年第 4 期。

周敏、韩景泉：《语段理论下汉语关系结构的生成》，《外国语》2012 年第 3 期。

周统权、郑伟、舒华、杨亦鸣：《汉语宾语关系从句加工优势论—来自失语症研究的证据》，《语言科学》2010 年第 3 期。

Adams, Catherine, "Syntactic comprehension in children with expressive language impairment", *International Journal of Language & Communication Disorders,* Vol. 25, No. 2, 1990.

Adani, Flavia, "Rethinking the acquisition of Relative Clauses in Italian: towards a grammatically based account", *Journal of Child Language,* Vol. 38, No. 1,

2011.

Adani, Flavia, Shem, Marie, & Zukowski, Andrea, "How do German children and adults deal with their relatives", In Stavrakaki, S., X. Konstantinopoulou & M. Lalioti, eds. *Advances in Language Acquisition*, Newcastle: Cambridge Scholars Publishing, 2013.

Adani, Flavia, Stegenwallner-Schütz, Maja, Haendler, Yair, & Zukowski, Andrea, "Elicited production of Relative Clauses in German: Evidence from typically developing children and children with Specific Language Impairment", *First Language,* Vol. 36, No. 3, 2016.

Adani, Flavia, van der Lely, Heather K. J., Forgiarini, Matteo, & Guasti, Maria Teresa, "Grammatical feature dissimilarities make Relative Clauses easier: A comprehension study with Italian children", *Lingua,* Vol. 120, No. 9, 2010.

Alloway, Tracy Packiam, Gathercole, Susan Elizabeth, Willis, Catherine, & Adams, Anne-Marie, "A structural analysis of working memory and related cognitive skills in young children", *Journal of Experimental Child Psychology,* Vol. 87, No. 2, 2004.

Alloway, Tracy Packiam, & Gathercole, Susan Elizabeth, "The role of sentence recall in reading and language skills of children with learning difficulties", *Learning and Individual Differences,* Vol. 15, No. 4, 2005.

Ambridge, Ben, Kidd, Evan, Rowland, Caroline F, & Theakston, Anna L, "The ubiquity of frequency effects in first language acquisition", *Journal of Child Language,* Vol. 42, No. 2, 2015.

Aoun, Joseph, & Li, Yen-hui Audrey, *Essays on the Representational and Derivational Nature of Grammar: The Diversity of Wh-constructions*, Cambridge: MIT Press, 2003.

Archibald, Lisa MD, & Gathercole, Susan Elizabeth, "Nonword repetition in Specific Language Impairment: More than a phonological short-term memory deficit", *Psychonomic Bulletin & Review,* Vol. 14, No. 5, 2007.

Archibald, Lisa MD, & Gathercole, Susan Elizabeth, "Visuospatial immediate memory in specific language impairment", *Journal of Speech, Language, and Hearing Research,* Vol. 49, No. 2, 2006.

Archibald, Lisa MD, & Joanisse, Marc F., "On the sensitivity and specificity of nonword repetition and sentence recall to language and memory impairments in children", *Journal of Speech, Language, and Hearing Research,* Vol. 52, No. 4, 2009.

Arnon, Inbal, "Relative clause acquisition in Hebrew: Towards a processing-oriented account*",* Paper delivered to the 29th Boston University conference on language development, Boston, 2005.

Arnon, Inbal, "Rethinking child difficulty: The effect of NP type on children's processing of Relative Clauses in Hebrew", *Journal of Child Language,* Vol. 37, No. 1, 2010.

Arosio, Fabrizio, Adani, Flavia, & Guasti, Maria Teresa, "Grammatical features in the comprehension of Italian Relative Clauses by children", In J. M. Brucart, G. Anna & J. Solà, eds., *Merging Features: Computation, Interpretation, and Acquisition,* Oxford: Oxford University Press, 2009.

Arosio, Fabrizio, Panzeri, Francesca, Molteni, Bruna, Magazù, Santina, & Guasti, Maria Teresa, "The comprehension of Italian Relative Clauses in poor readers and in children with Specific Language Impairment", *Glossa: a Journal of General Linguistics,* Vol. 2, No. 1, 2017.

Arosio, Fabrizio, Yatsushiro, Kazuko, Forgiarini, Matteo, & Guasti, Maria Teresa. "Morphological information and memory resources in children's processing of Relative Clauses in German", *Language Learning and Development,* Vol. 8, No. 4, 2012.

Bavin, Edith L., Wilson, Peter, Maruff, Paul, & Sleeman, Felicity, "Spatio-visual memory of children with Specific Language Impairment: Evidence for generalized processing problems", *International Journal of Language & Communication Disorders,* Vol. 40, No. 3, 2005.

Belletti, Adriana, "Notes on passive object relatives", In P. Svenonius, ed., *Functional Structure From Top to Toe: The Cartography of Syntactic Structures,* Oxford: Oxford University Press, 2009.

Belletti, Adriana, ed., *Structures and Beyond. the Cartography of Syntactic Structures Vol. 3,* New York: Oxford University Press, 2004.

Belletti, Adriana, Friedmann, Naama, Brunato, Dominique, & Rizzi, Luigi, "Does gender make a difference? Comparing the effect of gender on children's comprehension of Relative Clauses in Hebrew and Italian", *Lingua,* Vol. 122, No. 10, 2012.

Bencini, Giulia M. L. & Valian, Virginia V., "Abstract sentence representations in 3-year-olds: Evidence from language production and comprehension", *Journal of Memory and Language,* Vol. 59, No. 1, 2008.

Bishop, Dorothy V. M., "The underlying nature of Specific Language Impairment", *Journal of Child Psychology and Psychiatry,* Vol. 33, No. 1,1992.

Bock, Kathryn, "Syntactic persistence in language production", *Cognitive Psychology,* Vol. 18, No. 3, 1986.

Bock, Kathryn, "Closed-class immanence in sentence production", *Cognition,* Vol. 31, No. 2, 1989.

Bock, Kathryn, & Loebell, Helga, "Framing sentences", *Cognition,* Vol. 35, No.1, 1990.

Booth, James R., Mac Whinney, Brian, & Harasaki, Yasuaki, "Developmental differences in visual and auditory processing of complex sentences", *Child Development,* Vol. 71, No. 4, 2000.

Botwinik, Irena, Bshara, Reem, & Armon-Lotem, Sharon, "Children's production of Relative Clauses in Palestinian Arabic: Unique errors and their movement account", *Lingua,* Vol. 156, 2015.

Brandt, Silke, Kidd, Evan, Lieven, Elena, & Tomasello, Michael, "The discourse bases of relativization: An investigation of young German and English-speaking children's comprehension of Relative Clauses", *Cognitive Linguistics,* Vol. 20, No. 3, 2009.

Branigan, Holly, "Syntactic priming", *Language and Linguistics Compass,* Vol. 1, No. 1-2, 2007.

Branigan, Holly P., Pickering, Martin J., & Cleland, Alexandra A., "Syntactic co-ordination in dialogue", *Cognition,* Vol. 75, No. 2, 2000.

Branigan, Holly P., Pickering, Martin J., Liversedge, Simon P., Stewart, Andrew J., & Urbach, Thomas P., "Syntactic priming: Investigating the mental representation of language", *Journal of Psycholinguistic Research,* Vol. 24, No. 6, 1995.

Branigan, Holly P., Pickering, Martin J., McLean, Janet F., & Stewart, Andrew J., "The role of local and global syntactic structure in language production: Evidence from syntactic priming", *Language and Cognitive Processes,* Vol. 21, No. 7-8, 2006.

Cao, Shane Xuexin, Goodluck, Helen, & Shan, Xingyuan, "Double-gapped Relative Clauses in Chinese: Grammar and processing", Paper delivered to the Sixth Tokyo Conference on Psycholinguistics, Tokyo, 2005.

Caplan, David, "Syntactic competence in agrammatism-a lexical hypotheses", In M. Studdert-Kennedy, ed., *Psychobiology of Language*, Cambridge, MA: MIT Press, 1983.

Chang, Hsing-wu, "The comprehension of complex Chinese sentences by children: Relative Clause", *Chinese Journal of Psychology,* Vol. 26, No. 1, 1984.

Chao, Yuanren, *A Grammar of Spoken Chinese*, Berkeley: University of California Press, 1968.

Chen, Jidong, & Shirai, Yasuhiro,"The acquisition of Relative Clauses in spontaneous child speech in Mandarin Chinese", *Journal of Child Language,* Vol. 42, No. 2, 2015.

Chen, Zongli, *The Syntax of Restrictive Relative Constructions,* Ph.D. dissertation, Guangdong University of Foreign Studies, 2005.

Cheng, Sherry Ya-Yin, *The Acquisition of Relative Clasues in Chinese,* MA thesis, National Taiwan Normal University, 1995.

Cheung, Hintat, Chang, Chien-ju, Ko, Hwa-wei, & Tsay, Jane, *Taiwan Corpus of Child Mandarin*, 2011.

Chomsky, Noam, "On Wh-movemnt", In P. Culicover, T. Wason & A. Akmajian eds., *Formal Syntax*, New York: Academic Press,1977.

Chomsky, Noam, *The Minimalist Program,* Cambridge, MA: MIT Press,1995.

Chomsky, Noam, "Minimalist Inquiries, the Framework", In R. Martin, D. Michaels & J. Uriagereka eds., *Step by Step, Essays on Minimalist Syntax in Honor of Howard Lasnik,* Cambridge, MA.: MIT Press, 2000.

Chomsky, Noam, "Derivation by Phase", In M. Kenstowicz, ed., *Ken Hale. A Life in Language,* Cambridge, MA.: MIT Press, 2001.

Chomsky, Noam, "Beyond Explanatory Adequacy", In A. Belletti ed., *Structures and Beyond. The Cartography of Syntactic Structure Vol 3,* Oxford: OUP, 2004.

Chomsky, Noam. "On phases", In R. Freidin, C. Otero & M. L. Zubzarreta, eds., *Foundational Issues in Linguistic Theory: Essays in Honor of Jean-Roger Vergnaud,* Cambridge, MA.: MIT Press, 2008.

Cinque, Guglielmo, *Adverbs and Functional Heads,* New York: Oxford University Press, 1999.

Cinque, Guglielmo, *Functional Structure in DP and IP. The Cartography of Syntactic Structures vol. 1,* New York: Oxford University Press, 2002.

Clahsen, Bartke, Susanne, & Göllner, Sandra, "Formal features in impaired grammars: a comparison of English and German SLI children", *Journal of Neurolinguistics*, Vol. 10, No. 2, 1997.

Clahsen, Harald, & Dalalakis, Jenny, "Tense and agreement in Greek SLI: a case study", *Essex Reports in Linguistics,* No. 24, 1999.

Clahsen, Harald, "Linguistic perspectives on specific language impairment", In W. Ritchie & T. Bhatia, eds., *Handbook of Child Language Acquisition,* San Diego, CA: Academic Press, 1999.

Clay, Marie M., "Sentence repetition: Elicited imitation of a controlled set of syntactic structures by four language groups", *Monographs of the Society for Research in Child Development,* Vol. 36, No. 3, 1971.

Cleland, Alexandra A., & Pickering, Martin J., "The use of lexical and syntactic information in language production: Evidence from the priming of noun-phrase structure", *Journal of Memory and Language,* Vol. 49, No. 2, 2003.

Coady, Jeffry A. "Rapid naming by children with and without Specific Language Impairment", *Journal of Speech, Language, and Hearing Research,* Vol. 56, No. 2, 2013.

Coco, Moreno I., Garraffa, Maria, & Branigan, Holly, *Subject Relative Production in SLI Children during Syntactic Priming and Sentence Repetition*, In N. Miyake, D. Peebles, & R. P. Cooper, eds., Proceedings of the 34th Annual Conference of the Cognitive Science Society, Austin, TX: Cognitive Science Society, 2012.

211

Collins, Chris, "Economy of derivation and the generalized proper binding condition", *Linguistic Inquiry,* Vol. 25, No.1, 1994.

Collins, Chris, "A smuggling approach to the passive in English", *Syntax,* Vol. 8, No.2, 2005.

Comrie, Bernard, "Typology and language acquisition: The case of Relative Clauses", In A. G. Ramat, ed., *Typology and Second Language Acquisition,* Berlin: Mouton de Gruyter, 2002.

Contemori, Carla, & Belletti, Adriana, "Relatives and passive object relatives in Italian-speaking children and adults: Intervention in production and comprehension*", Applied Psycholinguistics,* Vol. 35, No.6, 2014.

Contemori, Carla, & Garraffa, Maria, "Comparison of modalities in SLI syntax: A study on the comprehension and production of non-canonical sentences", *Lingua,* Vol. 120, No.8, 2010.

Conti-Ramsden, Gina, Botting, Nicola, & Faragher, Brian, "Psycholinguistic markers for Specific Language Impairment", *Journal of Child Psychology and Psychiatry,* Vol. 42, No.6, 2001.

Corrêa, Letícia M. Sicuro. "An alternative assessment of children's comprehension of Relative Clauses", *Journal of Psycholinguistic Research,* Vol. 24, No.3,1995.

Costa, João, Lobo, Maria, & Silva, Carolina, "Subject–object asymmetries in the acquisition of Portuguese Relative Clauses: Adults vs. Children", *Lingua,* Vol. 121, No.6, 2011.

Crain, Stephen, McKee, Cecile, & Emiliani, Maria, "Visiting relatives in Italy", In L. Frazier & J. der Villiers, eds., *Language Processing and Language Acquisition,* Dordrecht: Kluwer, 1991.

Crain, Stephen, & Thornton, Rosalind, *Investigations in Universal Grammar: A Guide to Research on the Acquisition of Syntax and Semantics,* Cambridge, MA: MIT Press, 1998.

Cromer, Richard F., "Hierarchical disability in the syntax of aphasic children", *International Journal of Behavioral Development,* Vol. 1, No.4, 1978.

De Villiers, Jill G., "Defining SLI: A linguistic perspective", In Y. Levy & J. Schaeffer eds., *Language Competence across Populations: Toward a*

Definition of Specific Language Impairment, Mahwah: Lawrence Erlbaum Associates, 2003.

De Villiers, Jill G, Tager Flusberg, Helen B., Hakuta, Kenji, & Cohen, Michael, "Children's comprehension of Relative Clauses", *Journal of Psycholinguistic Research,* Vol. 8, No.5, 1979.

Deevy, Patricia, & Leonard, Laurence B., "The comprehension of wh-questions in children with Specific Language Impairment", *Journal of Speech, Language, and Hearing Research,* Vol. 47, No.4, 2004.

Del Gobbo, Francesca, *Appositives at the Interface,* Ph.D. dissertation, University of California at Irvine, 2003.

Diessel, Holger, "On the role of frequency and similarity in the acquisition of subject and non-subject Relative Clauses", In T. Givon & M. Shibatani, eds., *Syntactic Complexity: Diachrony, Acquisition, Neuro-cognition, Evolution,* Amsterdam: John Benjamins, 2009.

Diessel, Holger, & Tomasello, Michael, "The development of Relative Clauses in spontaneous child speech", *Cognitive Linguistics,* Vol. 11, No.1/2, 2000.

Diessel, Holger, & Tomasello, Michael, "A new look at the acquisition of Relative Clauses", *Language,* Vol. 81, No.4, 2005.

Dowty, David, "Thematic proto-roles and argument selection", *Language,* Vol. 67, No.3, 1991.

Dromi, Esther, Leonard, Laurence B., & Blass, Anat, "Different methodologies yield incongruous results: a study of the spontaneous use of verb forms in Hebrew", In Y. Levy & J. Schaeffer, eds., *Language Competence across Populations: Toward a Definition of Specific Language Impairment*, Mahwah, NJ: Lawrence Erlbaum Associates, 2003.

Edwards, Jan, & Lahey, Margaret, "Auditory lexical decisions of children with specific language impairment", *Journal of Speech, Language, and Hearing Research,* Vol. 39, No.6, 1996.

Edwards, Jan, & Lahey, Margaret, "Nonword repetitions of children with Specific Language Impairment: Exploration of some explanations for their inaccuracies", *Applied Psycholinguistics,* Vol.19, No.2, 1998.

Estes, Katharine Graf, Evans, Julia L., & Else-Quest, Nicole M., "Differences in the nonword repetition performance of children with and without Specific Language Impairment: A meta-analysis", *Journal of Speech, Language, and Hearing Research,* Vol. 50, No.1, 2007.

Everitt, Andrea, Hannaford, Philip, & Conti-Ramsden, Gina, "Markers for persistent specific expressive language delay in 3-4-year-olds", *International Journal of Language & Communication Disorders,* Vol. 48, No.5, 2013.

Fox, Barbara A, & Thompson, Sandra A., "A discourse explanation of the grammar of Relative Clauses in English conversation", *Language,*Vol. 66, No.2, 1990.

Franck, Julie, Lassi, Glenda, Frauenfelder, Ulrich H, & Rizzi, Luigi, "Agreement and movement: A syntactic analysis of attraction", *Cognition,* Vol. 101, No.1, 2006.

Friedmann, Naama, Belletti, Adriana, & Rizzi, Luigi, "Relativized relatives: Types of intervention in the acquisition of A-bar dependencies", *Lingua,* Vol.119, No.1, 2009.

Friedmann, Naama, & Novogrodsky, Rama, "The acquisition of Relative Clause comprehension in Hebrew: A study of SLI and normal development", *Journal of Child Language,* Vol. 31, No.3, 2004.

Frizelle, Pauline, & Fletcher, Paul, "Relative clause constructions in children with Specific Language Impairment", *International Journal of Language & Communication Disorders,* Vol. 49, No.2, 2014.

Frizelle, Pauline, O'Neill, Clodagh, & Bishop, Dorothy V. M., "Assessing understanding of Relative Clauses: a comparison of multiple-choice comprehension versus sentence repetition", *Journal of Child Language,* Vol. 44, No.6, 2017.

Gabriel, Audrey, Maillart, Christelle, Guillaume, Melody, Stefaniak, Nicolas, & Meulemans, Thierry, "Exploration of serial structure procedural learning in children with language impairment", *Journal of the International Neuropsychological Society,* Vol. 17, No.2, 2011.

Garraffa, Maria, Coco, Moreno I., & Branigan, Holly P., "Effects of immediate and cumulative syntactic experience in language impairment: Evidence from priming of subject Relatives in children with SLI", *Language Learning and*

Development, Vol. 11, No.1, 2015.

Garraffa, Maria, & Grillo, Nino, "Canonicity effects as grammatical phenomena", *Journal of Neurolinguistics,* Vol. 21, No.2, 2008.

Gavarró, Anna, Cunill, Arnau, Muntané, Miriam, & Reguant, Marc, "The acquisition of Catalan relatives: Structure and processing", *Revue Roumaine de Linguistique-Romanian Review of Linguistics,*Vol. 57, No.2, 2012.

Gehrke, Berit, & Grillo, Nino. "How to become passive", In K. K. Grohmann ed., *Explorations of Phase Theory: Features, Arguments, and Interpretation at the Interfaces,* Berlin: de Gruyter, 2008.

Gibson, Edward, "Linguistic complexity: Locality of syntactic dependencies", *Cognition,*Vol. 68, No.1, 1998.

Gibson, Edward, "The dependency locality theory: A distance-based theory of linguistic complexity", In Y. Miyashita, A. Mirantz, & W. O'Neil, eds., *Image, Language, Brain:Papers from the First Mind Articulation Project Symposium,* Cambridge, MA: MIT press, 2000.

Goodall, Grant, "On the syntax and processing of Wh-questions in Spanish", In V. Chand, A. Kelleher, A. Rodrígues & B. Schmeiser, eds., *Proceedings of the West Coast Conference on Formal Linguistics,* Somerville, MA: Cascadilla Press, 2004.

Goodluck, Helen, & Tavakolian, Susan, "Competence and processing in children's grammar of Relative Clauses", *Cognition,*Vol. 11, No.1, 1982.

Gopnik, Myrna, "Feature blindness: a case study", *Language Acquisition,* Vol. 1, No.2, 1990.

Grela, Bernard G., & Leonard, Laurence B., "The use of subject arguments by children with Specific Language Impairment", *Clinical Linguistics & Phonetics,* Vol. 11, No.6, 1997.

Grillo, Nino, "Minimality effects in agrammatic comprehension", In Blaho, S., Schoorlemmer, E., Vicente, L. eds., *Proceedings of Console XIII,* 2005.

Grillo, Nino, *Generalized Minimality: Syntactic Underspecification in Broca's Aphasia,* Ph.D dissertation, University of Utrecht, 2008.

Grillo, Nino, "Generalized Minimality: Feature impoverishment and comprehension deficits in agrammatism", *Lingua,* Vol. 119, No.10, 2009.

Grodner, Daniel, & Gibson, Edward, "Consequences of the serial nature of linguistic input for sentential complexity", *Cognitive Science,* Vol. 29, No.2, 2005.

Grodzinsky, Yosef, *Theoretical Perspectives on Language Deficits*, Cambridge, MA: MIT press, 1990.

Grosu, Alexander, "A unified theory of standard and transparent free Relatives", *Natural Language & Linguistic Theory,* Vol. 21, No.2, 2003.

Guasti Maria Teresa, & Cardinaletti, Anna, "Relative clause formation in Romance child's production", *Probus,* Vol. 15, No.1, 2003.

Guilfoyle, Eithne, & Noonan, Máire, "Functional categories and language acquisition", *Canadian Journal of Linguistics,* Vol. 37, No.2, 1992.

Guo, Ling-yu, Tomblin, J. Bruce, & Samelson, Vicki, "Speech disruptions in the narratives of English-speaking children with Specific Language Impairment", *Journal of Speech, Language, and Hearing Research,* Vol. 51, No.3, 2008.

Gutierrez-Mangado, M. Juncal, "Children's comprehension of Relative Clauses in an ergative language: the case of Basque", *Language Acquisition,* Vol. 18, No.3, 2011.

Håkansson, Gisela, & Hansson, Kristina, "Comprehension and production of Relative Clauses: a comparison between Swedish impaired and unimpaired children", *Journal of Child Language,* Vol. 27, No.2, 2000.

Hamburger, Henry, & Crain, Stephen, "Relative acquisition", In S. A. Kuczaj ed., *Language Development* (Vol. 1), Hillsdale: Lawrence Erlbaum Associates, 1982.

Han, Chung-hye, "On the syntax of Relative Clauses in Korean", *The Canadian Journal of Linguistics/La revue canadienne de linguistique,* Vol. 58, No.2, 2013.

Hawkins, John A., "Processing complexity and filler-gap dependencies across grammars", *Language,* Vol. 75, No.2, 1999.

Hawkins, John A., *Efficiency and Complexity in Grammars*, Oxford: Oxford University Press, 2004.

Hawkins, Roger, "Do second language learners acquire restrictive Relative Clauses on the basis of relational or configurational information? The acquisition of French subject, direct object and genitive restrictive Relative Clauses by second language learners", *Second Language Research,* Vol. 5, No.2, 1989.

He, Xiaowei, *Specific Language Impairment Checklist for Pre-school Mandarin-speaking children*, Unpublished work, 2010.

Heim, Irene, & Kratzer, Angelika, *Semantics in Generative Grammar* (Vol. 13), Oxford: Blackwell, 1998.

Hesketh, Anne, "The use of Relative Clauses by children with language impairment", *Clinical Linguistics & Phonetics,* Vol. 20, No.7-8, 2006.

Hestvik, Arild, Schwartz, Richard G., & Tornyova, Lydia, "Relative clause gap-filling in children with Specific Language Impairment", *Journal of Psycholinguistic Research,* Vol. 39, No.5, 2010.

Hirsch, Christopher, & Wexler, Ken, "Children's passives and their resulting interpretation", In K. Deen, J. Nomura, B. Schulz, & B. Schwartz, eds., *The proceedings of the inaugural conference on generative approaches to language acquisition-North America*, Honolulu, Hawaii: University of Connecticut occasional papers in Linguistics 4, 2006.

Hoffman, LaVae M., & Gillam, Ronald B., "Verbal and spatial information processing constraints in children with Specific Language Impairment", *Journal of Speech, Language, and Hearing Research,* Vol. 47, No.1, 2004 .

Hsiao, Franny, & Gibson, Edward, "Processing Relative Clauses in Chinese", *Cognition,* Vol. 90, No.1, 2003.

Hsu, Chun-chieh Natalie, "Revisit Relative Clause islands in Chinese", *Language and Linguistics,* Vol. 9, No.1, 2008.

Hsu, Chun-Chieh Natalie, Hermon, Gabriella, & Zukowski, Andrea, "Young children's production of head-final Relative Clauses: Elicited production data from Chinese children", *Journal of East Asian Linguistics,* Vol. 18, No.4, 2009.

Hsu, Chun-Chieh Natalie, "The role of age in Mandarin-Speaking children's performance of Relative Clauses", *Concentric: Studies in Linguistics,* Vol. 40, No.2, 2014.

Hu, Shenai, *Intervention Effects and the Acquisition of Relativization and*

Topicalization in Chinese, Ph.D dissertation, Universitat Autònoma de Barcelona, 2014.

Hu, Shenai, Gavarró, Anna, Vernice, Mirta, & Guasti, Maria Teresa, "The acquisition of Chinese Relative Clauses: contrasting two theoretical approaches", *Journal of Child Language,* Vol. 43, No.1, 2016.

Hu, Shenai, Gavarró, Anna, & Guasti, Maria Teresa, "Children's production of head-final Relative Clauses: The case of Mandarin", *Applied Psycholinguistics,* Vol. 37, No.2, 2015.

Huang, C.-T. James, *Logical Relations in Chinese and the Theory of Grammar,* New York: Garland publishers, 1998.

Huang, C.-T. James, "Chinese passives in comparative perspective", *Tsing Hua Journal of Chinese Studies,* Vol. 29, No.4, 1999.

Huang, C-T. James, Li, Y-H. Audrey, & Li, Yafei, *The Syntax of Chinese,* Cambridge: Cambridge University Press, 2009.

Hulk, Aafke, & Müller, Natascha, "Bilingual first language acquisition at the interface between syntax and pragmatics", *Bilingualism: Language and Cognition,* Vol. 3, No.3, 2000.

Hulsey, Sarah, & Sauerland, Uli, "Sorting out Relative Clauses", *Natural Language Semantics,* Vol. 14, No.2, 2006.

Huttenlocher, Janellen, Vasilyeva, Marina, & Shimpi, Priya, "Syntactic priming in young children", *Journal of Memory and Language,* Vol. 50, No.2, 2004.

Jakubowicz, Celia, "The language faculty: (Ab)normal development and interface constraints", Paper delivered to the GALA 2005 meeting—Generative approaches to language acquisition, Siena, Italy, 2005.

Jakubowicz, Celia, "Measuring derivational complexity: New evidence from typically developing and SLI learners of L1 French", *Lingua,* Vol. 121, No.3, 2011.

Jefferies, Elizabeth, Ralph, Matthew A. Lambon, & Baddeley, Alan D., "Automatic and controlled processing in sentence recall: The role of long-term and working memory", *Journal of Memory and Language,* Vol. 51, No.4, 2004.

Jensen de López, Kristine, Sundahl Olsen, Lone, & Chondrogianni, Vasiliki, " Annoying Danish Relatives: Comprehension and production of Relative

Clauses by Danish children with and without SLI", *Journal of Child Language,* Vol. 41, No.1, 2014.

Kail, Robert, "A method for studying the generalized slowing hypothesis in children with Specific Language Impairment", *Journal of Speech, Language, and Hearing Research,* Vol. 37, No.2, 1994.

Kail, Robert, & Salthouse, Timothy A., "Processing speed as a mental capacity", *Acta Psychologica,* Vol. 86, No.2, 1994.

Kamhi, Alan G., & Catts., Hugh W., "Toward an understanding of developmental language and reading disorders", *Journal of Speech and Hearing Disorders,* Vol. 51, No.4, 1986.

Kidd, Evan, & Bavin, Edith L., "English-speaking children's comprehension of Relative Clauses: Evidence for general-cognitive and language-specific constraints on development", *Journal of Psycholinguistic Research,* Vol. 31, No.6, 2002.

Kidd, Evan, Brandt, Silke, Lieven, Elena, & Tomasello, Michael, "Object Relatives made easy: A cross-linguistic comparison of the constraints influencing young children's processing of Relative Clauses", *Language and Cognitive Processes,* Vol. 22, No.6, 2007.

Kim, Chae-Eun, & O'Grady, William, "Asymmetries in children's production of Relative Clauses: data from English and Korean", *Journal of Child Language,* Vol.43, No.5, 2016.

Klem, Marianne, Melby-Lervåg, Monica, Hagtvet, Bente, Lyster, Solveig-Alma Halaas, Gustafsson, Jan-Eric, & Hulme, Charles, "Sentence repetition is a measure of children's language skills rather than working memory limitations", *Developmental Science,* Vol. 18, No.1, 2015.

Kohnert, Kathryn, Windsor, Jennifer, & Miller, Ruth, "Crossing borders: Recognition of Spanish words by English-speaking children with and without language impairment", *Applied Psycholinguistics,* Vol. 25, No.4, 2004.

Kolk, Herman H. J., "Disorders of syntax in aphasia, linguistic descriptive and processing approaches", In B. Stemmer & H. Whitaker, eds., *Handbook of Neurolinguistics*, San Diego: Academic Press, 1998.

Kuno, Susumu, "Subject, theme, and the speaker's empathy, A reexamination of Relativization phenomena", In C. Li, ed., *Subject and Topic,* San Diego: Academic Press, 1976.

Labelle, Marie, "Predication, Wh-movement, and the development of Relative Clauses", *Language Acquisition,* Vol. 1, No.1, 1990.

Labelle, Marie, "The acquisition of Relative Clauses: movement or no movement?", *Language Acquisition,* Vol. 5, No.2, 1996.

Lee, Thomas Hun-Tak, "The inadequacy of processing heuristics: Evidence from Relative Clause acquisition in Mandarin Chinese", In T. H.-T. Lee, ed., *Research in Chinese Linguistics in Hong Kong,* Hong Kong: Linguistic Society of Hong Kong, 1992.

Leonard, Laurence B., "Language learnability and Specific Language Impairment in children", *Applied Psycholinguistics,* Vol. 10, No.2, 1989.

Leonard, Laurence B., "Functional categories in the grammars of children with Specific Language Impairment", *Journal of Speech, Language, and Hearing Research,* Vol. 38, No.6, 1995.

Leonard, Laurence B., "Characterizing Specific Language Impairment: A crosslinguistic perspective", In M. Rice, ed., *Toward a Genetics of Language,* Mahwah: Lawrence Erlbaum Associates, 1996.

Leonard, Laurence B., *Children with Specific Language Impairment,* Cambridge, MA: MIT press, 2014a.

Leonard, Laurence B., "Specific Language Impairment across languages", *Child Development Perspectives,* Vol. 81, No.1, 2014b.

Leonard, Laurence B., Deevy, Patricia, Fey, Marc E., & Bredin-Oja, Shelley L., "Sentence comprehension in Specific Language Impairment: A task designed to distinguish between cognitive capacity and syntactic complexity", *Journal of Speech, Language, and Hearing Research,* Vol. 56, No.2 , 2013.

Leonard, Laurence B., McGregor, Karla K., & Allen, George D., "Grammatical morphology and speech perception in children with Specific Language Impairment", *Journal of Speech, Language, and Hearing Research,* Vol. 35, No.5, 1992.

Lewis, Richard L., Vasishth, Shravan, & Van Dyke, Julie A., "Computational principles of working memory in sentence comprehension", *Trends in*

Cognitive Sciences, Vol. 10, No.10, 2006.

Li, Ke, *The acquistion of Bei-constructions in Mandarin-speaking children with specific language impairment,* MA. Thesis, Guangdong University of Foreign Studies, 2015.

Li, Y-H. Audrey, "Word order, structure, and relativization", In S. W. Tang & C. S. Liu, eds., *On the Formal Way to Chinese Languages*, Stanford: CSLI Publications, 2002.

Lin, Chien-Jer Charles, & Bever, Thomas G., "Subject preference in the processing of Relative Clauses in Chinese", Paper delivered to the 25th west coast conference on formal linguistics, Somerville, MA, 2006.

Lin, Jo-wang, "On restrictive and non-restrictive Relative Clauses in Mandarin Chinese", *Tsinghua Journal of Chinese Studies,* Vol. 33, No.1, 2003.

Liu, Xueman Lucy, de Villiers, Jill, Ning, Chunyan, Rolfhus, Eric, Hutchings, Teresa, Lee, Wendy, Zhang, Yiwen, "Research to establish the validity, reliability, and clinical utility of a comprehensive language assessment of Mandarin", *Journal of Speech, Language, and Hearing Research,* Vol. 60, No.3, 2017.

Locke, John L., *The Children's Path to Spoken Language,* Cambridge, MA: Harvard University Press, 1993.

Locke, John L., "Gradual emergence of developmental language disorder", *Journal of Speech and Hearing Research,* Vol. 37, No.3, 1994.

Lum, Jarrad A. G., Conti-Ramsden, Gina, Page, Debra, & Ullman, Michael T., "Working, declarative and procedural memory in Specific Language Impairment", *Cortex,* Vol. 48, No. 9, 2012.

Lust, Barbara, Flynn, Suzanne, & Foley, Claire, "What children know about what they say: Elicited imitation as a research method for assessing children's syntax", In D. Mc Daniel, C. McKee & H. Cairns, eds., *Methods for Assessing Children's Syntax* , Cambridge, MA: MIT Press, 1996.

MacDonald, Maryellen C., & Christiansen, Morten H., "Reassessing working memory: comment on Just and Carpenter (1992) and Waters and Caplan (1996)", *Psychological Review,* Vol. 109, No.1, 2002.

MacWhinney, Brian, "The emergence of grammar from perspective taking", In

D. Pecher & R. Zwann, eds., *Grounding Cognition,* Cambridge: Cambridge University Press, 2005.

Mak, Willem M., Vonk, Wietske, & Schriefers, Herbert, "The influence of animacy on Relative Clause processing", *Journal of Memory and Language,* Vol. 47, No.1, 2002.

Mak, Willem M., Vonk, Wietske, & Schriefers, Herbert, "Animacy in processing Relative Clauses: The hikers that rocks crush", *Journal of Memory and Language,* Vol. 54, No.4, 2006.

Marinellie, Sally A., "Assessing and facilitating complex sentence formulation in picture description tasks", *Advances in Speech Language Pathology,* Vol. 8, No.2, 2006.

Marinis, Theodoros, & van der Lely, Heather K. J., "On-line processing of Wh-questions in children with G-SLI and typically developing children", *International Journal of Language & Communication Disorders,* Vol. 42, No.5, 2007.

Marshall, Chloe, Marinis, Theodoros, & van der Lely, Heather. K. J., "Passive verb morphology: The effect of phonotactics on passive comprehension in typically developing and Grammatical-SLI children", *Lingua,* Vol. 117, No.8, 2007.

Mastropavlou, Maria, *The Role of Phonological Salience and Feature Interpretability in the Grammar of Typically Developing and Language Impaired Children,* Ph.D dissertation, Aristotle University of Thessaloniki, 2006.

Mastropavlou, Maria, & Tsimpli, Ianthi Maria, Complementisers and subordination in typical language acquisition and SLI, *Lingua,* Vol.121, No.3, 2011.

McDaniel, Dana, McKee, Cecile, & Cairns, Helen Smith, eds., *Methods for Assessing Children's Syntax,* Cambridge, MA: MIT Press, 1998.

Meisel, Jürgen M., & Müller, Natascha, "Finiteness and verb placement in early child grammars: Evidence from simultaneous acquisition of French and German in bilinguals", In J. Meisel, ed., *The Acquisition of Verb Placement,* Dordrecht: Kluwer, 1992.

Menyuk, Paula, "Comparison of grammar of children with functionally deviant and normal speech", *Journal of Speech, Language, and Hearing Research,* Vol. 7, No. 2, 1964.

Messenger, Katherine, Branigan, Holly P., & McLean, Janet F., "Evidence for (shared) abstract structure underlying children's short and full passives", *Cognition,* Vol. 121, No.2, 2011.

Messenger, Katherine, Branigan, Holly P., & Mclean, Janet F., "Is children's acquisition of the passive a staged process? Evidence from six-and nine-year-olds' production of passives", *Journal of Child Language,* Vol. 39, No.5, 2012.

Montgomery, James W., "Examination of phonological working memory in specifically language-impaired children", *Applied Psycholinguistics,*Vol.16, No.4, 1995.

Montgomery, James W., Magimairaj, Beula M., & Finney, Mianisha C., "Working memory and Specific Language Impairment: An update on the relation and perspectives on assessment and treatment", *American Journal of Speech-language Pathology,* Vol.19, No.1, 2010.

Ning, Chunyan, *The overt syntax of topicalization and relativization in Chinese,* Ph.D dissertation, The University of California, Irvine, 1993.

Ning, Chunyan, Liu, Xueman Lucy, & de Villiers, Jill., The Diagnostic Receptive and Expressive Assessment of Mandarin, Dallas, TX: Bethel Hearing and Speaking Training Center, 2014.

Norbury, Courtenay Frazier, Bishop, Dorothy V. M., & Briscoe, Josie, Production of English finite verb morphology: A comparison of SLI and mild-moderate hearing impairment, *Journal of Speech, Language, and Hearing Research,* Vol. 44, No.1, 2001.

Novogrodsky, Rama, & Friedmann, Naama, "The production of Relative Clauses in syntactic SLI: A window to the nature of the impairment", *International Journal of Speech-Language Pathology,* Vol. 8, No.4, 2006.

O'Grady, William, *Syntactic Development,* Chicago: University of Chicago Press, 1997.

O'Grady, William, "Relative Clauses: processing and acquisition", In E. Kidd, ed., *The Acquisition of Relative Clauses: Processing, Typology and Function,*

Amsterdam: John Benjamins, 2011.

Owen, Amanda J., & Leonard, Laurence B., "The production of finite and nonfinite complement clauses by children with Specific Language Impairment and their typically developing peers", *Journal of Speech, Language, and Hearing Research,* Vol. 49, No.3, 2006.

Özge, Duygu, Marinis, Theodoros, & Zeyrek, Deniz, "Comprehension of subject and object Relative Clauses in monolingual Turkish children", In S. Ay, Ö. Aydın, İ. Ergenç, S. Gökmen, S. İşsever & D. Peçenek, eds., *Essays on Turkish Linguistics*,Wiesbaden: Harrassowitz Verlag, 2009.

Pérez-Leroux, Ana Teresa, "Resumptives in the acquisition of Relative Clauses", *Language Acquisition,* Vol. 4, No.1-2, 1995.

Pan, Victor Junnan, *Resumptivity in Mandarin Chinese: A Minimalist Account*, Berlin: Mouton de Gruyter, 2016.

Paradis, Michel, & Gopnik, Mirna, "Compensatory strategies in Genetic Dysphasia: declarative memory", *Journal of Neurolinguistics,* Vol. 10, No.2-3, 1997.

Pickering, Martin J., & Branigan, Holly P., "The representation of verbs: Evidence from syntactic priming in language production", *Journal of Memory and Language,* Vol. 39, No.4, 1998.

Pickering, Martin J., & Ferreira, Victor S., "Structural priming: A critical review", *Psychological Bulletin,* Vol. 134, No.3, 2008.

Pinker, Steven, & Ullman, Michael T., "The past and future of the past tense", *Trends in Cognitive Sciences,* Vol. 6, No.11, 2002.

Pollock, Jean-Yves, "Verb movement, universal grammar, and the structure of IP", *Linguistic Inquiry,* Vol. 20, No.3,1989.

Pu, Ming-Ming, "The distribution of Relative Clauses in Chinese discourse", *Discourse Processes,* Vol. 43, No.1, 2007.

Radford, Andrew, "Small children's small clauses", *Transactions of the Philological Society,* Vol. 86, No.2, 1988.

Radford, Andrew, *Syntactic Theory and the Acquisition of English Syntax,* Oxford: Blackwell, 1990.

Radford, Andrew, Atkinson, Martin, Britain, David, Clahsen, Harald, & Spencer,

Andrew, *Linguistics: An Introduction,* Cambridge: Cambridge University Press, 2009.

Rakhlin, Natalia, Kornilov, Sergey A., Kornilova, Tatiana V., & Grigorenko, Elena L., "Syntactic complexity effects of Russian Relative Clause sentences in children with and without Developmental Language Disorder", *Language Acquisition,* Vol. 23, No.4, 2016.

Ramus, Franck, Marshall, Chloe R., Rosen, Stuart, & van der Lely, Heather K. J., "Phonological deficits in Specific Language Impairment and developmental dyslexia: towards a multidimensional model", *Brain,* Vol. 136, No. 2, 2013.

Reinhart, Tanya, "Wh-in-situ in the framework of the Minimalist Program", *Natural Language Semantics,* Vol. 6, No.1, 1998.

Rice, Mabel L., & Wexler, Kenneth, "Toward tense as a clinical marker of Specific Language Impairment in English-speaking children", *Journal of Speech, Language, and Hearing Research,* Vol. 39, No.6, 1996.

Rice, Mabel L., Wexler, Kenneth, & Cleave, Patricia L, "Specific Language Impairment as a period of extended optional infinitive", *Journal of Speech, Language, and Hearing Research,* Vol. 38, No.4, 1995.

Rice, Mabel L., Wexler, Kenneth, & Hershberge, Scott., "Tense over time: the longitudinal course of tense acquisition in children with Specific Language Impairment", *Journal of Speech Language, and Hearing Research,* Vol. 41, No. 6, 1998.

Riches, Nick G., "Complex sentence profiles in children with Specific Language Impairment: Are they really atypical?", *Journal of Child Language*, Vol. 44, No.2, 2017.

Riches, Nick G., Loucas, Tom, Baird, Gillian, Charman, Tony, & Simonoff, Emily., "Sentence repetition in adolescents with Specific Language Impairments and Autism: An investigation of complex syntax", *International Journal of Language & Communication Disorders,* Vol. 45, No.1, 2010.

Rizzi, Luigi, *Relativized minimality,* Cambridge, MA: MIT Press, 1990.

Rizzi, Luigi, "The fine structure of the left periphery", In L. Haegeman, ed., *Elements of Grammar,* Dordrecht: Kluwer, 1997.

Rizzi, Luigi, "Locality and left periphery", In A. Belletti ed., *Structures and*

Beyond: The Cartography of Syntactic Structures, New York: Oxford University Press, 2004.

Rizzi, Luigi, "On the form of chains: criterial positions and ECP effects", In L. L.-S. Cheng & N. Corver eds., *Wh-movement: Moving On,* Cambridge, MA: MIT Press, 2006.

Roediger, Henry L., "Memory metaphors in cognitive psychology", *Memory & Cognition,* Vol.8, No.3, 1980.

Roland, Douglas, Dick, Frederic, & Elman, Jeffrey L, "Frequency of basic English grammatical structures: A corpus analysis", *Journal of Memory and Language,* Vol. 57, No.3, 2007.

Rummer, Ralf, "Immediate and delayed recall of visually presented sentences: evidence for the involvement of phonological information", *Experimental Psychology,* Vol. 51, No.1, 2004.

Schütze, Carson, & Wexler, Kenneth, "Subject Case Licensing and English Root Infinitives*",* Paper delivered to the 20th annual Boston University conference on language development, Somerville, MA, 1996.

Schuele, C. Melanie & Dykes, Julianna C., "Complex syntax acquisition: A longitudinal case study of a child with Specific Language Impairment", *Clinical Linguistics & Phonetics,* Vol. 19, No.4, 2005.

Schuele, C. Melanie, & Nicholls, Lisa M., "Relative Clauses: Evidence of continued linguistic vulnerability in children with Specific Language Impairment", *Clinical Linguistics & Phonetics,*Vol. 14, No.8, 2000.

Schuele, C. Melanie, & Tolberrt, Leslie, "Omissions of obligatory relative markers in children with Specific Language Impairment", *Clinical Linguistics & Phonetics,* Vol.15, No.4, 2001.

Seeff-Gabriel, Belinda, Chiat, Shula, & Dodd, Barbara., "Sentence imitation as a tool in identifying expressive morphosyntactic difficulties in children with severe speech difficulties", *International Journal of Language & Communication Disorders,* Vol. 45, No.6, 2010.

Sheldon, Amy, "The role of parallel function in the acquisition of Relative Clauses in English", *Journal of Verbal Learning and Verbal Behavior,* Vol. 13, No.3, 1974.

Shimpi, Priya M., Gámez, Perla B., Huttenlocher, Janellen, & Vasilyeva, Marina.,

"Syntactic priming in 3- and 4-year-old children: evidence for abstract representations of transitive and dative forms", *Developmental Psychology*, Vol. 43, No.6, 2007.

Simpson, Andrew, "Definiteness agreement and the Chinese DP", *Language and Linguistics,* Vol. 2, No.1, 2001.

Simpson, Andrew, "On the status of modifying DE and the structure of the Chinese DP", In S.-W. Tang & C.-S. Liu eds., *On the Formal Way to Chinese Languages,* Stanford: CSLI Publications, 2002.

Smolík, Filip, & Vávrů, Petra, "Sentence imitation as a marker of SLI in Czech: Disproportionate impairment of verbs and clitics", *Journal of Speech, Language, and Hearing Research,* Vol. 57, No.3, 2014.

Sorace, Antonella, "Pinning down the concept of 'interface' in bilingualism", *Linguistic Approaches to Bilingualism,* Vol. 1, No.1, 2011.

Sorace, Antonella, & Filiaci, Francesca, "Anaphora resolution in near-native speakers of Italian", *Second Language Research,* Vol. 22, No.3, 2006.

Stavrakaki, Stavroula, "Comprehension of reversible Relative Clauses in Specifically Language Impaired and normally developing Greek children", *Brain & Language,* Vol. 77, No. 3, 2001.

Stavrakaki, Stavroula, "A-bar movement constructions in Greek children with SLI", In E. Fava, ed., *Clinical Linguistics: Theory and Applications in Speech Pathology and Therapy,* Amsterdam: John Benjamins, 2002.

Stokes, Stephanie F., Wong, Anita M. Y., Fletcher, Paul, & Leonard, Laurence B., "Nonword repetition and sentence repetition as clinical markers of Specific Language Impairment: The case of Cantonese", *Journal of Speech, Language, and Hearing Research,* Vol. 49, No. 2, 2006.

Su, Yi-ching, *Relatives of Mandarin Children*, Paper delivered to the Generative approaches to language acquisition in North America, University of Hawai'i, Manoa, 2004.

Su, Yi-ching, "Word order effect in children's garden path of Relative Clauses", *Concentric: Studies in Linguistics,* Vol. 32, No. 2, 2006.

Suzuki, Takaaki, "A case-marking cue for filler–gap dependencies in children's Relative Clauses in Japanese", *Journal of Child Language,* Vol. 49, No. 2,

2011.

Tallal, Paula, & Stark, Rachel E., "Speech acoustic cue discrimination abilities of normally developing and language impaired children", *Journal of the Acoustic Society of America,* Vol. 69, No. 2, 1981.

Tarallo, Fernando, & Myhill, John, "Interference and natural language processing in second language acquisition", *Language Learning,* Vol. 33, No.1, 1983.

Tavakolian, Susan, "The conjoined-clause analysis of Relative Clauses", In S. L. Tavakolian", ed., *Language Acquisition and Linguistic Theory,* Cambridge, MA: MIT Press, 1981.

Temperley, David, "Ambiguity avoidance in English Relative Clauses", *Language*, Vol. 79, No. 3, 2003.

Thornton, Rosalind, "Elicited production", In Dana McDaniel, Cecile McKee, & Helen Smith Cairns, eds., *Methods for Assessing Children's Syntax,* Cambridge, MA: MIT Press, 1996.

Tomblin, J. Bruce, Mainela-Arnold, Elina, & Zhang, Xuyang, "Procedural learning in adolescents with and without Specific Language Impairment", *Language Learning and Development,* Vol. 3, No. 4, 2007.

Traxler, Matthew J., Morris, Robin K., & Seely, Rachel E., "Processing subject and object Relative Clauses: Evidence from eye movements", *Journal of Memory and Language,* Vol. 47, No.1, 2002.

Tsai, Wei-tien, *On Economizing the Theory of A-bar Dependencies*, Ph.D dissertation, MIT, Cambridge, MA., 1994.

Tsimpli, Ianthi Maria, "LF-interpretability and language development: a study of verbal and nominal features in normally developing and SLI Greek children", *Brain and Language,* Vol.77, No.3, 2001.

Tsimpli, Ianthi Maria, & Stavrakaki, Stavroula, "The effects of a morphosyntactic deficit in the determiner system: The case of a Greek SLI child", *Lingua,* Vol. 108, No.1, 1999.

Ukrainetz, Teresa A., & Gillam, Ronald B., "The expressive elaboration of imaginative narratives by children with Specific Language Impairment", *Journal of Speech, Language, and Hearing Research,* Vol. 52, No.4, 2009.

Ullman, Michael T., & Pierpont, Elizabeth I., "Specific Language Impairment is not specific to language: The procedural deficit hypothesis", *Cortex,* Vol. 41, No.3, 2005.

Van der Lely, Heather K. J., "Specifically language impaired and normally developing children: Verbal passive vs. adjectival passive sentence interpretation", *Lingua,* Vol. 98, No.4, 1996.

Van der Lely, Heather K. J., "Canonical linking rules: Forward versus reverse linking in normally developing and specifically language-impaired children", *Cognition,* Vol. 51, No.1, 1994.

Van der Lely, Heather K. J., "SLI in children: Movement, economy and deficits in the computational-syntactic system", *Language Acquisition,* Vol. 7, No.2-4, 1998.

Van der Lely, Heather K. J., "Evidence for and implications of a domain-specific grammatical deficit", In Jenkins, L., ed., *The Genetics of Language,* Oxford: Elsevier, 2004.

Van der Lely, Heather K. J., & Battell, Jackie, "Wh-movement in children with grammatical SLI: A test of the RDDR hypothesis", *Language,* Vol. 79, No.1, 2003.

Van der Lely, Heather K. J., & Harris, Margaret, "Comprehension of reversible sentences in specifically language-impaired children", *Journal of Speech and Hearing Disorders,* Vol. 55, No.1, 1990.

Van der Lely, Heather K. J., & Stollwerck, Linda, "Binding theory and specifically language impaired children", *Cognition,* Vol. 62, No.3, 1997.

Van der Lely, Heather K. J., & Ullman, Michael T., "Past tense morphology in specifically language impaired and normally developing children", *Language and Cognitive Processes,* Vol. 16, No.2-3, 2001.

Wang, Zhe, *Investigation and Research on Acquisition of Relative Clauses of Mandarin-speaking Children,* MA. thesis, Hunan University, 2009.

Wanner, Eric, & Maratsos, Michael, "An ATN approach to comprehension", In Morris Halle, Joan Bresnan, & George A. Miller, eds., *Linguistic Theory and Psychological Reality*, Cambridge, MA: MIT Press, 1978.

Warren, Tessa, & Gibson, Edward, "The influence of referential processing on sentence complexity", *Cognition,* Vol. 85, No.1, 2002.

Weismer, Susan Ellis, Evans, Julia, & Hesketh., Linda J., "An examination of verbal working memory capacity in children with specific language impairment", *Journal of Speech, Language, and Hearing Research,* Vol. 42, No.5, 1999.

Wexler, Kenneth, "Lenneberg's dream: Learning, normal language development and specific language impairment", In Y. Levy & J. Schaeffer, eds., *Language Competence across Populations: Toward a Definition of Specific Language Impairment,* Mahwah, NJ: Erlbaum, 2003.

Wexler, Kenneth, "Theory of phasal development: Perfection in child grammar", *MIT Working Papers in Linguistics,* No. 48, 2004.

Willis, Catherine S., & Gathercole, Susan E., "Phonological short-term memory contributions to sentence processing in young children", *Memory,* Vol. 9, No.4-6, 2001.

Warren, Tessa, & Gibson, Edward, "The influence of referential processing on sentence complexity", *Cognition,* Vol. 85, No.1, 2002.

Wu, Fuyun, Kaiser, Elsi, & Andersen, Elaine, "Subject preference, head animacy and lexical cues: a corpus study of Relative Clauses in Chinese", In H. Yamashita, Y. Hirose & J. L. Packard, eds., *Processing and Producing Head-final Structures,* Dordrecht, NL: Springer, 2010.

Xu, Ting, & Yang, Xiaolu, *Children's Acquisition of Passives in Chinese,* Paper delivered to the proceedings of the Ninth Tokyo Conference on Psycholinguistics, Tokyo Hituzi Syobo, 2008.

Yu, Haopeng, "The grammar impairment of Mandarin Chinese SLI children: evidence from topic-comment structures", *Journal of Language Teaching & Research,* Vol. 7, No.2, 2016.

Zukowski, Andrea, "Elicited production of Relative Clauses in children with Williams Syndrome", *Language and Cognitive Processes,* Vol. 24, No.1, 2009.

Zwart, Jan-Wouter, "A head-raising analysis of Relative Clauses in Dutch", In A. Alexiadou, P. Law, A. Meinunger & C. Wilder, eds., *The Syntax of Relative Clause,* Amsterdam: John Benjamins, 2000.

Appendices

Appendix A

One example of the stimulus materials used in the elicitation production task

引导语：有两个小朋友，一个小朋友在推爸爸，一个小朋友在推妈妈。你喜欢哪个小朋友？

Lead in：'There are two children. One child is pushing the father. The other is pushing the mother. Which child do you like?'

Appendix B

One example of the stimulus materials used in the Priming production task

基线引导语：这是汽车（指着启动图片中的任意一个汽车），这个小朋友是？（指着目标图片中推小姐姐的小哥哥）

Baseline lead in：'This is a car (pointing to one of the cars in the prime picture), who is the boy? (pointing to the boy that is pushing the girl in the target picture)'

启动引导语：这是推汽车的小哥哥（指着启动图片中的推汽车的小朋友），这个小朋友是？（指着目标图片中推小姐姐的小哥哥）

Prime lead in：'This is a boy that is pushing the car (pointing to the boy In other words pushing the car in the prime picture), who is the boy? (pointing to the boy that is pushing the girl in the target picture)'

Example prime picture

Example target picture

Appendix C

One example of the stimulus materials used in the sentence-picture matching task

引导语：这里有三个小姐姐，指一下亲小哥哥的小姐姐。

Lead in：'There are 3 sisters, point to the sister that kissed the brother.'

A set of example pictures used in sentence-picture matching task

Appendix D

One example of the stimulus materials used in the character-picture verification task

引导语：这里有两个小哥哥，指一下亲小姐姐的小哥哥。

Lead in：'There are 2 brothers, point to the brother that kissed the sister.'

Example picture used in character-picture verification task

Appendix E

One example of the stimulus materials used in the repetition task

引导语：小朋友，我们现在来做一个游戏。我说一句话，你也说一句话，你要跟我说的一样，好吗？追小偷的警察戴着黑色的帽子。

Lead in：'XXX，Let's play a game. I say a sentence, then you repeat it, OK? 'The policeman that was chasing the thief wore a black cap.'

Acknowledgments

I would like to take this opportunity to thank all the individuals who have supported and enlightened me throughout the time it took me to complete this research and to write this book.

First and foremost, I would like to sincerely express my gratitude to Professor He Xiaowei for having ushered me into the study of SLI, for his contribution to the research design, for his detailed comments on my work, and for his expertise, encouragement, and patience over such a long period. I am also deeply indebted to all other generative linguists in Guangdong University of Foreign studies: Professor Wen Binli, Professor Han Jingquan, Professor Zhang Qingwen, Professor Ma Zhigang, and Professor Wu Zhuang. They have enlightened me a lot in numerous lectures, seminars and private talks. For the fruitful discussion on the research design, I remain in debt to Professor Ning Chunyan, Professor Thomas Hun-tak Lee, Professor Zeng Tao and Professor Su Yi.

I wish to thank the staff members of the organizations and kindergarten with which I collaborated, who contributed to the realization of this research, and helped me with the data collection. I must acknowledge as well all the participants and their families in this study and the team members who helped me to run the experiments.

I also wish to acknowledge the Chinese Fund for the Humanities and Social Sciences (14CYY013) for funding. Thanks to the Faculty of Foreign studies in Henan Normal University for allowing me to study for my doctorate at Guangdong University of Foreign Studies for so many years.

My deepest thanks go to my family members: my parents for always encouraging me and supporting me, my wife Wang Haiyan for nursing our baby

Yu Hangzhi, my brother and sister-in-law for taking care of our father and mother when they were in their last days.

    I dedicate this book to my parents.